Christian Perspectives

A Biblical View of Law and Justice

Books previously published in the Christian Perspectives series

Christian Perspectives on Law Reform
Christian Perspectives on Human Rights and Legal Philosophy
Christian Perspectives on Law and Relationism
Christian Perspectives on the Limits of the Law

Christian Perspectives

A Biblical View of
Law and Justice

David McIlroy

PATERNOSTER

British Library Cataloguing in Publication Data
A catalogue record for this book is available from the British Library

ISBN 1-84227-267-5

Cover Design by FourNineZero
Typeset by WestKey Ltd, Falmouth, Cornwall
Print Management by Adare Carwin
Printed and Bound in Norway by Rotanor

To Aunty Rosanna,
who always knew
I'd be a writer

'No fair-minded reader of the Bible can avoid being impressed by the prominence given to law (Torah), righteousness and justice both in human and divine relationships. The Torah was described as God's loving gift to his people because it pointed the way to justice without which there can be no peace (Shalom), those right relationships that should exist within creation and with its Creator. I read this book with admiration and gratitude not only because it illuminates these Christian essentials but locates them in the wider theological and doctrinal context in which they are properly to be understood. He highlights both the potential for good and the limitations of human law. This book will confirm the sense of vocation that those involved in law making or administration should have and will help others to see that this is a necessary sphere of work for God's people in God's world.'

Mr Justice Mark Hedley,
President of the Lawyers Christian Fellowship

'The triad of Scripture, justice and law has represented through the ages a persistent focus for lawyers, philosophers and theologians. In a society seeking to accommodate these within the additional context of human rights, this timely volume represents a valuable resource to guide and illuminate research and thought.'

Professor Norman Doe,
Director of the Centre for Law and Religion, Law School, Cardiff University

'I warmly welcome David McIlroy's thought provoking essays on a biblical view of law and justice. Their range is very wide, covering, for example, the nature of kingship considered in relation to authority, the prophetic call to justice and an intriguing chapter on "Law and the Spirit". This book should be read by lawyers but its scope is not narrowly legal and it will interest anyone concerned with the relationship between biblical teaching and contemporary legal issues. As Editor of *Law and Justice*, the Christian Law Review, I am delighted to commend David McIlroy's book as a most valuable contribution to the debate on some of the most pressing issues which concern Christians today.'

John Duddington,
Editor of Law and Justice

Contents

Foreword   ix
Preface   xi
Introduction   xiii

1. The Character of God   **1**
The Lord is the Good Creator   1
The Lord God is the Ultimate Reality   2
God is Love   5
The Lord is Sovereign   7
The Lord is Holy   8
The Lord is Light   10
The Lord is Just   10
The Lord is Merciful/Generous/Gracious   12
The Wrath of God   13
Conclusion: The Harmony of God's Characteristics   16

2. Law, Creation and the Fall   **17**
Creation   17
The Fall   18
Justice and the Good Gifts of God Before the Fall   20
The Consequences of the Fall Mitigated   26
The Good Gifts of God and the Concept of the   33
    Good after the Fall
The Christian Vision of a Just Society   35

3. The Mosaic Law   **41**
The Covenant and the Law   41
Israel as a Holy Nation   44
Shalom   48
Understanding the Torah   50
The Administration of Justice   62
Israel as a Light to the Nations   65
Conclusion   67

4. Kingship   **69**
Submission to Authorities   69
Justice and Deliverance   70
The Vision for the King in the Old Testament   71
The Exercise of Justice   78
Conclusion   87

5. **The Prophetic Call to Justice**   **89**
   The Importance of Justice in the Prophetic Message   89
   Justice and the Nations.   105
   Conclusion: The Contrast Between Current Injustice   112
   and Divine Justice

6. **Christ and Caesar**   **115**
   Jesus is King   115
   What Manner of King?   116
   The Kingship of Jesus and the Law of Moses   122
   The Kingship of Jesus and the Kings of this World   130

7. **Law and the Spirit**   **143**
   Law and the Holy Spirit   143
   Structural Sin   153
   Conclusion   156

8. **Submission to the Authorities**   **157**
   Reprise   157
   Government has a Role within God's Purposes   158
   The Proper Aims of Government   161
   Defining the Good and the Right   162
   The Dangers of a Christian Vision of the Good and the Right   174
   The Calling of Secular Authorities: The Common Good   175
   Social Justice and the Just Society: The Role of Government   177
   Order and the Practical Importance of Justice   178
   The Accountability of Government   180
   The Christian Witness to the True Role of Human Law   182
   Conclusions   187

9. **The Last Judgement**   **189**
   The Cross and the Injustice of Human Laws   189
   The Last Judgement   190
   The Last Judgement will be a Revelation   193
   Human Justice in the Meantime   199
   Conclusions   202

Postscript   205
Bibliography   207

Scripture Index   219
General Index   235

Foreword

When I read the manuscript of this book I was excited. It is a much needed analysis of what the Bible has to teach us about law and justice. The author is a lawyer and a committed Christian who takes the authority of Scripture seriously. He does not offer simplistic solutions but rather makes us think about the relationship between law and justice. All Christian lawyers should read this book in order to grapple for themselves with the question 'what does the Bible teach us about law and the role of lawyers in bringing about justice in society?'

This book is the fifth book to be published by Paternoster in the 'Christian Perspectives on Law' series. This series is supported by the Lawyers' Christian Fellowship (LCF), a body representing more than 1500 Christian lawyers in the UK. Information about LCF can be found on its website < www.lawcf.org > or by contacting the LCF Secretary:

Hilary Lyndon,
Church Villa,
29 Church Lane,
Temple Normanton,
Chesterfield
S42 5DB
(Tel. 01246 856783; email: admin@lawcf.org ; DX 720377 Chesterfield)

The previous four books were all edited books comprising papers from LCF Academic Conferences and if not available from your Paternoster stockist can be obtained from LCF. Those books used Christian principles derived from the Bible to analyse a wide range of issues: legal philosophy, human rights, environmental law, family law, criminal law, contract, trusts, corporate governance, employment law, legal history, euthanasia, religious freedom, public international law, regulatory law, relationism, education law and land law.

Christian Perspectives on Law Reform, edited by Paul R. Beaumont (Carlisle: Paternoster, 1998)
Christian Perspectives on Human Rights and Legal Philosophy, edited by Paul R. Beaumont (Carlisle: Paternoster, 1998)
Christian Perspectives on Law and Relationism, edited by Paul Beaumont and Keith Wotherspoon (Carlisle: Paternoster, 2000)
Christian Perspectives on the Limits of Law, edited by Paul Beaumont (Carlisle: Paternoster, 2002)

The previous four books provide a wealth of ideas about how to apply a Christian worldview to particular areas of law. Although the law changes rapidly many of the ideas in those books are of lasting value. However, David's book adds several important new dimensions to the series:

1   The first single-authored book. This is obvious, but the added value of a single-authored work is that it provides a much more sustained and coherent analysis than even the best edited collections.
2   It gives a systematic account of a biblical view of human laws that will remain a reference work for a very long time to come. It is not another book explaining that the Old Testament Law has been transformed by New Testament grace. Rather, it is a book about the role of law in society.
3   It takes forward the difficult task of addressing the relationship between law and justice in Christian thought.

Gary Haugen's *Good News About Injustice* (IVP, 1999) has excited a new generation of Christian lawyers about the need to use their legal training to counteract severe injustice in several countries in the world. Gary Haugen has founded International Justice Mission that helps to release children from prostitution and slavery and to defeat other undoubted evils: see < www.ijm.org >.

David McIlroy's book helps to lay a clear biblical foundation for the Christian lawyer to be excited about his or her task in bringing about justice within the legal system that he or she has been called to serve. It is a 'must read' for all Christian lawyers!

Professor Paul Beaumont
Head of School of Law and Professor of European Union
and Private International Law, University of Aberdeen.
Adviser to the Department of Constitutional Affairs
and the Scottish Executive on Private International Law.
Vice Chairman of Lawyers' Christian Fellowship.

Preface

There are many to whom thanks is due, because without their assistance this book would never have come to completion. First and foremost must come the Lawyers' Christian Fellowship, whose support has enabled its publication. Steve Sanderson first encouraged me to dream that this book could and should be written. Paul Beaumont's editorial skills helped to refine it. Numerous other members of the Lawyers' Christian Fellowship listened to and commented on the ideas developed here. Among them, and without any pretence that this is an exhaustive list, are Jonathan Burnside, Christine John, James Griffiths, Ian Miller, Mark Mullins, Chris Pain, Julian Rivers, John Scriven, James Wakefield and Gary Watt.

I am also especially grateful to John Duddington, editor of *Law & Justice*, Alan Duce, editor of *Justice Reflections*, and Eric Owen, editor of *Graya*, first for printing some of the thoughts brought to fruition here in the form of articles, and secondly for allowing them to be incorporated into this book.

Thanks also go to my clerks and colleagues in Chambers at 3 Paper Buildings for tolerating my absences either researching or writing, and to the staff at the libraries of the London Institute for Contemporary Christianity and Spurgeon's College, where much of the research has taken place.

Over and above those contributions, however, I have benefited from the support of my church, Bedford Hill Baptist Church, where the quest after God is a way of life, and of my family, my parents, and my brothers and sisters (both by blood and wedlock), Doug, Joy, James and Fiona. Finally, and most importantly, I am grateful to those whose sacrifice has been the greatest and whose love and encouragement the most appreciated, Rebecca, Emily and Joshua.

Introduction

The Bible was not written as a handbook for lawyers, policemen, or civil servants setting out a theology of human law. It is concerned with the dealings of God with human beings, and of human beings with God. Its focus is on the relationship between God and men: on how that relationship has been disrupted, on the consequences of that disruption, and on the steps taken by God to restore that relationship. So, it may seem that when reading the Bible to find out why human laws should be obeyed, and what ends human legal systems should be serving, we are asking the Bible to answer questions which it does not address.

However, halfway through the second book of the Bible, Exodus, we are confronted by what look to us like a mass of laws, and this continues, with only brief interruptions, until the end of the fifth book, Deuteronomy. Later, we find the curious phenomenon of love poems to the Law in the Psalms; followed by the prophetic cry for justice against Israel, Judah and the surrounding nations. In the New Testament, we find first Jesus and then Paul talking again about the Law, and the Bible concludes, in the book of Revelation, with the Last Judgement.

Law as a category is to be found throughout the Bible. To treat it, as the early Reformers have sometimes been accused of doing, as *the* controlling category of the Bible may have been an over-emphasis, but equally to ignore it, as has been the more modern preference, is an overreaction.

The main question theologians have asked about Law in the Bible is: how does this relate to grace, and what part does it play in God's plans of salvation? But for lawyers, policemen and civil servants, in fact for anyone, an important question for our daily lives is: what, if anything, does the Bible say about human laws and legal systems?

First, it says that they are God-given as a restraint on the worst excesses of human sinfulness. The biblical writers would be in substantial agreement with Hobbes, the philosopher, in his vision of life without authority as one which would be nasty, brutish and short.[1]

Secondly, the Bible teaches us that God is concerned not only with our relationship with him but also with our relationships with one another. To the first great commandment 'Love the Lord your God',[2] is added the second, 'Love your Neighbour as yourself.'[3] Human laws

---

[1] T. Hobbes, *Leviathan* (1651) pt. 1, ch. 13.

[2] Mark 12:30; Deuteronomy 6:4–5.

[3] Mark 12:30; Leviticus 19:18.

have a part to play in promoting harmonious relationships between people, and to provide peaceful dispute resolution mechanisms when those relationships break down.

How those principles are worked out through the Bible is the subject of this book.

1

The Character of God

The Bible contains a record of God's revelation of his character to human beings. That character is revealed through his relationship with them. Although aspects of God's character can be, and will be in this chapter, stated in propositional form, it must be remembered that 'God is personal, and, as such, he cannot be *reduced* to a series of propositional statements; persons cannot be *reduced* to propositions.'[1]

In a sense, this chapter ought to come at the end of this book, because the God of the Bible revealed his character to his people through his interactions with them in their history. What is set out below is not intended to be an exhaustive character sketch; it would be impossible to produce such a thing in respect of an infinite God. But certain aspects of who God is have profound implications for the place of law, including the place for human laws, within his plans for humanity.

The Lord is the Good Creator

In its canonical form, the Bible begins by asserting that the Lord God is the Creator God.[2] The concern of the biblical writers in describing the act of creation is not so much with the production of matter *ex nihilo* (although this is part of the truth which they express[3]) but rather with the creation of order out of chaos.[4] The act of creation is also an act of ordering.

The first chapter of Genesis tells us that when God had created the world, and everything in it, culminating in his creation of human beings, he saw that it was very good.[5] The writer of Genesis clearly intends his readers to understand that the Creator God is a good God, who creates good things and delights in them. He is interested in his creation and capable of being pleased by it (or saddened by it, as the biblical story later reveals).

---

[1] J.E. Colwell, *Living the Christian Story: The Distinctiveness of Christian Ethics*, 79 (emphasis mine). See also C.E. Gunton, *A Brief Theology of Revelation: The 1993 Warfield Lectures*, 100, 109. The distinction to be drawn is between *expressing* a personal relationship in propositional form, and *replacing* the personal relationship by a series of propositions.

[2] Genesis 1:1; also e.g., Isaiah 40:12, 21–22, 26.

[3] O. O'Donovan, *Resurrection and Moral Order: An Outline for Evangelical Ethics*, 63.

[4] E. Lucas, *Ezekiel: The People's Bible Commentary*.

[5] Genesis 1:31. In fact, God expresses a similar satisfaction about the goodness of what has been created on each day of creation after the first (cf. Gen. 1:10, 12, 18, 25).

The creation was intended to reflect the goodness of the Creator. It contains within it beauty and form, patterns and artistry. It forms a coherent whole because it is bound together by principles which human beings have been able to explore and which we call the 'laws' of physics (although what we mean by that term is our approximations to the divine pattern). There is strangeness and infinity built into our world, illustrated by the fact that pi, indispensable to accurate calculations regarding a circle, is an infinitely complex number.

The goodness of the Creator issues forth from his being into a creation which is both separate from him and yet encompassed by him.[6] And the Bible tells us that into that creation God placed his crowning glory: human beings. Somehow, into the world he had created, God chose to make space for humankind. In fact, the Bible teaches the remarkable message that human beings are at the heart of the divine creation.[7] God made human beings in his own image.[8] What precisely constitutes the image of God (*imago Dei*) has been a matter of considerable argument among theologians, but it includes the idea that human beings are meant to reflect God's character.[9]

God acted out of love in creating human beings. He did not have to make us in order to satisfy some internal craving within himself. He exercised a free choice to make us because his nature is love.

That love comes to its culmination in the incarnation of the Son of God who came to carry out a humiliating, self-sacrificial act of rescue in order to restore the *imago Dei* when the rest of humanity had defaced it. What is unique and distinctive about the Christian doctrine of creation 'is that the universe is the creation of *this* God, the one who has made himself known in the history of his people, the one who has defined himself in the gospel story as Father, Son and Spirit.'[10]

The Lord God is the Ultimate Reality

The biblical God is answerable to no one and to nothing but himself. He is not bound by anything other than his own nature. This state of affairs must follow as a matter of logic. If God is to be God he must be the ULTIMATE – the ultimate reality, the ultimate truth, and so on.[11]

---

[6] Acts 17:28.
[7] Genesis 1:26–30.
[8] Genesis 1:26–27.
[9] N.T. Wright, *What Saint Paul Really Said*, 148.
[10] Colwell, *Living the Christian Story*, 88.
[11] Cf. O'Donovan, *Resurrection*, 132, where he makes the point: 'If [divine authority] is to command us as absolute authority, it must command us as supreme reality.' See also 103, 227.

The theologian and Archbishop of Canterbury, Anselm, argued that God is the being greater than which nothing can be imagined. God can also be seen as the principle bound by no higher principle.

This state of affairs can be contrasted with the theology to be found in the fantasy novels, *The Dragonlance Chronicles*, in which the wizard Raistlin inhabits a world ruled over by three principal gods: a good god, a neutral god and an evil goddess. Throughout the books Raistlin slowly increases his powers by discovering and casting magic spells. In one of the later books, he goes into the realms of the gods and fights the evil goddess. In the course of this battle, Raistlin discovers that, *despite herself*, the evil goddess is bound to answer the spells that he casts in her name. It becomes clear, therefore, that the controlling principle in this imaginary universe is not the principal gods but the rule that they must answer spells cast in their name. It is that principle which is the ultimate reality. The rules rule the gods.

When Moses met the Lord God at the Burning Bush, he wanted to know the name, the character, of the god with whom he was dealing. The Lord's answer was 'I AM WHO I AM' (Exod. 3:14). 'I am' is part of the verb 'to be'. God was expressing his existence as the ultimate reality. You cannot define him by reference to anything else. *There is nothing to compare him with*. Before creation, he existed. He is the Great, Omnipotent Being. He is the Ultimate, the One, the Only. Christians do not believe in a pantheon of gods, but in one sovereign God over the whole universe. He has no rivals. He stands alone.

But the Lord's answer could also be translated 'I WILL BE WHAT I WILL BE'. This possible interpretation makes it clear that God is dynamic and not static. He identified himself to Moses as the God of Abraham, Isaac and Jacob (Exod. 3:6) – i.e. as the God who had been in relationship with Abraham, Isaac and Jacob – and in revealing himself to Moses he was promising that he would reveal himself to Moses through his words and actions into the future.[12]

The Christian God is the ultimate reality in our universe.[13] The Bible is insistent about that. He has no rivals. There is no one to compare him to.[14] There is no higher order principle to which he is answerable. *There is no rule above his rule*.

This is scary – because it means that we are totally dependent on him, on his will, on his character, and on his nature. And, indeed, that is what the Bible teaches: 'in him we live and move and have our being' (Acts 17:28). He created us and he sustains us.[15]

If all this is true, and it is of the utmost importance for our daily lives that it is, then the vital question is: what is the God of our universe like?

---

[12] Colwell, *Living the Christian Story*, 90.
[13] O'Donovan, *Resurrection*, 227.
[14] Isaiah 40:18–20, 25.
[15] Hebrews 1:3.

The answer is contained in the Bible's pages and, above all, in the face/person of Jesus.[16]

But how can we rely on his nature? The biblical answer is that God's self-revelation is reliable because God is the same yesterday, today and forever.[17] In fact, the Bible says this both about God[18] and about Jesus[19] (lest there be any doubt about the divinity of Jesus).

The fact that God's nature is constant is of the utmost importance to our relationship to him. The Christian God is not like some pagan deity, whose moods swing unpredictably and who is capricious. He is not subject to whims or fancies. On the contrary, he is a God who is pursuing in history the purposes which he had planned from before the creation of the world.[20] A God who was faithless would simply be unworthy of trust. He might even become unbelievable!

The Lord is the God who is by nature reliable and constant (Mal. 3:6). That is revealed in his deeds; they always correspond to his words (Ps. 111:7).[21] The Lord is constantly true to his nature. He is, in that limited sense, a law unto himself.[22] Although 'God is free to command *whatever* he wills ... this freedom is specifically to command whatever *he wills*. ... God is not arbitrary; he "cannot disown himself" (2 Tim. 2:13); he cannot be other than himself as defined in the gospel story.'[23]

God is living proof that, as William Shakespeare put it, 'To thine own self be true, and it must follow, as the night the day, thou canst not then be false to any man.'[24] The expressions of God's will, from creation, to redemption, to judgement, are always consistent with God's nature.

Frédéric de Coninck puts it this way:

[16] John 14:9.

[17] To say that God's nature is constant is *not* to swallow the pill of immutability wholesale. The traditional doctrine of immutability is not only inconsistent with the biblical witness, but an unwarranted theological restraint on God's freedom to choose to be in relationship with his creation: see K. Barth, *Church Dogmatics* II/1 493f.

[18] Malachi 3:6.

[19] Hebrews 13:8.

[20] Psalm 33:11.

[21] J.E. Goldingay, *Daniel*.

[22] O. O'Donovan, *The Desire of the Nations: Rediscovering the Roots of Political Theology*, 40, says: 'There is ... a theme of legal and cosmic stability in Israel's faith; yet it is not self-standing, but rests on the self-consistency of Israel's God, his *emeth* and *emunah*, truth and faithfulness, in confirming and upholding his own judgments.'

[23] Colwell, *Living the Christian Story*, 118, commenting on the thought of Karl Barth.

[24] *Hamlet* act 1, sc. 3, 1.76. Though there have to be considerable doubts as to whether this maxim can be applied equally to humans, despite Shakespeare's views on the subject.

What remains constant ... is the love of God. God does not change, in the sense that he always remains faithful to his love, to his promises, to his covenants. Therefore the permanence in his nature is to be found in his relational side. Under the influence of Greek philosophy we have sought to define a God whose substance is unchangeable, when in fact it is his love, the relationship he has with the world, which is unchangeable.[25]

God is Love

Although God's constancy is of some comfort, having a God who was constantly malicious would be of limited benefit to his creatures. This is not the picture of God that the Old Testament presents. Psalm 145 declares:

> The LORD is gracious and compassionate,
>   slow to anger and rich in love.
> The LORD is good to all;
>   he has compassion on all he has made. ...
> The LORD is faithful to all his promises
>   and loving towards all he has made.
> The LORD upholds all those who fall
>   and lifts up all who are bowed down.
> The eyes of all look to you,
>   and you give them their food at the proper time.
> You open your hand
>   and satisfy the desires of every living thing.
> The LORD is righteous in all his ways
>   and loving towards all he has made.
> (Ps. 145:8, 9, 13b–17)

Hence, the Apostle John was keen to emphasise that God is Love.[26] Please note, that John said 'God is Love', not that 'Love is God'. John's point is that God defines what love is. If we want to know what love is like, look at God.[27] Look at his character, look at his actions, look at his emotions and you will see what love is like. As humans we must avoid the temptation to make God in our image. He defines us; it is not for us to define him.

God's love led him to make a world in which there were creatures with free will, who could choose to accept or to reject him. God's love led him to persevere with the human race, despite its wickedness, and to

---

[25] F. de Coninck, *La justice et le pardon*, 6. Translation mine.
[26] 1 John 4:8, 16.
[27] 1 John 3:16: 'This is how we know what love is: Jesus Christ laid down his life for us.'

recommit himself to ensuring its future after the Flood through the promise of the rainbow.[28]

God's love led him to choose a man, Abraham, so that through him and his descendant(s), all the peoples on earth would be blessed. God's love led him to call the people of Israel out of slavery in Egypt, under the leadership of a reformed murderer, to become a holy nation and a kingdom of priests.[29]

God's love led him to persevere with the people of Israel despite their rebellion and sinfulness; it led him to tolerate their request for a human king and to transform it, beyond the predicted failure of the kings of Israel and Judah, into a promise of a righteous king whose reign would last forever.[30]

God's love manifested itself as *hesed*, which 'means his abiding loyalty to his covenant, his unshakeable will to keep his gracious promise. … The translation *"steadfast love"* (RSV) gets nearer the true meaning'[31] than the translations 'kindness' or 'love' which fail to capture its full flavour.

God's love for his people meant that he desired their holiness and could not tolerate their continued, unrepentant sinfulness. It led him to take them into exile and back again, to demonstrate his desire that they should be wholly devoted to him.

God's love led him to send his own Son to resolve the problem of human sin which had bedevilled the people of Israel. God's love led him to the cross, to an ignominious death and a glorious resurrection. It was a self-giving love that transcends in its scope any possible act of love which a human could exhibit.

This is how we know what love is: we look at what God has done in the history which the Bible records for us, and then we look supremely at the example of Jesus.

The paradigm of love

The biblical paradigm of love is not disinterested benevolence. Although a high form of love, it is not the ultimate expression of it. God displays even-handed benevolence through his *common grace*. In his *redemptive* purposes, which even his common grace serves, God displays a different form of love, which can be compared to the ideal of fatherly/motherly love. This is love that is offered unconditionally to the child, which takes the initiative and perseveres, which maintains the bond until the moment of death. But such love is not disinterested. It desires relationship; it seeks

---

[28] Genesis 8:20–9:17.

[29] Exodus 19:6.

[30] Isaiah 9:6–7.

[31] C.J.H. Wright, *Living as the People of God: The Relevance of Old Testament Ethics*, 135.

a free response which will lead to intimacy and communion.[32] That is the paradigm of *redemptive love* that is presented in the Bible, above all in the teachings of Jesus and the writings of the Apostle John:

> God so loved the world (John 3:16), despite its estrangement from and hostility to God's self, that God spared no cost to be reconciled to humanity (Rom. 5:6–11, 2 Cor. 5:18–20). God was not content with displaying a superior one-way love toward humanity; God sought a wholehearted relationship of committed, covenant love from humankind in return.[33]

The Lord is Sovereign

The Lord is God. The history of the people of Israel, from Moses to Malachi, is written to demonstrate the fact that there is only one true God, who is, despite outward appearances, the sovereign ruler of the universe.[34] His sovereignty arises from the fact of creation. The world belongs to him because *he* made it, because *he* ordered it.[35] The nature of his kingly rule becomes evident through his dealings with the world at the time of Noah (Gen. 6–9). He is a good God, who does not break faith with the creation that he has made,[36] but he is also a just and holy God who cannot endure human wickedness indefinitely, because of the moral pollution it causes to his world and, according to the writer of Genesis 6, the pain it causes him (Gen. 6:6).

The Lord's sovereignty is universal (Ps. 9:7; 22:8; 96:10).[37] From the ten plagues sent as a judgement on the gods of Egypt;[38] to the confrontation between Elijah and the prophets of Baal on Mount Carmel; via the historical books of Kings and Chronicles; to the prophecies of the exile from Jeremiah, Ezekiel and Isaiah 40ff., the message of the Old Testament is the same: the Lord, the God of Israel is not merely the national deity of an insignificant tribe but the rightful ruler of the whole universe.[39]

---

[32] L. Woodhead, 'Love and Justice', *Studies in Christian Ethics* 5.1 (1992), 44–63.

[33] C.D. Marshall, *Beyond Retribution: A New Testament Vision for Justice, Crime and Punishment*, 27, commenting on the thought of Woodhead.

[34] 'To the Lord your God belong the heavens, even the highest heavens, the earth and everything in it … [f]or the Lord your God is God of gods and Lord of lords, the great God, mighty and awesome …' (Deut. 10:14, 17).

[35] O'Donovan, *Desire*, 34.

[36] O'Donovan, *Desire*, 32.

[37] O'Donovan, *Desire*, 34.

[38] Exodus 12:12.

[39] See, for example, 1 Chronicles 16:31; 29:11–12; Psalm 9:7–8; 45:6; 47:7–9; 93:1–2; 103:19; 145:11–13; Isaiah 37:16; 40:15–17, 22–24.

At the moment of the destruction of the Temple and the exiling of Judah from the Promised Land, the prophet Ezekiel has a vision. Its location is not accidental. The fact that it occurred on the plains of Chebar in Babylonia[40] is a theological statement of great significance. It is a demonstration that God is not limited to Israel's borders.[41] The oracles against the nations that are the fulcrum of the book may also have the same function.[42]

The Lord is Holy

Love is not the only one of God's characteristics. God is also holy (*qodesh*). His holiness first of all denotes his other-ness.[43] Thus it is an aspect of his transcendence. God is other.[44] The Lord is different from, separate from, his creation. Unlike the gods of Egypt, Assyria, Babylon and the other surrounding nations, God could not be captured or represented by the image of something created. It was not possible to make an idol of him.

'Holiness' at its origin means 'set apart'. God's holiness is simply expressed in the Song of Hannah: 'There is no Holy One like the LORD, no one besides you' (1 Sam. 2:2). Holiness is 'the conception that God is wholly other than man and the universe that he has made'.[45] When applied to God, holiness 'became an attempt to express the conception of that total otherness which is the mark of what is neither mortal nor created'.[46]

Our God stands apart from his creation. God is not the creation but is above or upon it. He is not a nature-deity like the Egyptian gods were. He is not tied in to the cycle of the seasons or the rhythm of the day. He stands above and beyond his creation. But he does not remain transcendent, aloof. He comes down to earth to meet with men and the places where he is present are transformed and become holy. Wherever God and men meet, there is holy ground.[47]

The book of Ezekiel begins with an ecstatic vision of the majesty of the Lord God.[48] What marks out Ezekiel's vision is its strangeness. What he describes is like nothing in the created order, although there are elements that he recognises.

---

[40] Ezekiel 1:1.
[41] J.B. Taylor, *Ezekiel: An Introduction and Commentary*, 23, 41; B.C. Birch et al, *A Theological Introduction to the Old Testament*, 340.
[42] Ezekiel 25:1–32:32. Taylor, *Ezekiel*, 184, 198–9.
[43] Lucas, *Ezekiel*, 195.
[44] Taylor, *Ezekiel*, 40–1.
[45] G.A.F. Knight, *A Christian Theology of the Old Testament*, 78.
[46] Knight, *Christian Theology*, 80.
[47] Exodus 3:5; Joshua 5:15.
[48] Ezekiel 1–3.

'Holiness' also carries with it the idea of purity. The holiness of our God is pure, a brilliant blinding whiteness, a perfection, a spotlessness, it is a spiritual and moral quality of his being. The Lord God is not a pagan Zeus or Jupiter, a sort of divine 'Superman' subject to the same temptations and whims as humans, only more powerful. He is an awesome judge, a consuming fire, a terrible perfect being. He has nothing in common with *Superman*, the hero in blue and red, played by Christopher Reeve (and latterly Dean Cain), who was reduced to impotence by kryptonite.

'The "holiness" of God is not just an awesome "religious aura", it is a moral passion.'[49] This purity is often expressed in the Bible through the image of fire.[50] It is through a burning bush that God appears to Moses;[51] it is through fire that many of the offerings laid down in the Mosaic Law are to be presented; it is the total consumption of the bull, the wood, the water and even the stones of the altar which demonstrates on Mount Carmel that the Lord alone is the true God.[52]

The purity of God's holiness is further revealed by his abhorrence of sin: 'God is not separated from the world by distance ... He is separated from it by the sin with which it is diffused.'[53] As the prophet Habbakuk puts it: 'He is of such a pure countenance that he cannot even look upon sin' (Hab. 1:13).[54]

In his process of creation, God set humans apart as special, thus chosen or indeed holy. After sin entered the world humans were still set apart, but were now separated from God's holiness by their sin. By establishing the covenant and the religious systems with Israel God gave them an opportunity to regain that special relationship with him. When applied to God's people, the command 'Be holy, because I am holy' (Lev. 11: 44–45)[55] was a call to live a distinctive life of obedience and service.

For Israel, therefore, the fire of God's holiness became an image of both purification and judgement (Isa. 33:14; Heb. 10:31; 12:29). The furnace of God's holiness could burn off the impurities in his people, leaving them pure and shining like a precious metal.[56] But for others, nothing but useless slag would be left.[57]

---

[49] Lucas, *Ezekiel*, 119.
[50] Lucas, *Ezekiel*, 60–1. See also Ezekiel 10:7; Isaiah 6:5.
[51] Exodus 3:1–6.
[52] 1 Kings 18:16–39.
[53] Knight, *Christian Theology*, 82.
[54] Translation of D.M. Lloyd-Jones in *Romans: Atonement and Justification*, 9.
[55] Quoted and applied to Christians in 1 Peter 1:16.
[56] Cf. Isaiah 1:21–31; 48:10; Malachi 3:2–3; 1 Corinthians 3:10–15.
[57] Ezekiel 22:17–22.

God's burning purity can be either a threat or a promise. For those who re-cognise their moral state and throw themselves on God's mercy, wanting to live in his ways, the burning coals of God can purify and restore. However, those who refuse to recognise their impurity ... find that those same burning coals produce a conflagration that consumes and destroys them.[58]

The Lord is Light

To change the metaphor, God is Light.[59] Light dispels darkness. Darkness evaporates in the presence of Light. Darkness is swallowed up by Light. This is one of the great images with which the Apostle John begins his Gospel. He describes the advent of Jesus, the divine *Logos* into the world and declares: 'The light shines in the darkness, but the darkness has not understood it' (Jn. 1:5).[60]

John's Gospel provides an explanation for this lack of understanding: 'Light has come into the world, but men loved darkness instead of light because their deeds were evil. Everyone who does evil hates the light, and will not come into the light for fear that his deeds will be exposed' (Jn. 3:19–20). The light of God's purity reveals the blackness of human hearts and the wickedness of human deeds.

Looking forward to the future, Paul describes the Last Judgement as the moment when everything will be brought into the light (1 Cor. 3:12–15; 4:5; Eph. 5:8–13). At this point, sin, sickness, death and dark-ness will be dispelled from the universe and all creation will rejoice in the light of God's presence.

The Lord is Just[61]

The American theologian, Carl Henry, described the Christian God as 'the God of justice and of justification'.[62] Deuteronomy 32:4 declares: 'He is the Rock, his works are perfect, and all his ways are just. A faith-ful God who does no wrong, upright and just is he.' Christopher Wright goes so far as to say, rightly as we shall see in the following chapters, that, 'No idea is more all-pervasive in the Old Testament than that God is a God of righteousness and justice.'[63] It is upon

---

[58] Lucas, *Ezekiel*, 61.

[59] 1 John 1:5.

[60] R.A. Burridge, *John: The People's Bible Commentary*, 34. See also John 8:12; 12:35.

[61] Isaiah 30:18; see also Malachi 2:17.

[62] Quoted by John Stott in his foreword to G.A. Haugen, *Good News About In-justice: A Witness of Courage in a Hurting World*, 10.

[63] Wright, *People of God*, 133.

'righteousness and justice' that the very throne of God is built (Ps. 89:14; 97:2).[64]

'The Lord of all the earth does justice ... It is an unrelinquishable affirmation of biblical faith ... that it is he who determines the right, upholds and establishes it, and rules the world of history by it. He is the Lord of the right.'[65] As Elihu, one of Job's comforters, puts it in the final speech of the book before God himself speaks to Job: 'The Almighty is beyond our reach and exalted in power; in his justice and great righteousness, he does not oppress' (Job 37:23).

When Jehoshaphat instituted judicial reforms in Israel, he warned the newly appointed judges: 'let the fear of the Lord be upon you. Judge carefully, for with the Lord our God there is no injustice or partiality or bribery' (2 Chr. 19:7).

But what is justice? What does justice mean? The first thing to note is that 'justice' is related to 'righteousness'. Indeed, in French, one word 'justice' is used to cover both concepts.

As with love, we must let God's character and actions define our vision of justice rather than letting our vision of justice define our expectations of God. Much of the Old Testament is either an explanation to an unbelieving people of how their experiences are actually a demonstration of God's justice,[66] or alternatively a heartfelt questioning of God's justice in the face of his apparent inactivity in the face of unjust suffering.[67]

God's sovereignty gives him the authority to define what is good and right for human beings living in society. God's laws are not only an expression of his will for human beings; they are a reflection of his nature. God's laws are a revelation of his heart for justice and mercy; and of his love for his creation.

God's justice does not show favouritism. He treats everyone fairly. In the words of Psalm 36:

> Your love, O Lord, reaches to the heavens,
>   your faithfulness to the skies.
> Your righteousness is like the mighty mountains,
> Your justice like the great deep.
> O Lord, you preserve both man and beast.
> How priceless is your unfailing love!
> Both high and low among men
>   find refuge in the shadow of your wings.

---

[64] See also Psalm 9:16; 33:5; 99:4; 101:1. In the words of Elihu, Job's comforter, in Job 34:12: 'It is unthinkable that God would do wrong, that the Almighty would pervert justice.' See also Job 8:3; 34:17; 36:3.

[65] J. Muilenburg, *The Way of Israel: Biblical Faith and Ethics*, 65.

[66] E.g., the prophecies of Isaiah 1 – 36; Jeremiah and Ezekiel.

[67] The books of Job and Habbakuk, and Jeremiah 12:1, as well as various Psalms, e.g. Psalm 73.

They feast in the abundance of your house;
You give them drink from your river of delights.
For with you is the fountain of life;
In your light we see light.
(Ps. 36:5–9)

The Israelites were told: 'The Lord your God is ... the great God, mighty and awesome, who shows no partiality and accepts no bribes. He defends the cause of the fatherless and the widow, and loves the foreigner, giving him food and clothing' (Deut. 10:17–18).[68] God's love for all human beings expresses itself in a special concern for the most vulnerable – the orphan, the widow and the foreigner. God's justice is therefore displayed when he intervenes to protect and provide for them.

God's justice is displayed in his righteous actions to bring about the state of total rightness, shalom, in which the harmony of the created order, and the peace between God and the people he has created is restored. It is therefore characteristic of God's justice that it seeks to restore relationship.

But God's justice also holds human beings accountable for their actions. Within the moral order which God has established, there is going to be a day of reckoning. We instinctively respond to the idea of 'just deserts', to rewards that are merited and punishments that are warranted. The Bible teaches that there will be a day when God judges on this basis.[69]

The Lord is Merciful/Generous/Gracious

We tend to regard justice and mercy as if they were at least partially contradictory. But in biblical thought the contrast is between mercy and *judgement*, not justice. James 2:13 says, 'Mercy triumphs over judgement (*krisis*).'

Justice and mercy are seen in the Bible as concepts linked through the idea of deliverance. Therefore, the prophet Isaiah can write, 'Yet the Lord longs to be gracious to you; he rises to show you compassion. For the Lord is a God of justice' (Isa. 30:18). God's justice is seen by the Old Testament writers in his acts of delivering his people from oppression. But God's mercy is also seen at work by the Old Testament writers in his acts of delivering his people *even when they do not deserve it.*

Both God's justice and mercy are demonstrations of his love. God's justice is the demonstration of his love for the oppressed, vindicating them and rescuing them from their oppressors. God's mercy is the demonstration of his love even for the oppressors, giving them the

---

[68] See also Psalm 103:6; 140:12.
[69] Matthew 16:27; 25:31–46; Romans 14:10–12; 1 Corinthians 3:10–15; 2 Corinthians 5:10.

opportunity to turn away from evil, and enter into right relations with their victims and with their God.

In the most surprising context, we find the merciful nature of God reaffirmed. The prophet Jonah was summoned by God to prophesy against the Assyrian capital, Nineveh. Although the message was ostensibly one of judgement and impending destruction, Jonah ran away and had to be persuaded to return to his task by memorable means. Jonah's explanation for his actions was not, apparently, fear but rather a deep concern he had about the character of the God with whom he was dealing. Jonah says, 'O Lord, is this not what I said when I was still at home? That is why I was so quick to flee to Tarshish. I knew that you are a gracious and compassionate God, slow to anger and abounding in love, a God who relents from sending calamity' (Jonah 4:2).[70]

Jonah was painfully aware of all the destruction and deaths Assyria had caused to the northern kingdom of Israel, which was his home. He had been looking forward to Nineveh's destruction. The last thing he wanted was for his message to be heeded and for God to suspend his judgement. Yet that is exactly what happened.

The book of Jonah is conclusive proof, from within the Old Testament, that judgement is not God's preferred approach to dealing with human beings. But God takes persistent, inveterate rejection of himself with the utter seriousness one would expect of a deity who was committed to giving his creatures *real* free will.

Whether God's justice is experienced by us as judgement or mercy depends on our own attitudes. 'Judgement … is the form God's love assumes when it is resisted'.[71] But coercion and force are not God's preferred methods of interaction with human beings. Judgement is the consequence of humanity's rejection of God. We bring it upon ourselves.

The Wrath of God

'God is love' is a meaningful statement because love is essential to God's nature. A Christian could not write, 'God is wrath'. It is not fundamental to God's nature to be wrathful or to be angry.[72]

> Wrath is not a chronic case of ill temper on God's part but a measured commitment to act against evil and injustice in order to contain it and destroy it. Wrath is not, therefore, an ontological attribute of God's nature or a function of God's personality. It is an expression of God's will that is contingent

---

[70] See also Numbers 14:18.
[71] Colwell, *Living the Christian Story*, 93.
[72] J.M. Gundry-Volf, 'Expiation, Propitiation, Mercy Seat' in *Dictionary of Paul and his Letters*, 282.

upon the existence of evil. If there were no sin in the world, there would be no occasion for wrath.[73]

However, it is an uncomfortable truth that, faced with a sinful world, God's wrath is an inexorable manifestation of his love and his holiness.[74] A holy God, a good God, cannot be true to himself and tolerate the presence of evil in his creation indefinitely. 'God would not be God if He did not hate sin.'[75] God's wrath is nothing other than his hatred of sin and its consequences.

Christopher Marshall characterises the biblical picture of the wrath of God as revealed in the Old Testament as 'double-sided': 'It is positive insofar as it is directed at evil and oppression that hinders God's purposes of deliverance for the covenant people; it is negative in that God's people, both corporately and individually, suffer under punishment for their own sinfulness and injustice …'.[76]

As we will see in chapter 2, human beings have chosen to rebel against God – to reject his sovereignty, to refuse his love, to ignore his goodness, to flout his holiness, to hide from his light, to despise his justice and mock his mercy. For all these things and more, God has pronounced the sentence of death that hangs over each and every one of us:

> [The] wrath of God has been 'revealed against all ungodliness and unrighteousness of men'. … It was revealed in the Garden of Eden. Here is man created perfect, given a helpmeet equally perfect; and here they are, enjoying a life of communion with God. Man is the acme, the highest point of God's perfect creation, and He puts the man and the woman in Paradise. But they disobeyed Him, rebelled against Him, and listened to the Tempter. Then God came down and spoke to them in His wrath against sin, and turned them out of the Garden and told them of the consequences that they were going to reap.[77]

God created a perfect world, but human beings have damaged it and marred its beauty. Ultimately, the rebels, the criminals, who are disturbing, defacing, devastating and destroying his creation must be called to account and dealt with.

> God's wrath stands as a corollary to God's righteousness: 'since God's fidelity to covenant demands human response and responsibility, wrath is what one experiences when one rejects God's offer of justice'.[78] It is imperative to recognize, however, that for Paul divine wrath is not a divine property, or essential attribute, but the active presence of God's judgement toward 'all ungodliness and wickedness' (Rom. 1:18). The wrath of God is not

---

[73] Marshall, *Beyond Retribution*, 171.
[74] Lucas, *Ezekiel*, 59.
[75] Lloyd-Jones, *Romans*, 8–9.
[76] Marshall, *Beyond Retribution*, 170.
[77] Lloyd-Jones, *Romans*, 10.
[78] A.J. Tambasco, *A Theology of Atonement and Paul's Vision of Christianity*, 33.

vindictive indignation or the anger of divine retribution, but the divine response to human unfaithfulness.[79]

The wrath of God is not merely a matter of cause and effect. The biblical truth is that morality is relational. Ultimately morality is personal.[80] The moral order of the universe is not an abstract, impersonal, standard; it is expressed in the moral personality of a holy God.[81]

As participants in sinful rejection of our Creator and of his purposes for our lives, human beings are rebels against our king, prodigal children who have disowned our heavenly father. We deserve destruction, and that destruction is mediated by God's wrath.

However, God does not wish to destroy human beings. Instead, he longs to restore us to our rightful place, enjoying good, wholesome, productive relationships with himself, with one another and with his creation. For sinful humanity, God's wrath was his first word not his last word.

God the Father sent his special envoy, Jesus, the Son of God, to earth to deal with the rebels. But how he did so was surprising. Jesus revealed the extent of God's hatred of sin, not by the destruction of the rebels, but by dying for them.

His was a true war of liberation. When Jesus came to earth 2,000 years ago, he came to offer an amnesty to the rebels. He came to announce that if any of the rebels wished to switch sides, to join the liberating forces, then they would be welcomed and their past rebellion would be forgiven. And he confirmed his offer of amnesty by writing it in his own blood.

For the biblical writers, the wrath of God is not something that is equally apparent at all moments in time and in all places at once. Rather, it is hidden and constrained, awaiting that awful day when it will be released. The punishment of death which God pronounced on the human race is suspended over each one of us, and we are being given time in which to return to God and to experience his mercy and grace rather

---

[79] J.B. Green, 'Death of Christ' in *Dictionary of Paul and his Letters*, 206.

[80] Marshall, *Beyond Retribution*, 195.

[81] C.E.B. Cranfield, *A Critical and Exegetical Commentary on the Epistle to the Romans*, 1:109. Cf. Lloyd-Jones, *Romans*, 12: 'We must get this clear, and especially at the present time, because such a scholar as Professor C.H. Dodd in his Commentary on the Epistle to the Romans denies this altogether. He does not believe in the wrath of God against sin. He teaches that what this really means is that sin always brings its own punishment. If you put your finger into the fire you will have pain, you will burn yourself. He does not believe that God, in addition to the immediate consequences, metes out punishment in a "wrath to come". But God says that He is going to do so, and in some cases He has done so already. That is the wrath of God, and it has been manifested.'

than his wrath. Because God's wrath is only partially disclosed at the present time, it is proper to speak in terms of *God's gracious wrath*, that partial revelation of his condemnation of evil, whereby God withdraws his restraining hand, so that people experience something of the full consequences of their sins for themselves, in the hope that, as a result, they will repent and further judgement might be avoided (cf. Ezra 9:13–15).

Conclusion: The Harmony of God's Characteristics

The characteristics of God must not be seen as if they somehow work against one another. God is no schizophrenic. On the contrary, he is a God of integrity and integration. His personality is not disintegrating; it is integrated. Any action of God's is inevitably, inexorably, an action of all his characteristics working together.

God is perfectly loving but also perfectly just. He is perfectly holy. His holiness and justice demands that our sins be paid for, that a punishment be served for them. His love declared that punishment served, and the price paid, when Jesus Christ died in our stead on the cross. This was necessary because God is consistent to himself. In all his ways he has to be loving, holy and just. To do otherwise would be to be flawed, to be imperfect, and that is something he is not. He is an integrated being, a whole, a unity. In him there is no incongruence; there are no shades of dark; all is light and purity.

The cross is a demonstration of his holiness, in his judgement on human sinfulness. The cross is a demonstration of his justice, in that sin is not allowed to go unpunished. The cross is a demonstration of his love, in that God paid the price of sin himself.

Why does all of this matter in a book about human laws? Because if we want to know how God feels about human laws and legal systems, we need to have some idea of what God is like. If the God with whom we had to contend was a war god, like the Roman god, Mars, then we could expect him to approve of a legal system which encouraged strength, aggression and brutality. But as the God we have to deal with is loving, just and holy we would expect him to prefer laws and legal systems which promote such virtues.

It also matters because, 'It is God's own self who models and gives content to those qualities of character and conduct that are ethically most important for God's people, such as holiness, love, justice, mercy and compassion (Mic. 6:8).'[82]

---

[82] Marshall, *Beyond Retribution*, 260.

2

Law, Creation and the Fall

Creation

The creation narratives of the book of Genesis are not written as a scientific textbook. The fundamental concern of the writer was to stress that the world was planned, designed and built by one unique Creator God.[1] In a region dominated by the pagan pantheons of Mesopotamia and Egypt, such an assertion was revolutionary. And the work of this God, says the writer of Genesis 1, was to bring order out of chaos. This was what was revealed to the writer of the creation narratives as he reflected on the creation which God had made.

The writer of Genesis would have agreed with the Apostle Paul, who wrote in 1 Corinthians 14:33, in a wholly different context, that 'God is not a God of disorder but of peace.' Out of chaos and formlessness, says the writer of Genesis, the Lord God created a world of order and peace (shalom), a world in which everything was harmonious and in which everything had its proper place. The 'natural' reality of the created world which God made was an ordered reality, and part of that order was a moral order.

The Genesis narratives tell us that God looked at his creation and saw that it was good. It was worthy of its Creator and a testimony to his character, to his love, his generosity and his greatness.

Genesis 1–2 contains two differing, and possibly parallel, creation accounts. Each has its own distinct point to make. Genesis 1 emphasises the place of humankind as the pinnacle of God's creation, uniquely ennobled by bearing the *imago Dei*, the image of God. Genesis 2 lays stress on the place of humankind as part and parcel of the created order. So, from the beginning, and even in our unfallen state, humans partook of the nature of both heaven and earth.

Humans are created beings, created by God, for God. The Westminster Confession elaborating on this theme says, 'The chief end of Man is to glorify God and enjoy him forever.' However, men and women have not been created as robots, but as beings with free will, capable of freely choosing to love God or to reject God. We have been made as independent moral agents.

God looked at human beings, as he created them, and saw that they were good. The world was originally a created perfection. It is obviously not so today. What happened? The Bible's answer to that question is that the Fall has happened.

---

[1] See also Psalm 96:5.

The Fall

The apple

Even in its perfect state, the world contained a Law. God told Adam: 'You are free to eat from any tree in the garden; but you must not eat from the tree of the knowledge of good and evil, for when you eat of it you will surely die' (Gen. 2:16–17). God, the good Lawgiver, created a perfect world, in which Adam had any number of trees from which to eat. Only one was denied him. There was a Law, and attached to that Law, there was a penalty: death.

In the Garden of Eden, before the Fall, Adam was in relationship with God. Within the context of that relationship, God had entrusted Adam with dominion over the earth. But God had also given Adam a command, an instruction. God placed before Adam a choice: Adam could choose to obey God or to disobey God.

Love must be free to be love. Robots cannot love. They can be programmed to exhibit signs that could be mistaken for affection but they cannot offer spontaneous, free, genuine love. For love to be *real*, the possibility of rejection, of hatred, must also be *real*. Even in the perfect world he had created, God left that possibility open.

When the devil disguised as a serpent came to tempt Eve, he focussed on the negative in the divine law. The question he asked Eve was: 'Did God really say, "You must not eat from *any* tree in the garden?" '[2] In fact, what God had said was that Adam and Eve were free to eat the fruit of any of the many trees in the garden, except one. The area of what was permitted to them was far greater than the one thing that they had been forbidden.

The second thing the serpent did when tempting Eve was to deny the reality of the penalty: 'You will not surely die', he said,[3] as if God would not be true to his word, and carry out the threatened punishment.

Thirdly, the serpent suggested that God was withholding from Eve something good, something desirable, the chance to be 'like God, knowing good and evil' (Gen. 3:5). The bitter irony was that human beings' godlikeness, the *imago Dei* that we bear, was horribly marred and defaced as a result of the decision to eat the apple. Our moral judgements became skewed. The consequences of giving in to the temptation were the opposite of what the devil suggested.

The issues at stake can be explored from a number of different perspectives: the command can be seen as a test to see whether Adam and Eve truly believed that God was good. Alternatively, the question was what mattered most to Adam and Eve: was it their relationship with God or was it grasping towards equality with God? The essence of Adam and Eve's sin can be seen as faithlessness, idolatry or greed. But it was also an

---

[2] Genesis 3:1.
[3] Genesis 3:4.

act of rebellion. It was a rejection of God's authority; a deliberate, defiant breaking of his law.[4] Therefore, one of the New Testament writers could say: 'Everyone who sins breaks the law; in fact, sin is lawlessness' (1 Jn. 3:4).' From its very beginnings, human sinfulness expressed itself in lawlessness and law breaking. Adam and Eve wanted to be a law unto themselves.

William Wilberforce, the great campaigner against slavery, described it this way: 'Sin is considered in Scripture as rebellion against the sovereignty of God, and every different act of it equally violates his law, and, if persevered in, disclaims his supremacy.'[5]

God's response to the original sin was one of judgement, but of judgement tempered by grace. Adam and Eve were evicted from the garden; they were denied access to the tree of life but their lives were not ended instantly.

The Hebrew name *adam* means 'the Man'. *Adam* was not just any old person; he was the first man. His actions set the tone for human behaviour down the years. His choices have become ingrained into the character of every human being born since. All of us have individually chosen to follow in his footsteps: rejecting God and God's good laws. Theologians call this the doctrine of original sin. As G.K. Chesterton dryly observed, 'original sin ... is the only part of Christian theology which can really be proved.'[6]

Through the doctrine of original sin, humankind is identified as having universally rebelled against God and thus merits God's disfavour. As a result of Adam's sin, God as Creator has the absolute right to destroy his creatures, he could execute the punishment for sin: death, at any moment he chooses. Death is a universal fact of life. It is the ultimate statistic: one out of every one people born dies. We are all mortal. But the sentence is not carried out immediately. It is suspended. In his mercy, God allows us to endure only limited punishment throughout our mortal lives, and a commutation of the penalty is available to us.

Humankind's Fall in the Garden of Eden was over an apple which carried the promise of 'being like God, knowing good and evil' (Gen. 3:5). In other words, it carried the promise of being able to make your own decisions about what was good and evil, of no longer having to rely on God's judgement, of no longer being under his authority. Adam and Eve grasped at the opportunity of escaping from God's authority.

On the other hand, humankind's salvation was a direct result of Jesus' choice to obey authority, to submit to the will of the Father when wrestling with temptation in the Garden of Gethsemane (Mt. 26:36–46).

---

[4] Wright, *People of God*, 71.
[5] W. Wilberforce, *A Practical View of Christianity*, 149. See also Norman Anderson who notes the significance of *anomia* ('lawlessness') as one of the biblical definitions of sin: *Freedom under Law*, 23.
[6] G.K. Chesterton, *Orthodoxy*, 10.

In so doing, Jesus became the founder of a new humanity, a Second Adam, if you will, and all who are associated with him, all who are 'in Christ', will not be permanently separated from God by death (1 Cor. 15:22; Rom. 5:12–19). In Christ, the *imago Dei* has been expressed, restored and fulfilled (Phil. 2:6–11).

Sin as slavery; sin as disease

The Bible teaches that sin is the result of deliberate wrong moral choices made by human beings. But it also teaches that sin is more than that. Sin is an enslaving power; it is a cancer of the human soul. Ziesler says: '[sin] is both what we do by choice, voluntary action, and also a power whose grip we cannot escape simply by deciding to'.[7] It is not just that we sin; we are sinful (sin-full). We are like alcoholics, who both choose to have drink after drink, and yet also find ourselves compelled to do so by something inside.

The doctrine of total depravity

The theologian John Calvin taught that we are so full of sin that each and every part of our personality is affected by it (the doctrine of 'total depravity'). Now Calvin did not mean that all parts of every human being are as bad as they could possibly be; rather what he meant was that if the human character is like a book, each page is stained. Not all are illegible, but each aspect of our personalities is marked by sin.

After the Fall, the world is a sick and sinful place, but it retains within it the impression of the good gifts of God before the Fall. The *imago Dei* is defaced, but it is not destroyed. Creation is fallen but it is not annihilated.

Justice and the Good Gifts of God Before the Fall

As we saw in chapter 1, the biblical vision of justice is that true justice is God's justice. It flows from his character. Although human beings have invariably chosen to do evil, they inhabit a world which was originally created by God to be good. It was a world in which God endowed human beings with a certain status, capacity and opportunities in which they could discover and fulfil their potential. It was a world that would have been characterised by justice and peace (shalom).

One of the most enduring formulations of justice is to be found in Justinian's Digest 'Give to each what is due to him'.[8] It is also to be found in Christian thought in the writings of Thomas Aquinas who said: 'Acts

---

[7] J.A. Ziesler, *Pauline Christianity*, 75–6, 92.

[8] The complete Justinian formula is *honeste vivere, neminem laedere, suum cuique tribuere.*

of justice are ordered to keeping the peace among men which comes about when everyone has what is his.'[9]

The problem with this formulation is that without an independent account of what is due to people it can be used to justify the most inhuman treatment of people; indeed, in its German translation, *Jedem das seine*, it was the motto above the gates of the Buchenwald concentration camp.[10]

In his clarion call for Christians to rediscover a ministry of justice, *Good News about Injustice*, Gary Haugen says this: 'Justice occurs when power and authority is exercised in conformity with God's standards. Injustice occurs when power is misused to take from others what God has given them, namely, their life, dignity, liberty or the fruits of their love and labour.'[11]

The vital content for the formulation – give to each what is due to him – is that what is due to people is what God has given to them. Haugen suggests that this includes people's lives, their dignity, their liberty and the right to the fruits of their love and labour. While this list is not exhaustive, because God gave each of these good gifts to human beings before the Fall, they have a claim to be regarded as primary.

God has given human beings life

The Bible teaches us that God gave life to the human race as a whole and gives life to us as individuals.[12] Christianity values life as God's gift, which is why Cain, though a murderer, was granted God's protection,[13] and why the commandment says 'Do not murder'. This is also the reason why Christianity attacks abortion and euthanasia as depriving the 'innocents' of their God-given life.[14] Apart from the use of sword by governing authorities, for defined purposes and as a proportionate response to evil,[15] no one has authority to take that life away.

[9] Aquinas, *Summa Contra Gentiles* book 3, chapter 34, quoted from *Selected Writings*, 278.

[10] Observation of J.W. Montgomery, 'Why a Christian Philosophy of Law?', in P. Beaumont (ed.), *Christian Perspectives on Human Rights and Legal Philosophy*, 84. See also B. Wortley, 'The Christian Tradition in English Law', *Law & Justice* 150 (2003), 11, for a discussion of how this formula was interpreted as limited to the rights of freemen in the ancient world.

[11] Haugen, *Good News*, 72; see also J. Ellul, *Le Fondement Théologique du Droit*, 28: '… dans l'Ecriture est juste seulement ce qui est conforme à la volonté de Dieu'.

[12] Psalm 139.

[13] Genesis 4:15. See J. Witte, *Law and Protestantism: The Legal Teachings of the Lutheran Reformation*, 300.

[14] J.W. Montgomery, 'Whose Life Anyway? A Re-examination of Suicide and Assisted Suicide', in P. Beaumont (ed.), *Christian Perspectives on Law Reform*, 83.

[15] Such a proportionate response might include, in increasing order of controversy, the maintenance of civil order, the waging of 'just wars' and the execution of capital punishment.

When Adam and Eve were evicted from the Garden of Eden, God could have made an end of the human race there and then. We were, and still are, individually and as a race, deserving of instant death for our sins (Gen. 2:17; 3:17–19; Rom. 6:23). That God stays his hand, and does not destroy us immediately is an act of immeasurable forbearance on his part.

For these reasons, humanity has no rights against God.[16] Nonetheless, God does not destroy us in an instant, as we deserve, but continues to bless us. He causes his rain to fall on both the just and the unjust (Mt. 5:45). In fact, every good gift that we enjoy comes from God (Jas. 1:17). We are, even in our sinful states, recipients of 'common grace', i.e. God's indiscriminate showering of temporal (and therefore temporary) blessings.

God has given human beings dignity[17]

God gave human beings dignity by making us in his image. The creation narratives teach us that human beings are special, that they are created in the image of God (Gen. 1:27). Because all human beings are made in the image of God, each and every human being is infinitely valuable.[18] All have the right to opportunities and to be given the potential to flourish. The biblical view of justice is not utilitarian, in that it seeks the good of each and every one, not just the greatest happiness of the greatest number.

As the writers of the *Evangelical Contribution On Northern Ireland* report on human rights put it: 'human being is defined by humanity's creation in God's image … human beings [therefore] have dignity, value and worth … Human dignity is given … as part of human createdness in the divine image.'[19]

How humans behave to one another matters not just because of who we are but also because of the God who made us. Because human beings are made in God's image, an assault on another human being is virtually an assault on God himself.[20]

Moreover, a Christian vision of the dignity of human beings rests not only on the fact that we are all created in the image of God, but also

[16] A.J. Rivers, 'A Bill of Rights for the United Kingdom?', in Beaumont (ed.), *Law Reform*, 42. Cf. R. Forster, *The Kingdom of Jesus*, 40.

[17] Article 5 of the Lausanne Covenant; F. Catherwood, *A Better Way: The Case for a Christian Social Order*, 36–52; M. de Blois, 'The Foundation of Human Rights: A Christian Perspective', in Beaumont (ed.), *Human Rights*, 14–18; M. Schluter and D. Lee, *R Factor*, 267; J.R.W. Stott, *Issues Facing Christians Today*, 154–6; P. Marcel, 'La Vraie Révolution: L'Intelligence du Coeur', in *Esprit Révolutionnaire et Foi Chrétienne*, 81; Wortley, 'Christian Tradition', 12; Witte, *Law and Protestantism*, 299.

[18] Haugen, *Good News,* 29.

[19] A. Thompson and C. McAdam, *A Shared Vision? Human Rights and the Church*, 30.

[20] W.J. Dumbrell, *Covenant and Creation: A Theology of the Old Testament Covenants,* 28; see also Rivers, 'Bill of Rights?', 42. See chapter 4.

on the fact that Jesus, the Son of God, became incarnate as a man,[21] God dignified human beings by becoming incarnate as one himself! And Jesus himself was conspicuous by the dignity with which he treated the outsiders in his society.[22] Ultimately, he demonstrated how much he thought individuals were worth by being willing to die for us.[23]

William Temple summed up the Christian position in the following words:

> The primary principle of Christian Ethics and Christian politics must be respect for every person simply as a person. If each man and woman is a child of God, whom God loves and for whom Christ died, then there is in each a worth absolutely independent of all usefulness to society.[24]

Therefore, all human beings have inherent dignity because they are created in the image of God, and because of their inherent worth, all human beings are possessed of intrinsic rights which no other human being can legitimately take away.[25]

The Bible acknowledges the truth in Kant's assertion that 'Human beings are ends not means'.[26] As members of the human family, we are under an obligation of love for others as worthy of equal care and respect as fellow creations of God.

As all human beings are created in God's image, with dignity and worth, so there is a powerful Christian argument for the fundamental equality of all people.[27] But Christian equality is different from secular ideas of equality, which at worst mean nothing other than that all people

---

[21] Stott, *Issues*, 155.

[22] Catherwood, *Better Way*, 36. See, for example, his treatment of the Samaritan woman at the well (Jn. 4:1–42), of Zacchaeus the tax collector (Lk. 19:1–9), of the ten lepers (Lk. 17:11–19) and his general reputation for eating with 'sinners' (Mt. 9:9–13; Mk. 2:13–17; Lk. 5:27–32).

[23] It is currently popular to see Jesus' death as representative, i.e. the one for the many. While that is certainly true, the biblical message is also that Jesus died for each and every one of us as individuals, i.e. that he died as our substitute. He paid the price for my sin.

[24] W. Temple, *Christianity and Social Order*, 67, quoted by Denning in *The Influence of Religion on Law*, 27.

[25] R.J. Neuhaus, 'The Catholic Difference', in C. Colson and R.J. Neuhaus (eds.), *Evangelicals and Catholics Together: Toward a Common Mission*, 177. See also D.H. McIlroy, 'A Christian State?', *Law & Justice* 120 (1994), 32 at 36; J.W. Montgomery, *Human Rights and Human Dignity*; Rivers, 'Bill of Rights?', 41–2; Stott, *Issues*, 149–62.

[26] I. Kant, *Foundations of the Metaphysics of Morals*, 47. O'Donovan explores how this proposition ought to be understood from a Christian perspective in *Resurrection*, 234–6.

[27] de Blois, 'Foundation of Human Rights', 18–21; see also Stott, *Issues*, 156–9; P. Brown, 'L'élitisme païen', *Histoire de la vie privée* Tome I, 239–41; O'Donovan, *Resurrection*, 228–9.

(usually with the conspicuous exception of the theory's proponent) are equally expendable. Christianity teaches that all are *equally valuable*.[28] The Christian idea of equality is given expression in the emphasis placed on equal land holding in the Mosaic Law and the prophets.[29]

God has given human beings liberty

When he created us, God gave human beings liberty.[30] We were not created as robots, obliged to do his bidding, but as creatures with free will able to choose to love him or to disobey him. In the Garden of Eden, Adam and Eve were given the choice to obey God or to eat the forbidden fruit.[31] Of course, Christians believe that obeying biblical morality is good, and knowing/loving God is the supreme good. But Christians also recognise that God has created human beings with free will and that it is a voluntary response that he desires of them.[32]

The Christian vision of liberty is that it is having the capacity and the opportunity to make meaningful moral choices.[33] It also involves being held responsible for those choices.[34] It is therefore different from the idea of freedom in so-called 'free love', where what is meant is the ability to choose without facing the consequences. Each of us will answer to God one day for the decisions we have taken in our lives.[35]

William Temple expounds upon the impact of the idea of liberty on relationships between the government and the citizen in his classic work, *Christianity and Social Order.*

[28] Temple, *Christianity and Social Order*, 37; see also B. Griffiths, *Morality and the Marketplace*, 37, 95.

[29] See Numbers 26:52–56; Joshua 13–18; Isaiah 5:8–10; Jeremiah 22:13–17; Micah 2:1–5, 4:4, Amos 5:11–12; Ezekiel 45:1–10; Zechariah 3:10. These themes are explored further in 'That there might be equality: An examination of the biblical perspective on economic equality, and its missiological relevance', Mohan Seevaratnam (unpublished dissertation, Ware, Herts: All Nations Christian College, 1998). See also Acts 4:32–35.

[30] Aquinas, *Summa Theologice* I–II, Prologue; O'Donovan, *Resurrection*, 109.

[31] Genesis 2:16–17.

[32] See Temple, *Christianity and Social Order*, 37.

[33] I have deliberately used the term 'liberty' here in its political sense. It is a very different concept from 'Christian freedom', as to which see O'Donovan, *Resurrection*, 109, 114, 120.

[34] J.D. Charles, 'Crime, The Christian and Capital Justice', *JETS* 38.3 (1995) 438n.31: '... to be punished ... because we in fact deserved it is to be treated as a dignified human moral agent, created in the image of God'; see also J.A. Kirk, *The Meaning of Freedom: A Study of Secular, Muslim and Christian Views*, 86, 244.

[35] It is part of the Christian understanding of human dignity that it involves having our decisions taken seriously by God, including, in the final analysis, our decision to reject him.

The person is primary not the society; the State exists for the citizen, not the citizen for the State. The first aim of social progress must be to give the fullest possible scope for the exercise of all powers and qualities which are distinctly personal; and of these the most fundamental is deliberate choice. Consequently society must be so arranged as to give to every citizen the maximum opportunity for making deliberate choices and the best possible training for the use of that opportunity ... it is the responsible exercise of deliberate choice which most fully expresses personality and best deserves the great name of freedom.[36]

It is central to Christianity's anthropology (if it may be called that), that human beings are autonomous moral agents, and that God gave us that autonomous moral capacity and does not seek to deny it to us despite our sinfulness. We are not destined to be robots, pre-programmed to obey him; other courses of action are equally possible.

But, we are all, in the end, accountable to God for how we have used our freedom. We are all accountable to God for the choices we have made. Each one of us is made in the image of God. We are accountable for the damage we have done to that image in ourselves and in others. Each one of us will be judged by him for our own sins,[37] and on the basis of our own response to his love for us expressed through his Son, Jesus Christ.[38]

God has given human beings the capacity for rewarding work and meaningful relationships

Despite the Fall, the creation ordinances, identified by Ernest Reisinger as the procreation command to be fruitful and multiply (Gen. 1:27–28), the Sabbath command to rest on the seventh day (Gen. 2:2–3), the work command (Gen. 2:15) and the marriage command (Gen. 2:24)[39] remain valid as both divine commands and divine blessings. In spite of the Fall, and the difficulties and frustrations which it entails, marriage and having children, work and rest are all good and God-given.

God gave human beings the capacity and the responsibility to work. Human work should be so structured in a way that it is rewarding, meaningful and can be seen to be valuable.[40] Human working patterns should include time off, rest, to prevent it becoming oppressive. When work is organised in this way, it becomes a good, to the extent that the writer of Ecclesiastes could say: 'A man can do nothing better than to eat and drink and find satisfaction in his work' (Eccl. 2:24).[41]

---

[36] Temple, *Christianity and Social Order*, 67. See also Griffiths, *Morality and the Marketplace*, 92–3.
[37] Ezekiel 18; Romans 3:23.
[38] John 3:16.
[39] E. Reisinger, *The Law and the Gospel*, 13–14.
[40] Catherwood, *Better Way*, 38.
[41] Ecclesiastes 2:24.

God gave human beings the capacity and the responsibility to love. The human condition is social.[42] As Aristotle put it: 'He who is unable to live in society, or who has no need because he is sufficient for himself, must be either a beast or a god.'[43] 'The first pages of the Bible make clear that people are not created only as individuals to live on their own ... people are created in communion with other people. Not only the individual, but also the communities of individuals, such as marriage and families, deserve respect.'[44] Human society should be so organised that good, loving relationships have a conducive climate in which to grow and develop.

Christianity recognises that:

> human being is fundamentally relational. Human identity and purposes is found and grounded in a threefold set of relationships – with God, with other human beings and with the rest of creation. These relationships are central to what it means to be human and to the extent to which these relationships are damaged, human beings fail to know the fullness of their identity and purpose. Thus any concept which privileges the notion of the human being as a self-defining individual prior to his or her relational identity is flawed.[45]

The Bible places the highest value on relationships. God chose the Father-Son relationship in order to explain the relationship between God the Father and the incarnate Jesus (e.g. Jn. 3:16). God chose the marriage relationship to express the union between Christ and his church (Eph. 5:22–32). Relationships are fundamental to who we are as human beings. We do not exist only as individuals; we are people, with both our individual traits and our networks of relationships that impact on who we are.

The Consequences of the Fall Mitigated

As created, the natural world was a pointer to the nature of its Creator. The vastness of its oceans, the splendour of its mountains, the beauty of its woods and fields, the diversity of its fauna and flora, all of these were intended to be a testimony to the awesome nature of its maker. Human beings, engaged in rewarding work, enjoying loving relationships, making positive choices, and treating one another with dignity, were to

---

[42] de Blois, 'Foundation of Human Rights', 15; see also Temple, *Christianity and Social Order*, 63.

[43] Aristotle, *Politics* Book 1, 1256b.

[44] de Blois, 'Foundation of Human Rights', 15; O'Donovan, *Desire*, 266.

[45] Thompson and McAdam, *A Shared Vision?*, 30; see also Schluter and Lee, *R Factor*, 176; Temple, *Christianity and Social Order*, 69, 71; and Preston's 1976 'Introduction' in *Christianity and Social Order*, 15.

be the high point of this expression. Nature, including humanity, was imprinted with the moral nature of the Creator.

The biblical picture is that the Fall of humankind disrupted the moral order of creation. This disruption of shalom, this fracturing of relationships between God and humankind had consequences. Some of those consequences are expressed in Genesis 3:14–19. The dislocation in the vertical relationship between God and human beings was reflected in a disruption of the horizontal relationships between men and women.

But just as human beings were the pinnacle of God's creation, so their descent into sin has affected the world around us. Just as we are no longer perfect; so the world in which we live is marred and scarred. Famines, floods and droughts are not just 'natural phenomena', they are an expression, an outworking of the fallen nature of our world.

However, there is enough of the original beauty and design in nature still visible for it to point beyond itself to the God who created it. Although nature contains enough clues to lead men to God and to a grasp of the moral nature of the universe,[46] and although 'the requirements of the law are written on [the] hearts [of men]', in their consciences,[47] these are unreliable guides, because human beings 'suppress the truth by their wickedness'.[48] But the fault for our failure to discern truth about God from nature lies not with God for failing to reveal himself and his requirements, but with us for our wilful, sinful blindness.

The problem with discerning morality from nature is not, as Hume believed, that it is impossible or impermissible to derive an 'ought' from an 'is'. Even a legal positivist like H.L.A. Hart started from an 'is'; it *is* a fact that people want to survive, in order to derive an 'ought'; therefore the law *ought* to be framed so as to enable them to do so.[49] The problem with discerning morality from nature is that creation is fallen; so nature is no longer a perfect reflection of God's character, and human beings are sinful; we no longer have perfect vision to discern the pattern from what we observe.[50]

Natural law

The Apostle Paul wrote this in Romans 2:14–15:

> Indeed, *when Gentiles*, who do not have the law, *do by nature things required by the law*, they are a law for themselves, even though they do not have the law,

---

[46] 'For since the creation of the world God's invisible qualities – his eternal power and divine nature – have been clearly seen, being understood from what has been made, *so that men are without excuse*', men have 'become filled with every kind of wickedness, evil, greed and depravity' (Rom. 1:20, 29).

[47] Romans 2:15. See O'Donovan, *Resurrection*, 114–19, for a discussion of the meaning of 'conscience' in Paul's Greek and its subsequent evolution in moral discourse.

[48] Romans 1:18; O'Donovan, *Resurrection*, 82, 88.

[49] H.L.A. Hart, *The Concept of Law*, 191–200.

[50] Marshall, *Beyond Retribution*, 172.

since *they show that the requirements of the law are written on their hearts*, their consciences also bearing witness, and their thoughts now accusing, now even defending them.[51]

Within the Christian Church throughout the Middle Ages, thinkers such as Thomas Aquinas and others were concerned to come up with a universal 'natural' law applicable to all humanity by virtue of its irresistible appeal to central concepts of the good accepted as valid by everyone, and clearly related to the essential nature of humankind.

The problem with 'natural law' down the years has been that because of our sinfulness and the fallen nature of our intellect,[52] there is very little universal agreement as to what is good.[53] In order to defend natural law as an inherent product of human rationality, either one has to retreat with John Finnis to such a high level of abstraction that the concepts derived are of only tenuous practical application,[54] or one has to concede that the moral principles to be derived from nature are not in fact universally known, but only capable of being universally known. Once that concession has been made, it is both possible and arguably necessary to locate natural law principles within the context of revelation.[55]

On this view of natural law, the ethical revelation from nature, the clearer exposition of God's requirements in the Ten Commandments and the rest of the Mosaic Law, and finally the definitive exploration of the demands of God's law by Jesus relate to one another as different degrees of light illuminating the same ethical landscape. The first as the first light before dawn, when indistinct shadowy outlines are all that can be discerned, the second like the dawning sunlight, as colours emerge and shapes become clearer, and the last like the noonday sun when features and forms are at their brightest.[56]

[51] Italics mine. In understanding this passage I side with those scholars who reject Barth's reading of 'Gentiles' as referring to 'Gentile Christians', and understand it in the usual sense of meaning those unbelieving non-Jews: see J.W. Montgomery, 'Law and Justice', *Law & Justice* 120 (1994), 18, and F.F. Bruce, *The Epistle of Paul to the Romans: An Introduction and Commentary*, 86.

[52] Which, following Calvin's doctrine of total depravity, must logically be affected just as much as any other part of our make-up. Cf. Marshall, *Beyond Retribution*, 172.

[53] M. Mead, 'Some Anthropological Considerations Concerning Natural Law', *Natural Law Forum* 6 (1961), 51.

[54] J. Finnis, *Natural Law and Natural Rights*, 86–90: There is only a minimum of normative content in Finnis' seven basic goods: life, knowledge, play, aesthetic experience, sociability, practical reasonableness and religion.

[55] This requires an account of the action of the Holy Spirit as mediator of the revelation of God and of his will for human beings as expressed in the created order. Cf. Gunton, *Revelation*, 33–4, 46, 55, 61, 108.

[56] This view can be traced back to Gratian, the great eleventh-century codifier of canon law. It differs from the traditional conception of natural law in

Common grace

Human beings are in a moral mess. We no longer agree about what is good and right, nor do we pursue the good and practise the right even when we can identify them. And yet, things are not universally as bad as they could be. The Bible does not support the view of Pangloss, whom Voltaire rightly ridiculed for adopting the naïve view that everything is as good as it can possibly be in this world. Instead, the biblical emphasis is on the fact that things are not as bad as they could be. The devastating consequences of human sinfulness are not exhibited, in all places and at all times. God has held back his judgement against sin, so that individuals and nations are not subject to the sentence of death that could be imposed instantaneously. Equally significantly, the Bible teaches that God is at work in the world, *restraining the consequences of sin*. Therefore, while judgement *is* a personal act of God as opposed to a merely intrinsic consequence of the moral order of the universe, it is conceived of by the biblical writers primarily in the form of God withdrawing his protection from the sinful so they experience to a greater extent the fruits of their actions.[57] As Paul wrote: 'The wages of sin is death' (Rom. 6:23), and when God withdraws his protection then it is payment time.

Despite our wickedness and sinfulness, God has not put an end to the human race. In fact, he continues to sustain us, and in an extraordinarily generous way, which theologians describe as 'common grace'. Jesus taught, in the Sermon on the Mount, that: 'Your Father in heaven causes his sun to rise on the evil and the good, and sends rain on the righteous and the unrighteous' (Mt. 5:45). Paul told the people of Lystra that God 'has shown kindness by giving you rain from heaven and crops in their seasons; he provides you with plenty of food and fills your hearts with joy' (Acts 14:17). Some of God's blessings are indifferently administered, and are in no way dependent on belief in and faith in him.[58] In fact, the Bible says God pays special attention to the needs of the weak and the vulnerable.[59] His concern to bless all leads him to a particular focus on those who are in most need of blessing.

[56] (*continued*) that natural law is no longer an ethical standard *independent* of the Bible's teaching, and therefore sidesteps the objection raised by Yoder and Ellul to natural law: J.H. Yoder, *Christian Witness to the State*, 82–3; J. Ellul, 'Concerning the Christian Attitude Toward Law', *Christian Scholar* 42.2 (1959), 139ff.; and *Le Fondement Théologique du Droit*, 45–53. To regard, as Ellul does, the presence of ideas of 'justice' within the non-Christian community as nothing other than brute fact, seems to me to be a failure to reflect adequately on the role of the Holy Spirit as revealer of divine truth, both within and apart from Scripture.

[57] Marshall, *Beyond Retribution*, 148, 173, 198.

[58] Belief in him is the acceptance that a god exists, and faith in him takes us from the realm of Deism into that of Religion.

[59] F. de Coninck, *La justice et la puissance*, 16–17.

God has invested human governments with authority

The Bible teaches that government is, or at least has the potential to be, an instrument of God's common grace.[60] In the Old Testament, the book of Judges contains an almost unreadable account of the depravity and violence which can occur when there is no effective authority and everyone is free to do as he or she sees fit.[61] From idolatry[62] to fratricide,[63] civil war[64] to unprovoked military aggression[65] and the use of death squads,[66] gang rape[67] and forced marriages,[68] it is a haunting indictment of the chaos which can ensue when everyone makes up their own rules to live by without any regard for others. Written or edited in the time of the kingdom, the commentator's analysis of the reasons for the Israelites' disarray was 'In those days Israel had no king'.[69]

The existence of governmental authority *can* act as a brake on the evil that men do and preserve some semblance of social order:

> The law exists to constrain selfishness and distribute penalties. It is there to control the human tendency to destroy. This is its God-given right, and to fail to do this is to fail in its duty. God has ordained government so that we may live in a harmonious community.[70]

> Therefore Government is, or can be, a means through which God acts to restrain the consequences of sin from reaching their full destructive potential within human communities.

Secular theory struggles with the State: is it simply a handy name for the collective will of the people (as Rousseau thought) or is it fundamentally the province of a sovereign who gives commands (as Austin and the early Utilitarians believed) or is there something else to it? Did it come about or can it be justified as the result of a social contract, as Locke, Hobbes or Rawls posit?

[60]   O'Donovan, *Desire*, 149, identifies 1 Peter 2:13–17 as one of the passages in which this idea is expressed.
[61]   Judges 17:6; 18:1; 19:1; 21:25.
[62]   Judges 2:12–3, 17, 19; 3:7; 8:33; 10:6; 17:1–13.
[63]   Judges 9:5; 20:1–48.
[64]   Judges 9:30–57.
[65]   Judges 18:27.
[66]   Judges 21:10–12.
[67]   Judges 19:22–28.
[68]   Judges 21:20–23.
[69]   Judges 17:6. See also Judges 18:1; 19:1; 21:25.
[70]   Patricia Voute, 'In Sickness & Health', *Third Way* (October 2002), 9. One of the two justifications for the necessity of human law put forward by Aquinas was the need for compulsion to force selfish people to act reasonably: *Summa Theologiae* I–II q.90 a.3 ad.2; q.95, a.1c and ad.1; q.96, a. 5c.

The Christian justification for government is: 'there is no authority except that which God has established' (Rom. 13:1). The origin of all authority is God. Government is a means appointed by God for restraining human wickedness and for bringing about order in human societies. The witness of Scripture is that there are spiritual realities behind the human power and authority structures which are visible to us. Government is more than the sum total of its people. It has an authority from God. Those who govern have a mandate from God to do so.

Government is an instrument given to restrain the Fall, but it is administered by sinful human beings who are prone to the temptation to misuse the power that it carries with it. Throughout the Bible, human governors are held accountable to God for the way in which they have governed.

In acting to restrain evil and preserve social order, government is acting in accordance with God's character. Government has faults, but it is still necessary.

1. Government is necessary because order requires authority

For order to be established and maintained it requires authority.[71] Someone has to make the decisions. The buck has to stop somewhere. Order needs to be enforced to be effective. Someone has to be in charge and take final responsibility for what happens, although this recognition does not preclude a balancing of authority and division of powers.

2. Order is desirable because it tends to bring peace

Why is God a God of order? Because order promotes peace. Order is better than anarchy because God loves peace (shalom*)*. Law, in the sense of a commonly understood set of rules providing the minimum standards of behaviour, is necessary for any society to function.[72] Law is the form of order that regulates relationships and makes good relationships possible.[73] In any family there have to be rules, for example, about who buys the food and cooks the meals, how long you spend in the bathroom, what programmes are watched on television, what time you have to be back by in the evening, etc. In wider society, too, law is better than anarchy. It is better than anarchy because it allows communication, and therefore allows the gospel to be spread more effectively.

---

[70] *(continued)* was the need for compulsion to force selfish people to act reasonably: *Summa Theologice* I–II q.90 a.3 ad.2; q.95, a.1c and ad.1; q.96, a. 5c.

[71] 'There are, in the final analysis, only two ways of making a choice between alternative ways of co-ordinating action to the common purpose of common good of any group. There must be either unanimity, or authority. There are no other possibilities.' Finnis, *Natural Law*, 232; O'Donovan, *Desire*, 18.

[72] A point made by Anderson, *Freedom under Law*, 8.

[73] J. Cundy, (ed.), *Law – Some Christian Perspectives* (Glasgow: Lawyers' Christian Fellowship, 1990), 4.

Human government is part of the divine pattern of 'common grace' extended unconditionally to all human beings.[74] Human justice is thus an example of divine grace.

'With respect to evil, [government] functions as a medium of divine wrath ... God's way of providentially controlling human sin by permitting its deadly consequences to fall back on its perpetrators'[75] instead of spilling over to destroy the community as a whole. However, government's role is not limited to dealing with criminals. There is more to justice than penal justice.

Government has a legitimate role in maximising people's opportunity to enjoy the good gifts which God has given them in creation. 'In God's order the State exists because of the basic social needs of people living together in society. God invests government with authority so that it can be the servant of all in furthering our common good.'[76] In exercising its duty to further the common good of all, the State must act justly; it is under a duty to do justice.

Grace and judgement

The theological truth that human government is a manifestation of God's grace is problematic because it combines together judgement and grace. We live in a world in where, in an act of immeasurable grace on the part of the only wholly (and holy) just judge, the death sentence which our sins deserve is not administered immediately; but, nonetheless, it is an act of God's grace that *some* forms of human sinfulness are dealt with by means of immediate punishment administered by human agency.

There is a purpose to God withholding the full force of his judgement now. 2 Peter 3:9 tells us: 'The Lord is not slow about his promise, as some think of slowness, but is patient with you, not wanting any to perish, but all to come to repentance.' The withholding of the full implementation of the divine sentence upon human sinfulness is an act of grace because *it gives us time to repent*, to turn away from our sins, to step off the highway that leads to death, and to choose to walk the road that leads back to God and to life.

However, despite the fact that God's judgement is not fully manifest at the present time, it is present in part. 'We live in a world where there are consequences to our actions. There are moral laws at work.'[77] Often our pursuit of what we want carries its own terrible consequences. As the prophet Hosea put it: 'For they sow the wind, and they shall reap the whirlwind' (Hos. 8:7).[78] 'God's judgement is a judgement of grace – a

---

[74] F. Catherwood, *Pro-Europe?*, 24–5.

[75] Marshall, *Beyond Retribution*, 148.

[76] J. Gladwin, *The Good of the People: A Christian Reflection on Living with the Modern State*, 62.

[77] Lucas, *Ezekiel*, 71.

[78] See also Psalm 81:11–12; 106:13–15.

judgement in that it confronts and condemns, rather than ignores or excuses, the destructiveness of present human conduct, and a work of grace in that it aims at repentance, transformation, and restored communion.'[79] This partial manifestation of God's judgement is an act of God's grace because it shows us the consequences of the way we are heading, *it demonstrates to us the need to repent.*[80] All the various forms through which God's judgement in this fallen world is mediated can communicate this truth to those who have ears to hear. They are manifestations of God's *gracious wrath.*[81]

The Bible's witness is that God calls us to repent, to turn back to him. But the Bible also emphasises that God himself has taken the first steps in order to make that repentance possible. He has been active in the world he created, seeking to bring about his redemptive purposes. In some theological schemes, redemption has been played off against creation. This is unfortunate because we need a word like 'redemption' or 'renewal' in order to encapsulate the flavour of God's plans for the world which he created and which has fallen because of sin. We need a word to describe God's good plans for *this* creation, restoring it not to its former glory but to a future glory that will surpass in beauty and splendour the original design. The Fall has happened and God did not try to pretend that it had never occurred; he did not attempt to wind the clock back; instead he bore in himself, on the cross, in the person of Jesus, the pain and the price of redeeming his creation, of taking the steps necessary in order to move from the fallenness of the present age, not back to the perfection of the primeval Eden, but instead forward to the perfection of the heavenly City.[82] This was done not because human beings deserved it, but in fact in spite of our unworthy nature (Rom. 5:6–11). It was the most awesome act of redeeming grace on the part of God.

The Good Gifts of God and the Concept of the Good after the Fall

Christianity has a clear account of the ultimate good to offer: to know and to love God.[83] This, Jesus says, is eternal life: 'that they may know you, the only true God, and Jesus Christ, whom you sent' (Jn. 17:3). But, Christianity also has space within its theology for earthly things that are good,

---

[79] Marshall, *Beyond Retribution*, 167–8.
[80] Marshall, *Beyond Retribution*, 165, 167.
[81] Cf. Marshall, *Beyond Retribution*, 198; O'Donovan, *Desire*, 258.
[82] Just as Haggai was promised that the glory of the second temple would surpass the glory of the first (Hag. 2:9), so Christians can confidently expect that the majesty of the new heaven and new earth will surpass even the perfection and beauty of Eden.
[83] John 10:10.

provided that they are kept in proper perspective and not absolutised, i.e. transformed into idols. In the creation narratives, Gary Haugen identifies five good gifts of God: life, dignity, liberty, love and labour.[84]

Any Christian theology, properly so-called, must not just give an account of creation but also of the difference Jesus makes, of the impact of the coming of Christ. These good gifts of God, given in creation, marred by the Fall, are taken up and redeemed by Christ. Jesus came to give life in all its fullness (Jn. 10:10). In his dealings with people, Jesus treated each and every one with dignity. Indeed, he paid special attention to the weak, the crippled, the blind, the leprous, the social outcasts (prostitutes and tax collectors), demonstrating by his actions and attitudes their value to God. Jesus came to proclaim freedom and he acted to free people trapped by sin and sickness. He declared, 'If the Son sets you free, you will be free indeed' (Jn. 8:36; Gal. 5:1). His followers grasped the implications of his teaching as laying the foundations for a new pattern of mutual service that was capable of transforming work and family relationships (Eph. 5:21–6:9; Col. 3:12–4:1; 1 Pet. 2:13–3:7).[85]

However, although they are capable of being redeemed, the Christian understanding is that even these natural goods are only relative goods. There is within Christian theology an understanding that it could be right to give up each and every one of them in order to pursue the ultimate good of knowing God and following Jesus (Mt. 10:39; 19:29; Mk. 8:35; 10:30; Lk. 9:24; 14:26; 17:33; 18:29–30).[86] Indeed, to absolutise any one of these natural goods is to make it an idol. Just as these goods find their origin in the work of God in creation so they find their coherence in the work of God in Christ, a work which will ultimately transcend their limitations: transforming abundant life into eternal life, dignity into glorification, liberty into release from sin, sickness and death and into worship, work into Sabbath rest, and relationships into perfect communion with God and the saints.

With regard to Christianity's vision of the ultimate good, this is not susceptible of enforcement by human laws. The Christian church should have recognised far sooner than it did that forced love of God is no love at all.[87] Governments and Christians have been given no divine mandate to enforce Christian conversion on individuals.[88] The Great Commission was given to the church not to the Government.

[84] Haugen, *Good News*, 72.

[85] O'Donovan, *Desire*, 183–5.

[86] O'Donovan, *Desire*, 254; *Resurrection*, 95: 'Discipleship … involves us in the suffering of exclusion from various forms of created good which are our right and privilege as Adam's restored children.'

[87] As to which, see for example, Temple, *Christianity and Social Order*, 69; O'Donovan, *Desire*, 224.

[88] Rivers, 'Bill of Rights?', 38–9, 'For the Christian, to be moral is to be perfect in Christ, and one can never be satisfied with anything short of perfection. If it is the aim of the state to make people moral, it is the aim of the state to make

But as well as the Christian vision of the ultimate good: knowing God; there is also a Christian vision of what is 'naturally' good, as a basis for a good society: that people might have their material and relational needs sufficiently supplied to be able to enjoy life in this world, and the opportunity to respond freely to the gospel, so that they might be able to enjoy life in the next world. Christianity can derive from the creation narratives a vision of what is 'naturally' good for human beings, whether they accept the Christian God as Lord or not. The good gifts of God given before the Fall remain good, though now imperfect, even after the Fall.

The vision of what is 'naturally' good for human beings set out in the creation narratives is reinforced in the book of Ecclesiastes: 'I know that there is nothing better for men than to be happy and do good while they live. That everyone may eat and drink, and find satisfaction in all his toil – this is the gift of God' (Eccl. 3:12–13).[89] 'Enjoy life with your wife, whom you love, all the days of this meaningless life that God has given you under the sun ...' (Eccl. 9:9).[90] If this life is all there is, then to be happy in your work, and with your wife, and to do good, makes for a 'good' life.

This is what you would expect if W.J. Dumbrell is correct in his assertion: 'the thought of the wisdom literature [in the Old Testament] reflect[s] a theology based upon the fact of creation.'[91] The key phrase in Ecclesiastes is 'under the sun', in other words, the writer is reflecting on how people should live, if this life is all there is.

A just and good society is, therefore, one in which the creation values of the sanctity of human life, the importance of human dignity and human liberty, and the opportunity for rewarding work, appropriate rest and meaningful relationships are upheld; and in which, people have the opportunity to respond freely to the love of God.

The Christian Vision of a Just Society

The Christian vision of a just society is built around a distinctive understanding of the nature of the common good and of obligations of social

---

88 (*continued*) people moral, it is the aim of the state to make people into mature followers of Christ, displaying his character, growing into perfection ... All are called to acknowledge Christ as Lord, so "Christian morality" must be universally binding, if not universally acknowledged. Love for one's neighbour is shown by a concern that he too grows up in Christ. So as a Christian voter, campaigner, legislator, governor, lawyer, judge, one's function is at root to see Christ glorified in each person's life ... [But] In propagating the gospel, Christians are to eschew the use of physical force, using argument and example to persuade others of the truth.'

89 See also Ecclesiastes 2:24.

90 See also Ecclesiastes 5:18; 8:15.

91 Dumbrell, *Covenant and Creation*, 205; see also J. Blenkinsopp, *Wisdom and Law in the Old Testament: The Ordering of Life in Israel and Early Judaism*, 23.

solidarity. Because human beings as individuals are infinitely valuable, the teaching of the Christian church is that the interests of one may not be sacrificed for the greater happiness of another.[92] Because human beings are called to live lives of responsible freedom, they ought to be given opportunities to make meaningful choices, and be called to account for their wrong choices. Because human relationships are fundamental to what it means to be human,[93] those in human societies have responsibilities towards one another. Law is relational; concerned with social wrongs and social order.

The common good

Governments owe a duty to be even-handed, to look after the interests of the common good.

Catholic Social Teaching even starts from the premise: 'The attainment of the common good is the sole reason for the existence of civil authorities.'[94] This notion of the common good is more inclusive than that of the utilitarians, as *Pacem in Terris* goes on to spell out:

> Hence every civil authority must strive to promote the common good *in the interests of all*, without favouring any individual citizen or category of citizen ... Nevertheless, considerations of justice and equity can at times demand that those in power pay more attention to the weaker members of society, since these are at a disadvantage when it comes to defending their own rights and asserting their legitimate interests.[95]

Despite their different conceptions of the person, this Christian idea is close to the idea of the philosopher John Rawls that the aim of government must be to maximise the resources available to the worst off (the maximin principle).[96] For Rawls, this is his second principle of justice, the first being that 'each person is to have an equal right to the most extensive basic liberty compatible with a similar liberty for others.'[97]

[92] John Casey identified precisely this distinction between Christian ethics and utilitarian ethics as being at the heart of the issues in the tragic case of the Siamese twins: *Re A (Conjoined Twins)* [2001] 1 FLR 1, 2 WLR 480 in an article in *The Daily Mail* on 5 September 2000, 10.

[93] J.W. Montgomery makes the point that the classical theologians of orthodox Christianity, such as Augustine, taught that man does not exist for himself alone, but for his God and for others: Montgomery, 'Whose Life Anyway?', 93.

[94] Papal Encyclical *Pacem in Terris*, 54 quoted in P. Vallely (ed.), *The New Politics*, 9, 50.

[95] Pacem in Terris, 56, quoted in Vallely (ed.), *New Politics*, 9. The same emphasis is to be found in the book of Proverbs, and is considered in chapter 4 of this book.

[96] Set out in J. Rawls, *A Theory of Justice*, 130–5, 266–7.

[97] Rawls, *Theory of Justice*, 53.

For Rawls, the two principles are arranged in lexical priority, i.e. that it is impermissible to give up basic liberties in exchange for social and economic goods.[98] For the Christian too, a person's rights to life, to dignity, to liberty and to intimate relationships are inviolable. This, of course, does not preclude an individual from choosing to lay down their life, dignity, liberty or intimate relationships for the sake of the gospel.[99] Nor does it prevent the State from depriving them of their life or liberty when such is the just response to the violation of another's rights for which they are responsible.[100]

On the issue of work, the libertarian right argue that the fruits of one's labour are inviolable, and whilst all should be charitable, none should be forced into giving. Taxation is therefore illegitimate because of its coercive element, where the person being taxed receives no personal corresponding benefit from the taxation.[101] Such a line of argument can even be Christianised on the basis that just as work is a God-given gift, so are its profits.[102]

However, all citizens benefit from the services provided by government. Indeed, it is those services, from the police force to the road sweepers, which make the earning of money possible. It is therefore just that those services should be paid for, and since all benefit from them, that all should pay for them. Moreover, those who profit in society do so because of the advantages which that society, through its government, offers to them, and by the grace of God.[103] No one is truly a 'self-made millionaire'. In a fallen world, just procedures do not guarantee just outcomes. The market may be the closest to a just procedure for human exchanges that it is possible to achieve, but that does not mean that it cannot operate injustice.

For the Christian, justice has to be prior to profit and there is therefore a legitimate place for redistribution of wealth through taxation.[104] If Romans 13:7 and 13:8 were not habitually separated in

[98] Rawls, *Theory of Justice*, 52–6.

[99] Matthew 10:39; 16:25; 19:29; Mark 8:35; 10:29; Luke 9:24; 18:29; 1 Corinthians 4:10; 2 Corinthians 4:11; Philippians 1:29; Colossians 1:24; 1 Peter 3:14.

[100] Romans 13:4.

[101] R. Nozick, *Anarchy, State and Utopia*, 167–74, 265–8.

[102] C.M. Gay, *With Liberty and Justice for Whom? The Recent Evangelical Debate over Capitalism*, 93.

[103] Deuteronomy 8:17–18; James 4:13–15.

[104] Finnis counters Nozick's argument against redistributive taxation set out in *Anarchy, State and Utopia*, ix, 167–74 by positing that '… in establishing a scheme of redistributive taxation, etc., the State need be doing no more than crystallise and enforce duties that the property-holder *already* had. Coercion, then, comes into play only in the event of recalcitrance that is wrongful not only in law but also in justice.': *Natural Law*, 186–7. The Christian would locate such pre-existing obligations in God's gift of the earth and its fruit to humanity as a whole before giving it to any individuals.

modern Bibl/es it would perhaps be clearer that this obligation to pay taxes and to respect government is a matter of debt, and that 'he who loves his fellow-man has fulfilled the law'.[105]

For the Christian, kindness to the poor is a theological given. Therefore, the Christian right has, by and large, sought to present its disagreement with the Christian left in terms of a disagreement about the best means to achieve the commonly desired ends of the elimination of poverty, the equitable distribution of resources, and so forth.[106] The question is whether the right is correct in its accusation that its theological opponents have confused the responsibilities of love and justice,[107] and whether either in theory or in practice, the two concepts can be so neatly divided as the right pretend.

Solidarity

The Bible quite clearly teaches about our obligations towards our fellow human beings. When God asked Cain about the killing of Abel, Cain replied, 'Am I my brother's keeper?' (Gen. 4:9). No, Cain was not his brother's keeper; he was his brother's brother. The obligations of social solidarity arise not because we are fellow Christians but because we are fellow humans.[108] Our obligations to one another cross the boundaries of class, status, nation and race. The poet and Dean of St Paul's, John Donne, was right when he wrote 'Any man's death diminishes me, because I am involved in Mankind; And therefore never send to know for whom the bell tolls, it tolls for thee.'[109]

Pope John Paul II spelt out solidarity in the encyclical *Sollicitudo Rei Socialis* as being 'a firm and persevering determination to commit oneself to the common good; that is to say, to the good of all and of each individual because we are all really responsible for all.'[110]

In the book of Leviticus, God's people were explicitly commanded to 'love your neighbour as you love yourself' (Lev. 19:18). In addition to the high value it places on the individual, Christianity lays stress on the idea that all men and women are due equal respect and have responsibilities to one another and to wider society.[111]

[105] de Coninck, *La justice et le pardon*, 57.
[106] Gay, *Liberty and Justice*, 83, 97.
[107] Gay, *Liberty and Justice*, 92.
[108] Catherwood, *Better Way*, 41; Stott, *Issues*, 161, 221–6; D. Burnett, *The Healing of the Nations*, 25; O'Donovan, *Resurrection*, 239–43. Nonetheless, there are also distinctive responsibilities which we owe to our natural families (1 Tim. 5:4) or to others within 'the household of faith' (Gal. 6:10).
[109] *Devotions on Emergent Occasions* (1624) Meditation XVII.
[110] *Sollicitudo Rei Socialis*, 38.
[111] MCD Westminster Declaration 1990. In recognising the obligations of social solidarity 'the biblical social model is multipolar, consisting of individuals in relationship with family, tribe and local community as well as with

There is a tension between individual responsibility and social solidarity, and the balance is a delicate one. Jesus calls us to himself as individuals, but he calls us into a new community, an *ecclesia*. His call may be deeply disruptive of our existing personal relationships,[112] but he calls us into a new relationship with himself, with others and with the created order.

Any account of justice which makes the rights of individuals primary prejudices against communitarian benefits and communal interests.[113] There is a valid place for individual rights, but tempered, although not obliterated, by our responsibilities towards one another as sharers of a common humanity.

Economic and social justice

A commitment to dignity, solidarity, and to the good of all necessitates a commitment to social justice. If all are made in the image of God then all have the right to participate in the riches of his creation, both economic and social.

Matthijs de Blois has argued:

> it is remarkable that in two of the three places in the Bible where the word 'equality' is used it refers to equality in, at least partly, a material sense … There are good reasons to defend, on the basis of the equal worth of human beings, social human rights, which are formulated to ensure a just social order in which there are real possibilities for development for all human beings.[114]

The creation ordinances provide a framework for human beings to fulfil their natural potential, albeit that its ultimate realisation is now frustrated by the Fall. In working out how that potential might be maximised even in our fallen world, Christopher Wright identifies four key creation values from the narratives in Genesis: the principle of shared access to and use of the land and natural resources; the privilege and responsibility of work; the principle that man has dominion over the land to make it fruitful (which Wright calls the principle of economic growth); and the principle of stewardship.[115] He could also have added the principle of shared rest. Wright concludes from the creation narratives that the principle of shared access is prior to the principle of private property,[116] although it serves only to set bounds on the latter rather than to negate it.

---

[111] (*continued*) central government': Richard Abbott, 'Human Rights and the Draft EU Constitution' *Engage*, issue 2, summer 2003, 7.

[112] Matthew 10:34–38; 12:48–50; 19:29; Mark 3:32–35; 10:29–30; Luke 12:51–53; 14:26.

[113] Rivers, 'Bill of Rights?', 43.

[114] de Blois, 'Foundation of Human Rights', 21.

[115] Wright, *People of God*, 85.

[116] Wright, *People of God*, 117. See also Temple, *Christianity and Social Order*, 48–9, where he buttresses his position by quoting Ambrose in support of it!

Already within the creation narratives of Genesis, the Bible contains a wealth of material with profound implications for the shape and nature of human law. Those principles are then developed within the context of the nation of Israel in the Torah, the Mosaic Law.

3

The Mosaic Law

The Covenant and the Law

The Mosaic Law (Torah) was neither God's first word to his people nor his last word to his people. Norman Anderson rightly stresses that 'it is essential to see the Mosaic law as a whole, and the Decalogue in particular, as the stipulations attached to a covenant originally made with Abraham, and renewed to Israel as a people redeemed by the Exodus from slavery in Egypt'.[1] The Mosaic Law was given to God's people, chosen and saved by grace, as guidance for right living in relationship with God. It was given 'in order to enable them to embody *creation* principles in their socio-political life'.[2]

The ten commandments

At the heart of the Sinaitic covenant lie the Ten Commandments. They alone were given directly by God. However, for all their importance, they were given *after* the sequence of events which began with Moses' encounter at the burning bush and culminates with the escape of the Israelites at the Sea of Reeds. The covenant begins with the Lord telling Moses to tell the people, 'You yourselves have seen what I did to Egypt, and how I … brought you to myself' (Exod. 19:4).

God renewed his covenant of grace with his people on Mount Sinai. The record of the Decalogue in Exodus 20 begins with the vital preface, 'I am the LORD your God, who brought you out of Egypt, out of the land of slavery' (Exod. 20:2).[3]

The Hebrew word for 'covenant' (*berit*) can refer to political treaties or to marriage, and either or both of those ideas are the inspiration for its application to the relationship between God and his people.[4] In all cases, 'the essence of the covenant is to be found in faithfulness'[5] to the other party to it. In marriage, this included sexual fidelity. In political arrangements, this included compliance with the terms of the treaty.

---

[1] Anderson, *Freedom under Law*, 105; see also Dumbrell, *Covenant and Creation*, 91; G. Goldsworthy, *Gospel and Kingdom: A Christian Interpretation of the Old Testament*, 61; Wright, *People of God*, 22.
[2] Wright, *People of God*, 113.
[3] Wright, *People of God*, 22.
[4] Lucas, *Ezekiel*, 129.
[5] Lucas, *Ezekiel*, 129.

The Sinaitic covenant resembles the suzerain-vassal form of covenant common in the Ancient Near East, in which a dominant ruler imposed on a subject a set of terms which would govern their future relationship.[6] 'The *form* of the covenant established between the Lord and Israel seems clearly to have made use of this protocol of international politics. It identified the Lord as the great king ("I am the LORD your God"), recounting his deeds ("who brought you out of Egypt"), and recording the stipulations of the commandments and laws he laid upon his 'vassal' people.'[7]

The Decalogue commences with the sovereign declaration: 'I am the LORD your God, who brought you out of Egypt, out of the land of slavery' (Exod. 20:2). 'As in other suzerain treaties, the Covenant is introduced by a description of the great King himself and his relationships to his vassals.'[8] The preamble and historical prologue are to be found in Exodus 20:1–2 and 19:3–6. The Ten Commandments then form the centrepiece of the people's obligations.

The obligation placed on the Israelites is one of full obedience and covenant keeping (Exod. 19:5). The demands imposed are set out in Exodus 20 and in the Book of the Covenant that follows (probably up to the end of Exodus 23). The Israelites are expected to display the loyalty a suzerain would expect from his vassal and more. The loyal love (*hesed*) required of them is spelt out in the first two of the Ten Commandments.[9] God will have no rivals.

The Law was the moral revelation given to a people already saved by grace. '[T]he Ten Commandments were never intended to institute a system of legal observances by which one could earn God's acceptance.'[10] 'As with the other major covenants (Noah, Abraham, David), the Sinai covenant is made with those who have already been elected and delivered and have responded in faith and worship.'[11]

In Deuteronomy 4:11–14, Moses recalls the event as follows:

> You came near and stood at the foot of the mountain while it blazed with fire to the very heavens, with black clouds and deep darkness. Then the LORD spoke to you out of the fire. You heard the sound of words but saw no form; there was only a voice. *He declared to you his covenant, the Ten Commandments*, which he commanded you to follow and then wrote them

---

[6] G.E. Mendenhall, *Law and Covenant in Israel and the Ancient Near East*, sets out the six elements that were usually present in such treaties. For a consideration of how closely the Sinaitic and other biblical covenants fit the typical pattern, see Anderson, *Freedom under Law*, 105–6.

[7] Wright, *People of God*, 111.

[8] Anderson, *Freedom under Law*, 107.

[9] Knight, *Christian Theology*, 221; Anderson, *Freedom under Law*, 107.

[10] W.S. LaSor, D.A Hubbard and F. Wm Bush, *Old Testament Survey: The Message, Form and Background of the Old Testament*, 75.

[11] Birch et al, *Theological Introduction*, 151.

on two stone tablets. *And the* LORD *directed me at that time to teach you the decrees and laws you are to follow in the land that you are crossing the Jordan to possess.*

Apart from the Ten Commandments, given directly by God, the rest of the Mosaic Law enjoys a dual character: it is both God-given law and human-made law (Exod. 20:19; Deut. 4:1–2; 28:1), just as the Bible as a whole is both the words of God and the words of the human authors.

God gave the Mosaic Law to his people, within the context of a pre-existing relationship between them.[12] Having said that, an essential part of the covenant relationship was the people's obligation to serve the Lord God alone in obedience to his declared will, as a response to what God had already done for them.[13]

The covenant with Moses transcends the suzerain-vassal treaty form which was its origin; in that the sovereign's purpose was not just to oblige the vassal towards him, but rather to deliver them from slavery! 'The Ten Commandments can be seen as given in order to preserve the rights and freedoms gained by the exodus, by translating them into responsibilities.'[14]

Having redeemed them, God did not:

> set [his people] loose in the world in the hope that a redeemed people would know how to live harmoniously without the need for laws, institutions and structures of social and political authority. The deliverance from the autocratic oppression of Egypt was not inspired by the anarchist's vision. On the contrary, the very freedoms and values that the exodus deliverance achieved were at once set within a protective framework of mutual responsibilities. The Ten Commandments particularly can be interpreted in that way.[15]

The book of the covenant: Exodus 20:22–23:33

Immediately after the Decalogue follows a wide spectrum of covenant laws. These range from cultic rules relating to the appropriate worship of the Lord God (Exod. 20:22–26) and the observance of sabbaths and the celebration of religious festivals (Exod. 23:10–19), to rules governing the treatment of slaves and women (Exod. 21:2–11; 22:16–17) and other vulnerable members of society (Exod. 22:21–27; 23:9), to rules relating to personal injuries (Exod. 21:12–36), to rules governing theft and other property disputes (Exod. 22:1–15), to rules regulating lawsuits and the administration of justice (Exod. 23:1–3, 6–8). As can be seen from the

---

[12] C.J.H. Wright, *God's People in God's Land: Family, Land, and Property in the Old Testament*, 21; *People of God*, 160.

[13] Dumbrell, *Covenant and Creation*, 98, 143; Wright, *God's People in God's Land*, 34; *People of God*, 23, 160.

[14] Wright, *People of God*, 142.

[15] Wright, *People of God*, 113.

variety of concerns addressed in the judgements (*mishpatim*) (Exod. 21:1), the command to be holy related to the whole of life. The ethical behaviour expected of the Israelites was to be a response of gratitude for God's saving acts in history, whose content would be modelled on the character of God as demonstrated in those saving acts,[16] 'the covenant require[d] nothing less than the "imitation of God" '.[17]

Israel as a Holy Nation

The book of Leviticus

This imitation of God, and in particular, of the holiness of God, is stressed throughout the Pentateuch, but above all, in the book of Leviticus:

> The book of Leviticus is the center of the Pentateuch. This placement conveys the importance of worship for the life and well being of the community. As God had been active in Israel's history, so God promises to be active in worship. Through these visible and tangible means, from sacrifices to dramatised festivals, God continues to overcome slavery and death and bestows life and salvation.[18]

The religious acts prescribed for the people, and officiated over by the priests, were designed to remind them of the covenant-love of God and to inspire them to obey the divine law as expounded to them by the priests.

The book of Leviticus, as well as significant portions of the books of Exodus and Numbers, describe a cultic system built around ritual and sacrifice, with the Tabernacle as the focal point for the demonstration of God's presence with his people.

Leviticus 17–26 contains the 'Holiness Code', which explains the emphasis on holiness that lies behind all of the laws, practices and systems set out in the preceding chapters and books. Israel was to maintain these systems in order to both acknowledge God's holiness and also to imitate that holiness. Leviticus 19:2 sets out God's 'reasoning' behind the laws: 'You shall be holy, for I the Lord your God am holy.'[19] The Lord gave Israel a legal-religious system in order that they themselves may be holy, a reflection of the covenant God had made with their ancestors that they are a chosen nation, set apart and holy.

Again, the laws cover a wide range of human activity: from sexuality (Lev. 18, 20) to social life generally (Lev. 19), to the specific regulations for the priests (Lev. 21–22), and for the celebration of the Sabbath, religious festivals and the year of Jubilee (Lev. 23–25). Obedience to these

---

[16] Marshall, *Beyond Retribution*, 5.
[17] Leviticus 11:45; Deuteronomy 10:17–19. Marshall, *Beyond Retribution*, 5.
[18] Birch et al, *Theological Introduction*, 135.
[19] Peter applies this command to the church in 1 Peter 1:16.

laws will lead to the blessings promised in Leviticus 26:1–13 and disobedience to the punishments decreed in Leviticus 26:14–43.

The Torah emphasises God's holiness through the process of sanctifying the Israelites. By obedience to its demands the Israelites were kept conscious of 'the holy'. 'Many departments of Israel's life had to be made holy unto the Lord; that is to say, they were set apart, or sanctified, and therefore regarded as belonging to Yahweh.'[20]

The people's worship, and the rituals that attended it, demonstrated the correct approach towards a holy God, and the need to be a 'holy', i.e. set apart, people. 'Strict measures associated with holiness exist not to protect God from contamination by the world, nor to protect the world from God, but to honour God's character as God and to assure a proper relationship with God in the midst of a world of disorder and sin.'[21]

The Israelites were called to be a holy people, and the food laws and other parts of the Mosaic Law were designed, in part at least, to highlight their distinctiveness. Within the Israelite community, the priesthood and the Levites, and also, in a different way, the Nazirites, were the living embodiment of this principle. The Levites had been 'set apart' as a result of their zeal for the Lord during the incident of the golden calf.[22] The Levites, the Nazirites, and the Levitical Priesthood were all to be examples to the rest of the people of the holiness of God.

However, most of Leviticus is addressed to the people, and even the parts specifically for the priests (Lev. 6:8–7:21; 16:1–28) were available for everyone to read.[23] The priests were the guardians of the sacred lore, not to keep it secret but to teach it to the people.[24] Moses' blessing to the Israelites in Deuteronomy 33 identifies three significant strands in the role of the Levites. They were the possessors of the sacred stones Urim and Thummim, used to discern God's will;[25] they were to teach the law to the Israelites; and they were to offer incense and offerings to God.[26] The order is significant because it places knowing and obeying the will of God above the sacrificial system.[27]

Therefore, although the Levites and the priests were to be exemplars of holiness; it was not to be their exclusive preserve. Rather, the intention was that the people as a whole would be taught and encouraged to live up to the standards of holiness set by the priests to such an extent that the entire nation could be regarded as holy, and as a kingdom of priests (Exod. 19:6). 'God chose and called Israel, not at the expense of the rest,

---

[20] Knight, *Christian Theology*, 172.
[21] Birch et al, *Theological Introduction*, 139.
[22] Exodus 32:25–29.
[23] Birch et al, *Theological Introduction*, 136.
[24] Cf. Ezra 7:10; Ezekiel 44:23.
[25] Deuteronomy 33:8.
[26] Deuteronomy 33:10.
[27] *The Lion Encyclopedia of the Bible*, 140.

but for the sake of the rest.'[28] The people were to be a holy nation, reflecting God's character in a distinctive manner for all the world to see. *The people were to be the book of Leviticus read by their neighbours.*

The book of Numbers

The book of Leviticus is followed in the Pentateuch by the book of Numbers. Through its largely narrative passages, the book of Numbers describes how, far from being models of obedience and holiness, the people were faithless and rebellious. The result is that the people wander in the wilderness for forty years, an entire generation passes away, and the conquest of Canaan is only marginally closer at the end of the book than it had been at the beginning. The unresolved issue for Israel at the end of Numbers is their entry into the Promised Land.

The book of Deuteronomy

In such circumstances, a renewal or repetition of the covenant between God and his people would seem prudent. That is precisely what one finds in the book of Deuteronomy. Whatever its date and authorship, the entire book of Deuteronomy can be seen as an extended covenant, or a commentary on the Mosaic covenant itself mimicking the covenant structure.[29] Meredith Kline again saw a close parallel with the Ancient Near East treaty form, dividing Deuteronomy as follows: preamble, with identification of Yahweh as the divine king (Deut. 1:1–5), historical prologue (Deut. 1:6–4:49), covenant stipulations (Deut. 5:1–26:19), covenant sanctions (Deut. 27:1–30:20), and provision for covenant continuity (Deut. 31:1–34:12).[30] Again, what is missing from the standard template, for obvious reasons, are the gods as witnesses.

What is heavily stressed in Deuteronomy, however, is the gracious nature of God's choice of Israel (Deut. 7:7f.; 8:17f.; 9:5), an idea seen earlier in Exodus 19:4 and Genesis 15:7.[31] God, the Lord of the universe, freely and graciously condescended to enter into a covenant relationship with a people.

Time and again, in Deuteronomy, the people are motivated to obedience to God's laws by being reminded of what the Lord has done for them by rescuing them from their slavery in Egypt.[32] Indeed, much of Deuteronomy is a reprise and an expansion upon key parts of the

---

[28] Wright, *People of God*, 110.

[29] Lasor et al, *Old Testament Survey*, 112; Wright, *People of God*, 115.

[30] M. Kline, *The Treaty of the Great King.* Christopher Wright identifies the same structure, although he identifies chapters 1 to 3 as the historical prologue, chapters 4 to 11 as the call to obedience, chapters 12 to 26 as the laws proper and chapters 27 to 28 as the concluding blessings and curses.

[31] Wright, *People of God*, 51.

[32] Wright, *People of God*, 29. See Deuteronomy 15:15; 8:2, 11.

book of Exodus. Chapters 4 to 6 centre around the Ten Commandments, while chapters 12 to 26 are an expansion or commentary upon the Book of the Covenant in Exodus 20:22–23:33. Around these focal points are woven other passages in both poetry and prose which stress the importance of keeping these laws as part of the covenant with Israel's God.

But the focus in Deuteronomy is not just upon the Exodus from Egypt (Deut. 13:5; 16:12), but now upon the entry into the Promised Land. The people are being reminded of the laws given by Moses in order that they may follow them 'in the land that you are crossing the Jordan to possess' (Deut. 4:14; 5:31; 12:1).

For the Deuteronomist, keeping the law is a matter of fidelity to the covenant and faithfulness to the God of the covenant. It is these things which will secure Israel's possession of the land.[33] Moses declares in Deuteronomy 4:1, 'Hear now, O Israel, the decrees and laws I am about to teach you. Follow them so that you may live and may go in and take possession of the land that the Lord, the God of your fathers, is giving you.'[34] It is the people's failure to keep the covenant and to obey the law that is understood by the prophets and the writers of Joshua through 2 Kings (often referred to as the Deuteronomic History) to lead, inexorably, to the exile, to the people of Israel being dispossessed of the land. This interpretation of Israel's history also accounts for the emphasis placed on teaching the law in post-exilic Judaism (of which Ezra is the prime example).

Disobedience to God's commands is not just important because it is a violation of divine law. Its prime significance is that it is a rejection of the divine overtures of love. At its worst, sin is a refusal of a relationship with him. In the New Testament just as much as the Old Testament, love of God expresses itself in obedience to his commands (Jn. 15:12–17), or to put it another way, *God calls a people of faith to live lives of faithfulness.* And, in the old covenant as well as the new covenant, those lives of faithfulness are to be lived out in the community of God's people.[35] In social terms, that faithfulness and its consequences could be expressed very simply as they were in Deuteronomy 16:20: 'Follow justice (*tsedeq*) and justice alone, so that you may live and possess the land the LORD your God is giving you.' Conversely, the wronging of another 'in any way' was characterised not only as a social wrong but also as unfaithfulness to the Lord (Num. 5:6):

> *Israel's righteousness* consists in exhibiting the ethical and religious conduct specified in the terms of the covenant, in the 'judgments' or 'laws' (*mishpatim*) codified in the Torah. Law, covenant, and righteousness are thus

---

[33] See also Psalm 37:27–29.

[34] See also Deuteronomy 4:5; Leviticus 20:22; 25:18; 26:3–35.

[35] G. Fee, *God's Empowering Presence: The Holy Spirit in the Letters of Paul*, ix, and especially chapter 6. See also de Coninck, *La justice et le pardon*, 53.

interpenetrating concepts. To be righteous is to be faithful to the law of the covenant-keeping God and thus to treat fellow members of the covenant community with justice. To be unrighteous is to act in ways that break covenant.[36]

This breaking of the covenant with God will, if persisted in, lead to the eviction of the people from the Promised Land and to the imposition of the punishments and curses set out in Deuteronomy 27 and 28. But even here, when God acts in judgement against his own people, it is 'a judgment mediated in covenant',[37] which seeks, ultimately, to restore the people to relationship with God.

Shalom[38]

Jesus summed up the teaching of the Law and the Prophets in the two great commandments: 'Love the Lord your God with all your heart and with all your soul and with all your mind' and 'Love your neighbour as yourself' (Mt. 22:37–40).[39] His analysis was not an alien intrusion into the logic of the Mosaic Law. On the contrary, the commandments he identified as the greatest are to be found in the Old Testament text itself, in Deuteronomy 6:5 and Leviticus 19:18 respectively.

The vertical obligation of 'Love for God' was to be matched by the horizontal obligation to 'Love your Neighbour'. The connection between the two dimensions of holiness was such that, the sabbath was understood as an obligation and responsibility towards God himself, to be expressed through one's land and one's relationship with impoverished fellow Israelites.'[40] 'You honoured God by keeping a law which benefited your poorer brethren.'[41]

---

[36] Marshall, *Beyond Retribution*, 47–8. In fact, the covenant includes obligations to demonstrate the same justice towards foreigners living within the covenant community.

[37] O'Donovan, *Desire*, 51, see also 130.

[38] There is an interesting comparison to be drawn between the biblical idea of shalom and the Ancient Egyptian concept of *maât*, a notion which encompassed the natural rhythm created in that land by the floods of the Nile, as well as the cohesion of the world, the harmony of the universe, and justice: de Coninck, *La justice et la puissance*, 25.

[39] 'Love your neighbour as yourself' is also identified as the heart of the law in Matthew 19:19, Luke 10:27, Romans 13:9, Galatians 5:14 and James 2.8.

[40] Wright, *God's People in God's Land*, 148. See also Isaiah 28:17, where the references to measuring line, to check the accuracy of the horizontal dimension and to plumb-line, to check the accuracy of the vertical dimension indicate the close link between right relations with God and right relations with others.

[41] Wright, *People of God*, 156.

In Leviticus 19, the command, 'Be holy because I, the LORD your God, am holy'[42] is followed by a chapter which demonstrates just how many dimensions of social life are to be affected by holiness. These include 'generosity to the poor at harvest time, justice for workers, integrity in judicial processes, considerate behaviour to other people, equality before the law for immigrants [and] honest trading'.[43]

All of these various laws and provisions are designed to create a state of shalom, of peace-order-harmony. 'The central concern of biblical law was the creation of shalom, a state of soundness or "all-rightness" within the community. The law provided a pattern for living in covenant, for living in shalom.'[44] Shalom is not just the absence of hostility but a positive state of order and harmony, based on justice and righteousness.[45] In the words of Isaiah 32:17: 'The fruit of righteousness (*tsedeqah*) will be peace (*shalom*).'

God's gracious actions towards Israel, his work in delivering them from oppression, were to be the inspiration for them to act justly in their relations with one another:[46]

> [Given] Israel's origins as liberated slaves, [shalom] necessarily required provision for the impoverished and oppressed, which is why so much biblical legislation is devoted to 'social justice' concerns, such as care for widows, orphans, aliens, and the poor, the remission of debts, the manumission of slaves, and the protection of land rights. In this connection, covenant justice could be understood as positive succor for, and intervention on behalf of, the poor and the oppressed.[47]

The ethics of the Torah are fundamentally theological: 'they are at every point related to God – to his character, his will, his actions and his purpose.'[48] Because of what God had generously done for his people, so they too were to be generous to one another. Because of God's holiness, they too were to be holy.

In Israel, just as holiness was too important to be left to the priests, so justice was too important to be left to the judges. The whole people were to be holy; and the whole people were to act justly.

---

[42] Leviticus 19:2.

[43] Wright, *People of God*, 27.

[44] Marshall, *Beyond Retribution*, 48.

[45] Lucas, *Ezekiel*, 175; R.T. France, *The Gospel According to Matthew: An Introduction and Commentary*, 207: 'The Old Testament scope of justice is wider than mere legal vindication, and denotes instead the setting right of whatever is not as it should be, "the complete establishing of the will of God".'

[46] Micah 6:3–5; Exodus 20:1–17. Marshall, *Beyond Retribution*, 5.

[47] Marshall, *Beyond Retribution*, 48.

[48] Wright, *People of God*, 21.

Understanding the Torah

Torah as guidance, rather than mere legislation

The Hebrew word for the 'Mosaic Law' is the Torah, and this word Torah, although it is invariably translated in English versions of the Bible as *Law*, is actually closer in meaning to *instruction, direction* or *guidance*. 'What is primarily involved in [the] Hebrew term [for law Torah] is direction for life within the framework of [a] presupposed relationship' not the idea of regulations imposed by authority and backed by sanctions, which is the connotation of the English word *law*.[49] Although the analogy is an imperfect one, the Torah is closer in nature to the Highway Code than to the Road Traffic Acts.

An appreciation that what is meant by Torah in the Old Testament is divine instructions for life, makes it easier to understand how the psalmists and others could regard it as a delight to meditate upon.[50]

The Torah does not purport to be a comprehensive legal code, covering every possible situation which would confront the people of Israel in the land of Canaan.[51] Such a task would be impossible. Rules always run out. Human law making is a reiterative failure to classify reality. Equally, 'many of the injunctions of the Torah are not enforceable legislation, but demands based on the presupposition of covenant obligation to the Lord and to one's neighbour.'[52]

Instead of being an exhaustive written legal code, Torah was intended to be a source of guidance for the Israelites.[53] The priests were to instruct them in it;[54] they were to teach it to their children;[55] they were to internalise it;[56] to grasp the gist of it; and meditate upon it; and to apply its guidance to the varying circumstances of their lives. It was not meant to operate as a graven written code but as a living, internalised source of ethical instruction. Obedience to Torah was meant to cultivate *character*, inform *values* and teach *wisdom*, so that a *wise* man would know how to apply the Torah in each of the circumstances of his life.

The Deuteronomist puts the following words into Moses' mouth: 'See, I have taught you decrees and laws as the Lord my God commanded

---

[49] Dumbrell, *Covenant and Creation*, 91.

[50] Psalm 119 is, in essence, a love poem to the Torah. See also Psalm 1:2; 112:1; Joshua 1:8 and Romans 7:22.

[51] In the following section I am heavily indebted to Jonathan Burnside for his helpful comments on an earlier draft of this chapter. The views expressed remain, however, my sole responsibility.

[52] Wright, *People of God*, 113.

[53] J.A. Thompson, *Deuteronomy: An Introduction and Commentary*, 12.

[54] Leviticus 10:11; see also Joshua 1:8.

[55] Deuteronomy 5:9; 6:7, 20–25; 11:19.

[56] Deuteronomy 6:6–9.

me ... *Observe them carefully, for this will show your* wisdom *and understanding to the nations'* (Deut. 4:5–6). Faithful observance of Torah was both to be informed by wisdom, and to be a demonstration of wisdom.

Even in its application by judges, the Torah required the use of wisdom. Torah was not legislation in the sense of a modern Act of Parliament. Rather, it is a set of precedents, or a list of test–cases.[57] Instead of performing philological gymnastics in order to decide whether the case before him fitted within the letter of the rule of Torah, the judge was to consider the similarities and dissimilarities between the facts before him and the test case contained in the Torah. From there he was to use his judicial creativity and wisdom in using the content of the Torah to devise a remedy that was appropriate to the situation with which he had to deal. 'The emphasis was on the imperative to do justice and act fairly without bribery or favouritism, but much was left to the discretion and judgement of those responsible (Deut. 16:18–20; 17:8–13)'.[58]

The content of the Torah

There is a long tradition of dividing the Mosaic Law into moral rules, ceremonial rules and judicial rules:[59] a division which has attractions for modern minds as we readily think in the categories of private morality, communal religious observance and public laws. This tradition asserts that some parts of the Mosaic Law set out moral principles, values which the people of Israel were called to live up to because they were God's people. Some provide details on a priestly, ritual, sacrificial system. Some are laws in the sense that modern lawyers would understand the term, in that they identify standards of behaviour and prescribe penalties to be applied by judges.

The difficulty with this theoretical distinction is in the way the material is presented in the Pentateuch, where the various rules are deeply interwoven not to say entangled.[60] After stoutly defending the distinction, Walter Chantry has to concede: 'It would be a mistake to read through Exodus or Deuteronomy attempting to label one verse ceremonial and another moral. In many instances all three are intertwined so that it is seldom possible to make such neat identifications. The glaring exception is the Ten Commandments.'[61]

---

[57] Marshall, *Beyond Retribution*, 219; O'Donovan, *Desire*, 39.

[58] C.J.H. Wright, *Walking in the Ways of the Lord: The Ethical Authority of the Old Testament*, 104.

[59] A division identified by Aquinas in one of his inaugural sermons in 1256: Aquinas, *Selected Writings*, 9. See also W.J. Chantry, *God's Righteous Kingdom*, 113; O'Donovan, *Resurrection*, 159–60.

[60] Reisinger, *Law and the Gospel*, 57; see also the fictitious exchange in the Prologue to Wright, *People of God*, 14.

[61] Chantry, *God's Righteous Kingdom*, 119; Christopher Wright would dispute the uniqueness of even the Ten Commandments in this regard: *People of God*, 158.

As a tool for *interpreting the Old Testament text*, the theoretical distinction between moral, ceremonial and civil law appears flawed.[62] What is valid, however, is the recognition that there are ceremonial, moral and civil aspects to the prescriptions of the Mosaic Law. The text cannot be neatly divided into the categories of ceremonial, moral and civil law, in which we tend to think today. Each prescription may have moral, ceremonial and civil aspects to it.[63]

The ceremonial rules in the Mosaic Law were demonstrations of God's holiness and his requirements for purity.[64] So all the sacrifices were simply shadows of the great sacrifice that Jesus would make on the cross.[65] Once he had died, the meaning of the sacrifices had been fulfilled. There was no longer any need for them. They were completed.[66] The judicial aspects of the Mosaic Law were rules specifically given to the Israelites 'to follow in the land that you are crossing the Jordan to possess' (Deut. 4:14). But the moral principles to be found throughout the Mosaic Law remain important today as illustrations of God's intentions for the organisation of society. The distinction between the ceremonial, the moral and the civil aspects of the Mosaic Law is to be found in their relationship to Christ, and is therefore proper to a *Christian* understanding of the Torah.[67]

1. Equality before the Law

Moses taught, 'You shall have one law for the alien and for the citizen'.[68] Unlike the laws of the surrounding nations, 'biblical law applied equally to persons of all classes: there was one standard for all, rich and poor, native and stranger.'[69] Even slaves were protected by the law from cruelty (Exod. 21:20f., 26f.) and oppressive working conditions (Lev. 25:39f.,

---

[62] Though I have argued elsewhere that it remains valid for understanding the approach of the New Testament writers to the Torah: 'The Relevance of Old Testament Law for Today: Part One', *Law & Justice* 148 (2002), 21 at 26ff.

[63] Although one of the proponents of the threefold distinction which Wright criticises, Calvin himself recognised that the division was not absolute and there were moral aspects to the ceremonial and judicial parts of the Mosaic Law: J. Calvin, *Institutes* Book IV, ch. 20, para. 14. See also O'Donovan, *Resurrection*, 160.

[64] Anderson, *Freedom under Law*, 111; Chantry, *God's Righteous Kingdom*, 115.

[65] Reisinger, *Law and the Gospel*, 52, 55; the technical theological word for these 'shadows' is 'types'.

[66] Chantry, *God's Righteous Kingdom*, 115–16; Reisinger, *Law and the Gospel*, 53–4.

[67] Cf. D.H. McIlroy, 'The Relevance of Old Testament Law for Today: Part One'; O'Donovan, *Resurrection*, 159–60.

[68] Leviticus 24:22.

[69] See also Deuteronomy 10:19. See Marshall, *Beyond Retribution*, 80. Marshall's comments are in the context of the *lex talionis*, but the principle of equality before the law is of more general application in the Torah. See also Wright, *People of God*, 166; Lucas, *Ezekiel*, 225.

43). Concern that the law should be applied equally expressed itself in the proclamation of a solemn curse on the one who withholds justice from the alien, the fatherless or the widow (Deut. 27:19). The Mosaic Law clearly upholds the dignity of all human beings.

This is in marked contrast to the other legal systems of antiquity, where the prospects of obtaining justice and the penalties imposed by the judges were graduated against the lower classes. At several points in the Torah, this obligation to treat foreigners (aliens) on an equal footing is based on the fact that Israel herself had been aliens in Egypt.[70]

2. Landholding and Jubilee

In Deuteronomy, to the fact that the Israelites are obliged to God because he brought them out of Egypt, is added the fact that they are obliged to him because he will bring them into the Promised Land.[71] '[T]he overarching theme of the ... history of the Pentateuch, on through the books of Joshua and Judges and up to the establishing of the territorial limits of the kingdom of David, is the promise and the possession of the land.'[72]

The land was so important to the Israelites that it can even be seen as the third point of the triangle of their relationship with God.[73] The land belonged to God and he had distributed among the people.[74] In Numbers 26 and 34, and in Joshua 13–19, the land is divided up 'according to their clans', i.e. to extended family-groups. Through the widely dispersed ownership of land between extended families, Israelite society preserved its egalitarian rather than hierarchical nature.[75] 'Given the variety of Palestinian geography, this did not mean that everyone should have the *same*, but that every family should have *enough* for economic viability.'[76]

'The household, with its landed property, stood as the basic unit at the centre ... of Israel's life.'[77] This emphasis on family life placed relationships at the heart of the nation. Extensive regulations existed in Israel in order to ensure that the land, which was the key to participation in the economic life of the country, did not pass permanently out of the hands of the family. Land could not be sold permanently (Lev. 25:23) because the seller or a kinsman could always redeem it and even if that did not happen, it had to be returned in the Year of Jubilee.[78] Whatever the ups and downs of a family's economic fortunes, at least once in its lifetime

---

[70] Exodus 23:9; 21:2–11, 20f., 26f.; Deuteronomy 15:15.
[71] Deuteronomy 9:5; 26:9.
[72] Wright, *People of God*, 46.
[73] Wright, *People of God*, 19–20; O'Donovan, *Desire*, 41–6; W.D. Davies, *The Gospel and the Land: Early Christianity and Jewish Territorial Doctrine*, 58.
[74] Leviticus 25:23.
[75] Wright, *People of God*, 37.
[76] Wright, *People of God*, 77.
[77] Wright, *God's People in God's Land*, 1.
[78] Wright, *People of God*, 83.

each generation would be given an opportunity to regain its place as an important stakeholder in the wealth of the nation.[79]

This system of widely dispersed landholding was reinforced and protected by the institution of Jubilee:

> The jubilee was designed to prevent the accumulation of the bulk of the land in the hands of a few. It protected a system of land tenure that was intended to be broadly equitable, with the ownership of land widely spread throughout the population. It was an attempt to impede, and indeed periodically to reverse, the relentless economic forces that lead to a downward spiral of debt, poverty, dispossession and bondage.[80]

If outright annexation or acquisition of a family's land was outlawed in Israel, so too was creeping encroachment. Deuteronomy 27:17 pronounces a curse on the man who moves his neighbour's boundary stone.[81] The rich and powerful were to respect the property of their poor neighbours. The practice of encroachment was, however, sufficiently notorious to have become a proverbial example of injustice by the time of the prophet Hosea.[82]

> [T]he concept of land as divine *gift* generated a strong set of *rights* for both the nations and individuals [and] on the other hand, the concept of the land as under continuing divine *ownership* generated a wide range of *responsibilities* ... to God; to one's family, to one's neighbours.[83]

3. Regulation of economic activity

The land was given to the people not to be left permanently fallow and unproductive, but to be used by them productively. 'Biblical teaching encourages industry and embraces wealth as a just reward for it.'[84] There was nothing wrong per se in building up one's wealth but it was not to be idealised (or indeed idolised).[85] The wealthy were encouraged to be generous not miserly (Prov. 11:24).[86]

Profit seeking was subject to controls. Trade was to be honest. Weights and measures were to be accurate (Deut. 25:13–16).[87] This was an issue of righteousness (*tsedeq*). Proverbs 16:11 even goes so far as to say: 'Honest scales and balances are from the Lord; all the weights

---

[79] Griffiths, *Morality and the Marketplace*, 80–5.
[80] Wright, *People of God*, 101.
[81] See also Deuteronomy 19:14.
[82] Hosea 5:10; see also Job 24:2f. and Proverbs 23:10. Wright, *People of God*, 84.
[83] Wright, *People of God*, 58.
[84] Nick Spencer LICC e-mail update, 'The price of everything and the value of nothing', 23 May 2003.
[85] Proverbs 16:19.
[86] Wright, *People of God*, 85.
[87] See also Leviticus 19:36; Proverbs 11:1; 20:10, 23; Ezekiel 45:10–12.

in the bag are of his making.' Producers were encouraged not to take advantage of food shortages in order to raise prices excessively (Prov. 11:26).

The laws about tithing,[88] resting and gleaning[89] were designed to prevent landowners from bleeding their land and their workers dry in the name of profit.[90] In place of profit maximisation there was an ethical framework for a form of profit optimisation.[91]

Justice was to be given a higher priority than the pursuit of ever-increasing profits.[92] The Bible has nothing against wealth creation, but it insists that everyone ought to be able to benefit from it.[93] De Coninck argues that 'prosperity' was an important part of the shalom which the Torah was intended to secure, but that 'prosperity' only partakes of the nature of shalom when it is a blessing to everyone.[94] 'Abundance is therefore conditioned by, and subordinated to, a just sharing of riches, to a social harmony which is opposed to oppression. And this means that in certain circumstances, God calls his people to frugality rather than to abundance.'[95]

4. Workers' rights

'Israel was founded on the revolutionary ideal of social and economic egalitarianism',[96] and this translated itself into a strong, practical concern for the rights of workers. Hired workers were to be paid promptly and fully.[97] All were to have a day of rest a week, whether employer, employee and even working animals![98] 'In addition to this regular weekly total rest, slaves and other residential and hired workers were to be allowed to enjoy all the benefits of the ... festivals ... which added several days' break from work throughout the agricultural year.'[99]

Even the institution of slavery, a cursed form of perpetual social non-existence at other times and in other cultures, was transformed in

---

[88] Leviticus 27:30–32; Deuteronomy 14:22–29.
[89] Leviticus 19:9–10; Ruth 2:2; Wright, *People of God*, 86.
[90] The Jubilee legislation also has obvious restrictive consequences on profit making.
[91] S. Copp, 'A Christian Vision for Corporate Governance', in P. Beaumont (ed.), *Christian Perspectives on Law Reform*, 129. If James 5:1–6 is anything to go by, this concern about profiteering is carried over into the new covenant era.
[92] F. de Coninck, *La justice et l'abondance*, 11.
[93] de Coninck, *La justice et l'abondance*, 23.
[94] de Coninck, *La justice et l'abondance*, 24.
[95] de Coninck, *La justice et l'abondance*, 27, translation mine.
[96] Wright, *God's People in God's Land*, 46.
[97] Leviticus 19:13; Deuteronomy 24:14f. See also James 5:4.
[98] Exodus 20:11; Deuteronomy 5:15.
[99] Deuteronomy 16:11, 14.

the Torah law into a limited, humane, form of bankruptcy or punishment, where at least a change of employer, if not outright freedom, could be obtained every six years, and from which an individual or his children were entitled to emerge in the Year of Jubilee.[100] For those slaves who ran away from their masters, unlike the harsh penalties imposed by Roman law or later, God commanded: 'If a slave has taken refuge with you, do not hand him over to his master. Let him live among you wherever he likes and in whatever town he chooses. Do not oppress him' (Deut. 23:15).

All in all, '... there was a deep and detailed concern in the Old Testament with work and employment, in respect of conditions and terms of service, adequate rest and fair pay.'[101] The Mosaic Law demonstrates a keen awareness of the need to provide a proper balance between work and rest, and to ensure that work was rewarding.

5. Balance between risk and reward

Consumer credit was strictly regulated in the Mosaic Law. Lending at interest was prohibited between Israelites.[102] Christopher Wright suggests that this did not apply to commercial loans, but rather to loans made to enable a poor man to purchase necessities, such as the annual supply of seed.[103] To the ban on usury (Exod. 22:25–27; Lev. 25:35–38; Deut. 23:19–20) was added restrictions on what could be taken as a pledge and retained as a pledge: so that the poor man should be left in possession of his millstones to be able to grind his flour,[104] and his cloak to sleep in overnight.[105]

The effect of these provisions was to shift the risk in lending from the poor borrower, to whom the inability to redeem the pledge or repay the loan would spell certain financial ruin, to the rich lender, whose investment would only be repaid if the poor man prospered. If the loan could not be repaid, the debtor was to be released from it in the seventh year.[106]

6. (Re)distribution of profits

In addition to the controls on the pursuit of economic activity, the Mosaic Law contains provisions for the (re)distribution of part of the fruits of it. It is almost impossible to ignore the plethora of biblical references which demonstrate that God has a special concern for the poor, but

---

[100] Exodus 21:1–6, 20f., 26f.; Leviticus 25:39–55. See Wright, *People of God*, 78; Lucas, *Ezekiel*, 218.
[101] Wright, *People of God*, 79.
[102] Exodus 22:25; Leviticus 25:36f.; Deuteronomy 23:19f.
[103] Wright, *People of God*, 84.
[104] Deuteronomy 24:6.
[105] Exodus 22:26–27; Deuteronomy 24:12–13.
[106] Deuteronomy 15:1–3.

they originate in the Torah.[107] Care for orphans and widows is part of a pure and undefiled religion before God (Jas. 1:27).[108]

Although, within Israel, the fact that they had been redeemed *as a people* from slavery in Egypt was to be their prime motivation for social justice, it also stemmed from a recognition of the obligation of solidarity which rests upon us simply by reason of our common, created humanity.[109]

'Every third year ... the tithe was collected and stored for the use of the poor in general – Levites, aliens, widows and orphans.'[110] And every seventh year, the land was to lie unploughed and unused so that 'the poor among your people may get food from it'.[111]

Reading the Mosaic Law, it is impossible to avoid the conclusion that 'concern for the poor [is seen in the Bible as] more than just an individual matter: it is legitimately a function of government acting on behalf of society as a whole and comparable to its mandate to maintain law and order.'[112]

There is considerable force in John Gladwin's assertion: 'The whole infrastructure of the modern State – Parliament, Government, the Courts, the various levels of political life, if they are to be seen as deriving their authority and meaning from God Himself, must attend to the impact of their work on the poor, the distressed, the vulnerable.'[113] Paul Oestreicher is no doubt right to claim: 'A society's maturity and humanity will be measured by the degree of dignity it affords to the disaffected and the powerless.'[114] Israel was meant to be a shining example of social justice in this regard.

Writing from Eastern Baptist Theological Seminary, Philadelphia, USA and revising his seminal account of Christians' international social obligations, Ronald Sider, author of *Rich Christians in an Age of Hunger*,[115] set out the following reflection:

> I never thought that biblical revelation demanded absolute equality of income and wealth. But I used to be more concerned than I am today with the proportion of income and wealth that different groups possess. I feel absolutely confident, however, that the biblical understanding of 'economic equality,' or equity, demands at least this: *God wants every person, or family, to*

---

[107] For example, Exodus 23:19; Leviticus 19:10 and 23:22; Deuteronomy 15:11; 1 Samuel 2:8; Job 5:15; Psalm 10:14 and 35:10; Jeremiah 5:28–29, 21:12; Amos 2:6–7; Luke 4:18; James 2:5–6.

[108] de Blois, 'Foundation of Human Rights', 21.

[109] Wright, *People of God*, 137.

[110] Deuteronomy 14:28f.; 26:12ff. Wright, *People of God*, 85–6.

[111] Exodus 23:11; Leviticus 25:6f. Wright, *People of God*, 86.

[112] Griffiths, *Morality and the Marketplace*, 36.

[113] Gladwin, *Good of the People*, 33.

[114] P. Oestreicher, *Thirty Years of Human Rights*, quoted in Stott, *Issues*, 157.

[115] R. Sider, *Rich Christians in an Age of Hunger*, xii.

have equality of economic opportunity at least to the point of having access to the
necessary resources (land, money, education) to be able to earn a decent living and
participate as dignified members of their community.[116]

The Mosaic Law was designed to create a society of relative equality, in which each family possessed adequate land resources to be able to earn a reasonable and acceptable living.[117] The thrust of the Old Testament Jubilee legislation was to ensure that everyone maintained a stake in society, by ensuring at least once in a lifetime, the return of the ancestral lands, which carried with them social status and the ability to earn a living.[118]

7. Social justice beyond the economic

But the Christian approach to the issue of social justice goes beyond mere economics.[119] Money is after all only a tool, and the love of money a root of all kinds of evil.[120] The Bible clearly teaches, 'A man's life does not consist in the abundance of his possessions' (Lk. 12:15).

Not entirely with his tongue in his cheek, R.H. Tawney urged the idea of an equal distribution of wealth, not 'because such wealth is the most important of men's treasures, but to prove that it is not'.[121] On the other hand, as Pope John Paul II has pointed out: 'It is possible to

---

[116] E. Van Der Heide, 'Justice in International Relations with Less Developed Countries', *Transformation* 1 (April–June 1984) identifies three scriptural requirements of a just society: (1) All families have access to the basic necessities of life; (2) All people have the opportunity to use and develop their labour resource; (3) There is a distribution of wealth and income sufficiently equitable to assure that each person can exercise his or her stewardship responsibility.

[117] Adam Scott argues that the Mosaic legislation provided for 'equality in kind, though not in degree', in P. Beaumont and K. Wotherspoon (eds.), *Christian Perspectives on Law and Relationism*, 170. Brian Griffiths' more conservative analysis was that while the Mosaic legislation provided for 'the ability of each family to retain a permanent stake in the economy, the mandate on the community [was] to relieve poverty rather than pursue equality ...'. *Morality and the Marketplace*, 9, see 81–3 and 94.

[118] In these comments I gratefully adopt the insights of Mohan Seevaratnam in 'That there might be equality'. See also de Coninck, *La justice et l'abondance*, 33.

[119] As too, to be fair, does Rawls' conception of justice: 'It is a mistake to believe that a just and good society must wait upon a high material standard of life.' *A Theory of Justice*, 257.

[120] 1 Timothy 5:10.

[121] R.H. Tawney, *The Acquisitive Society*, 291, quoted in C. Bryant, *Possible Dreams: A Personal History of the British Christian Socialists*, 192.

become repressive in your search for justice, if you are single-mindedly in pursuit of the justice of equality rather than the justice of God.'[122]

Such is the *mainmise* of capitalism in the West that when we think of the poor we think primarily if not exclusively of the economically poor. But more than the lack of money can impoverish people. People can be socially and relationally impoverished. God's concern for the poor is not just for those who are economically poor but also for those who are relationally impoverished.[123]

In the Mosaic vision of society, the 'clan' (extended family) was the basic social, economic and religious unit. It was through affiliation to one of these groups that the Israelite gained his or her status within the covenant community. Thus the poor identified in the Old Testament are typically the widow (relationally impoverished by the death of her husband), the orphan (relationally impoverished by the death of parent(s)) and the alien (relationally impoverished by separation from kin and culture).[124] Indeed, the Bible recognises that it is most often *because* of social and relational impoverishment that people become economically poor.

Some of the stranger provisions of the Mosaic Law, such as the institution of levirate marriage, were designed to combat this social exclusion by reintegrating the widow within a family group and seeking to maximise her chances of having a son who could inherit her dead husband's property.[125]

8. Civil and criminal justice

In a society in which the role of centralised authority was limited, and without anything that would be recognisable to modern eyes as a 'police force', the distinction between civil and criminal justice is difficult to maintain.

However, especially in comparison with other legal systems, what is most striking about the Mosaic rules on punishment and compensation is the priority given to people over property. It is offences against people which warrant the most serious punishment not infringements on other's property rights.[126]

The emphasis in the Mosaic rules on punishment and compensation is on restoration of harmony in the community. In order to achieve this, private vengeance had to be restrained. The *lex talionis* which prescribes a fracture for a fracture, an eye for an eye, a tooth for a tooth (Lev. 24:17–22)[127] is intended to operate in this way, to prevent *vendettas*. It is intended to prevent the destructive escalation of violence which

---

[122] Quoted in Vallely (ed.), *New Politics*, 88.

[123] O'Donovan, *Desire*, 98.

[124] See, for example, Zechariah 7:8–12.

[125] Deuteronomy 25:5–10 and the book of Ruth.

[126] Marshall, *Beyond Retribution*, 207.

[127] See also Exodus 21:22–25; Deuteronomy 19:15–21.

Lamech describes in Genesis 4:23 when he tells his wives that he has killed a man for wounding him, a young man for injuring him, and demands seventy-seven times vengeance for his own death.[128] The *lex talionis* made it impermissible to return the insult with interest.[129]

Ultimately, a community must either eliminate, exclude or reintegrate its offenders. In Israel, certain sorts of offenders were to be eliminated. A variety of offences were subject to the penalty of death. Christopher Marshall groups these capital offences into four categories: unlawful taking of human life, other interpersonal offences, sexual offences, and religious offences.[130] But, from the explicit mention in relation to murder, idolatry and perjury in capital trials, of the fact that substituting a lesser penalty was forbidden, it would seem that, at least in relation to *some* of them, the death penalty could be commuted.[131]

What links the four categories of capital offences together is their covenantal or sacral character.[132] Murder and the cognate offences of avenging a death despite an acquittal by the law (Deut. 17:12), perjury in relation to a capital crime (Deut. 19:16–19), and owning an animal which has killed before and kills again (Exod. 21:28–30) are all deliberate violations of the sanctity of human life.[133] Cursing, striking and rebelling against one's parents (Exod. 21:15–17; Lev. 20:9; Deut. 21:18–21) are a violation of the covenantal nature of family life. The kidnapping of a fellow Israelite for the purpose of selling him into slavery (Exod. 21:16; Deut. 24:7) is a violation of the covenant which the Lord God made with all his people. Adultery, bestiality, incest, homosexuality, rape of a married woman, prostitution by a priest's daughter; all these are violations of the sanctity and covenantal character of marriage. And the religious offences of blasphemy, sorcery, witchcraft, child sacrifice, idolatry, false prophecy, Sabbath-breaking, and refusal to accept a decision of a priest or a judge, all these are obviously sacral/covenantal in nature.

Murder is a violation of the *imago Dei* borne by each and every human being. It is a usurpation of the power of life and death, which rightly belongs to God alone. The fact that the death penalty could not be commuted in the case of murder, and that even for the killer who was adjudged to have been only a manslaughterer, the penalty was confinement to a city of refuge until the death of the high priest (Num. 35:6–34; Josh. 20:1–9) demonstrates the high value the Mosaic Law placed on human life.

---

[128] Marshall, *Beyond Retribution*, 204.
[129] O'Donovan, *Desire*, 112.
[130] Marshall, *Beyond Retribution*, 205–6.
[131] Marshall, *Beyond Retribution*, 218.
[132] Marshall hints at this in *Beyond Retribution* at 212 but does not expand upon the point.
[133] Marshall, *Beyond Retribution*, 241–2; E.A. Martens, 'Capital Punishment and the Christian', in J.H. Redekop and E.A. Martens (eds.), *On Capital Punishment*, 24; J.R.W. Stott, *The Message of Romans*, 345.

Where execution was carried out, part of its function was exemplary. It demonstrated what was not to be tolerated, under any circumstances, in Israel. The sin which had occurred was anathema to Israel as the holy people of God and the offender therefore was to be removed from Israel's society.[134]

In comparison, the Mosaic Law rarely prescribed exclusion. Imprisonment is not to be found as a form of punishment in the Torah. The cities of refuge operated as a partial exclusion, whereby a manslaughterer could escape the avenging family without leaving the covenant community entirely.[135]

In relation to minor crimes, the Torah's preference is for re-integration into society and restoration of relationships by way of monetary compensation. Many of the provisions of the Mosaic Law seek 'to restore shalom by "making good" the loss or debt incurred by the wrongdoer, both by punishment and by compensation to the injured party, where applicable'.[136]

It was only *in extremis* that shalom within the community as a whole would be restored by the elimination of the wrongdoer whose actions had so gravely disrupted it. But whatever the punishment meted out, it is clear that '... in the legal processes described in the Old Testament ... the goal of the whole forensic process is the restoration of fellowship within the community',[137] the re-establishment of the state of shalom.

Mosaic Law and the Fall: divorce law

Although the people of Israel were called to be an example of holiness to their neighbours, and although their social and economic institutions were designed to embody important creation principles: upholding the sanctity of human life, human dignity expressed through approximate social equality and equality before the law, and a focus on rewarding work and meaningful relationships, there was a recognition among biblical lawmakers and judges of the limitations of fallen human nature. Thus there are laws to cover a wide variety of forms of depravity, cruelty and violence. There was no pretension that the effects of the Fall were not still felt within Israel. One of the key functions of law is to manage and mitigate the effects of human sinfulness and failure.

One particularly vivid example of this is in relation to divorce law. Although there was provision whereby a man could divorce his wife

---

[134] Cf. Marshall, *Beyond Retribution*, 105, 213, 218, 240.
[135] Marshall, *Beyond Retribution*, 207.
[136] Wright, *People of God*, 143. Cf. Numbers 5:6: 'When a man or woman wrongs another in any way and so is unfaithful to the Lord, that person is guilty and must confess the sin he has committed. He must make full restitution for his wrong, add one fifth to it and give it all to the person he has wronged.'
[137] Marshall, *Beyond Retribution*, 48–9.

(Deut. 24:1), God declared through the prophet Malachi, 'I hate divorce' (Mal. 2:16) and the patient endurance of the prophet Hosea in the face of his wife's infidelities is a vivid example of the lengths to which God went to preserve his covenant relationship with his people.

When Jesus reaffirmed God's desire that the marriage relationship should be for life, the Pharisees asked him, 'Why then, did Moses command that a man give his wife a certificate of divorce and send her away?' (Mt. 19:7). Jesus replied, 'Moses permitted you to divorce your wives *because your hearts were hard*' (Mt. 19:8). In other words, Moses acted to mitigate the consequences of human sinfulness, requiring a husband to give his wife a written certificate of divorce, thereby setting her free to marry another man rather than simply expelling her from his household and so condemning her to a life of destitution and/or prostitution.

The Administration of Justice

1. Justice within the family unit

Just as it was the primary social, economic and religious unit, so the extended family was the primary judicial unit.[138] 'On many routine matters, and some larger ones, the head of the household could act on his own legal authority without recourse to civil law or to the external authority of a court of elders.'[139]

Even in today's Western society, parents still have a considerable scope with regard to the discipline of their children. In Israel, this power extended into adult life and could be exercised by the head of the household over all who were living within the family group. Equally, in British employment law, employers are allowed to specify, within certain ever-tightening limits, the offences for which discipline will be imposed within a corporate context, and the procedures that will be adopted. The head of the Israelite family had a combination of the powers recognised today in parents and employers over the members of his 'family', who were usually both his relations and his employees.

However, his rights were not total. A slave owner was liable to punishment if he killed one of his slaves, and a slave had the right to be released if his owner knocked out one of his eyes or teeth.[140] The family members were always free to leave the family grouping and even slaves had an expectation of departure in the Sabbath year. Moreover, the most serious penalty, that of death, could not be imposed by the head of the household.[141] It was reserved to the elders of the community, and the father's

---

138 Wright, *People of God*, 154.
139 Wright, *People of God*, 155.
140 Exodus 21:20–21, 26–27.
141 Deuteronomy 21:18–21.

accusations that his son was rebellious and uncontrollable had to be supported by the boy's mother and found proven before it would be carried out (Deut. 21:18–21).[142]

Although to our minds it appears strange to have the judge and the offender so intimately involved with one another's lives, it is of the essence of biblical justice that it is relational in nature. Furthermore, the localised nature of justice in Israelite society emphasises the biblical ideal that all within the community should be just in their dealings with one another.

Biblical justice extended beyond the courtroom. All Israelites were called to act justly towards their neighbours,[143] and kindly towards the poor.[144] As we have seen, these obligations translated into specific commands, such as allowing the poor to glean from the edges of your fields[145] and as to what could be taken as security in respect of loans to the poor.[146] In fact, the biblical ideal was that courts would be unnecessary because the people would obey the Torah and behave justly to one another.

2. Justice beyond the family unit

The initial hope was, no doubt, that no further institutions of justice would be necessary. However, the people quickly resorted to using Moses as a court of appeal or in order to resolve disputes between one clan and another. As Moses explained to his father-in-law, Jethro: '… the people come to me to seek God's will. Whenever they have a dispute, it is brought to me, and I decide between the parties and inform them of God's decrees and laws' (Exod. 18:15).

But even before the promulgation of the Decalogue, the stream of disputes had become so constant that Moses was sitting as judge from morning to night (Exod. 18:13). Jethro could see that it was wearing Moses out. Instead of Moses seeking to deal with all the disputes himself, Jethro suggested that Moses appoint capable men, 'men who fear God, trustworthy men who hate dishonest gain … as officials over thousands, hundreds, fifties and tens … [to] serve as judges for the people at all times' (Exod. 18:21). Instead of attempting to resolve every dispute personally, Moses was to delegate the responsibility to these judges. He would only be involved personally in the case of a dispute which the judges found too difficult to decide (Exod. 18:22, 26).[147]

---

[142] Wright, *People of God*, 167.

[143] Psalm 112:5: 'Good will come to him who is generous and lends freely, who conducts his affairs with justice.'

[144] Proverbs 28:8.

[145] Deuteronomy 24:19–21 and described in practice in Ruth 2.

[146] Deuteronomy 24:6.

[147] For a discussion of this passage, see B.S. Jackson, 'Historical Observations on the Relationship between Letter and Spirit', in R. O'Dair and A. Lewis (eds.), *Law and Religion* at 104–5.

Thus, from the outset, there was a body of judges within Israel with judicial functions. There was also a tradition of appeal to higher authority. In the years before the monarchy, that appeal was to the charismatic leadership of the nation, be it Moses or Joshua, or one of the judges in the book of that name.[148] At the end of the pre-monarchic period, it was Samuel who assumed that role. The assumption was that his sons would take over that role after him, but they proved to be unworthy of doing so. Indeed, one of the stated reasons given for the people's demands for a king was that Samuel's sons had 'turned aside after dishonest gain and accepted bribes and perverted justice'.[149]

In between the decisions of the head of the family and an appeal to the leadership of the nation, lay the courts of elders; the local village assembly where most disputes, accusations, trials and cases were resolved.[150]

But because the law was God's law, and because it required godly wisdom to reach right judgements, the priests were also competent to act as judges (Deut. 17:8–13; Ezek. 44:24). Deuteronomy 17:8 comes shortly after Deuteronomy 16:18–20 which envisages the appointment of non-Levitical judges. The role of the priestly judges was to act as a court of appeal or as a forum for especially difficult cases, whether categorised as disputes involving 'bloodshed, lawsuits or assaults'.

When, at the end of his reign, David nominated Solomon, the wisest judge of all, as his successor, the book of Chronicles also records that among the Levites he appointed six thousand 'to be officials and judges' (1 Chr. 23:4), some of whom at least were 'assigned duties away from the temple', dispensing local justice throughout Israel (1 Chr. 26:29).

When King Jehoshaphat instituted a programme of judicial reforms, he appointed judges in each of the fortified cities of Judah (2 Chr. 19:5) and also in Jerusalem, where he appointed both Levites and heads of Israelite families 'to administer the law of the Lord and to settle disputes' (2 Chr. 19:8). The task of these judges was not only to give judgements in the cases before them, whether involving bloodshed or other concerns of the law, but also to warn the litigants not to sin against the Lord (2 Chr. 19:10). Jehoshaphat placed over the judges 'Amariah the chief priest ... in any matter concerning the Lord, and Zebadiah, ... the leader of the tribe of Judah ... in any matter concerning the king' (2 Chr. 19:11). Even though Jehoshaphat had assumed responsibility for organising the whole judicial process[151] he maintained the distinction between things that were God's concern and things which were the king's.

---

[148] E.g., Deborah in Judges 4:5.

[149] 1 Samuel 8:3.

[150] Wright, *People of God*, 169.

[151] For which there was the precedent of David in 1 Chronicles 23:4, and probably also Solomon.

Israel as a Light to the Nations[152]

Part of God's intention was that the nature and quality of Israel's social life would be a challenge and an inspiration to the surrounding nations.[153] Just as Israel had been delivered from Egypt 'in the sight of the nations' (Lev. 26:45) so now it was to live in the Promised Land as a light to the nations (Deut. 28:1–14). Israel was intended by God to be a paradigm. 'Israel's socio-economic life and institutions [were meant to be] models ... of principles of justice, humaneness, equality and responsibility'.[154] 'God's purpose ... was not just righteous individuals, but a new community who in their social life would embody those qualities of righteousness, peace, justice and love which reflect God's own character and were his original purpose for mankind.'[155] *Those to whom the nature of God's requirements had been most fully revealed were to, in their lives, exhibit and reveal them to others.* They could only do so by being distinctive in their lifestyle. A similar obligation falls on the church today.

The universal nature of morality

But undergirding the Israelites' sense of their own distinctiveness was meant to be the recognition that there was nothing special about them other than the fact they had been chosen and that God's law had been revealed to them.[156] The Torah was simply an expression of the moral standards to which God would hold all people accountable.[157] The close link in Jewish thinking between *creation ethics* and *redemption ethics*, or to use different terms, *natural law* and *divine law*[158] is evident from the fact that the book of Genesis is just as much part of the Pentateuch as the books containing the Mosaic legislation.

> The God who, as their Redeemer, gave the law to Israel as his own people, was also known to be the Creator and Ruler of all mankind. The law is based on the assumption of Israel's accountability to the Lord as their covenant sovereign. But that in itself rests on the axiom of Old Testament creation faith that *all* people are morally accountable to God. In fact, canonically speaking, the creation narratives and their moral implications were *part* of 'the law', meaning the Pentateuch, to the Israelites.'[159]

---

152 Cf. Isaiah 49:6; 60:1–3.
153 Deuteronomy 4:6–8.
154 Wright, *God's People in God's Land*, xvii.
155 Wright, *People of God*, 35.
156 Deuteronomy 9:5.
157 O'Donovan, *Resurrection*, 189–90.
158 The latter distinction is that of Aquinas, *Summa Theologice*, qn 91, art 4.
159 Wright, *People of God*, 161.

For the writer(s) of Genesis, the Jews were God's special people precisely *because* the Torah was universally applicable and they alone were the law-keepers. Because their God was a holy God, a moral God, and because he alone was God it was inconceivable that his standards of justice and righteousness were not universally applicable. 'It is simply affirmed and assumed that the Torah and its commands pertain to all of creation and thus to human persons.'[160]

A similar view is apparent among the prophets: '[For Amos] Yahweh is a God of moral perfection, who requires moral behaviour of all people. God gives life to all, and all will be held accountable for their actions in the world.'[161] As we will see in chapter 5, the prophets clearly regard the nations as under God's judgement on the basis of objective criteria:

> [N]ations are accused by the God of Israel on the basis of moral criteria of universal human validity. They are not judged only for wickedness committed against Israel, God's people, but for wrongs done among themselves. Treaties had been broken, communities pillaged, captured and sold, atrocities committed, inhumanities perpetrated. And the Lord, *Israel's* God, had seen it and held these other nations accountable for their mutual behaviour.[162]

Israel's calling to be holy carried with it a terrible responsibility

The corollary of the universal nature of God's moral laws was that if Israel failed to show the distinctive moral character expected of her, she too would be judged for breaking them in just the same way as the other nations had been. Just as the land had 'vomited out' the Amorites because of their sins so the Israelites too could be expelled from it if they behaved no better.[163]

The later prophets explained to the people repeatedly how:

> God's sovereignty in the realm of history [was such that he] can use a pagan king like Nebuchadnezzar to carry out his purposes. A great empire and ... superpower like Babylon is like a sword in his hand, to wield as he pleases. In all this, his sovereignty is exercised with no hint of favouritism or unfairness. It is exercised according to principles of justice. If his own people are wicked

---

[160] W. Brueggemann, *Theology of the Old Testament: Testimony, Dispute, Advocacy*, 455.

[161] Lasor et al, *Old Testament Survey*, 251.

[162] Wright, *People of God*, 124. He was talking, in the passage quoted, about Amos. Other prophets who also prophesied against the nations include Isaiah (Isa. 13:1–21:17; 23:1–25:12; 34:1–17; 46:1–47:15), Jeremiah (Jer. 25:15–38; 46:1–51:64) Ezekiel (Ezek. 25:1–32:32; 35:1–15; 38:1–39:6), Joel (Joel 3:1–16), Obadiah, Jonah, Nahum, Zephaniah (Zeph. 2:4–15), and Zechariah (Zech. 9:1–8).

[163] Leviticus 18:24–28; 20:22–24.

and rebellious, [the LORD] will bring judgment upon them, even employing a pagan nation for this purpose.[164]

Conclusion

Christopher Wright says, 'If anything can be said to have been crucial to the relationship between Israel and Yahweh, it was the requirement of justice and the integrity of those who administered it.'[165] He is certainly right to emphasise both the importance of justice and the need for integrity on the part of those who administered it; but the high point of the biblical vision was for a state of shalom in which because of the righteousness (*tsedeq*) of the people, acts of delivering justice performed by judges were very much the exception rather than the rule.

---

[164] Lucas, *Ezekiel*, 117, commenting on Ezekiel 21:28–32.
[165] Wright, *God's People in God's Land*, 81.

4

Kingship

At its worst, the state is nothing more than an organisation 'with a comparative advantage in violence'.[1] In such a world, ' "just" or "right" means nothing but what is in the interest of the stronger party'.[2] Power is, therefore, inherently dangerous.

The Bible recognises that states have a tendency towards violence. But the Bible also recognises that governments can exert a restraining influence, bringing a degree of peace, order and justice to societies. The example of the famine relief programme organised by Joseph in Egypt (Gen. 41) is an early illustration of the good that can be achieved through the wise exercise of governmental authority.

Submission to Authorities

Human beings cannot exist in society with one another without some form of leadership in decision-making, dispute resolution and organisation. The book of Judges contains a graphic description of the chaos, lawlessness and moral bankruptcy of the Israelites before the establishment of the kingship. Maintenance of order is the *sine qua non* for government and administration,[3] but order alone falls far short of the biblical ideal for authority.

The general tenor of the biblical message is that governing authorities are to be submitted to.[4] Whenever God's people are living in foreign lands, their approach to the pagan authorities is respectful. In the biblical narratives, the point at which resistance was urged is when the price of obedience is religious compromise, participation in idol worship[5] or the banning of worship of the true God.

Even the Exodus, the great *leitmotiv* of the liberation theologians, is *not* a story of how Moses led a successful armed revolt against the authority of

[1] D.C. North, *Structure and Change in Economic History*, 21.

[2] Spoken by Thrasymachus in Plato's *The Republic*, Book 1, 338c.

[3] Proverbs 28:2: 'When a country is rebellious, it has many rulers, but a man of understanding and knowledge maintains order.'

[4] There are exceptions to this, e.g. Jehu who was anointed to execute God's judgement on the house of Ahab (2 Kgs. 9:7–10). However, Jehu's thirst for blood went beyond the bounds of the judgement he had been authorised to carry out, and in the end his own dynasty would be punished for the massacre at Jezreel which he carried out (2 Kgs. 10:1–11; Hos. 1:4). 'Jehu's *methods*, as a response to religio-political oppression, receive no commendation in the Old Testament': Wright, *People of God*, 129.

[5] As to which, see Daniel 3 and 6.

Pharaoh. Rather, it is a story of how Moses, as the representative of the people, presented a series of requests; accompanied by demonstrations of God's power; which resulted in Pharaoh agreeing to let the Israelites go. Pharaoh and his army were destroyed not at Moses' hands, but at God's.[6]

However, although the Bible urges submission to all governing authorities, it contains within its pages a model for kingship that was (and is) in stark contrast to the practices of the surrounding nations. Nor, as we shall see in the following chapter, is submission to authority to be equated with uncritical acceptance of social injustice.

Justice and Deliverance

In Hebrew thought, justice and deliverance are the actions *par excellence* of the king. From the beginnings of Israel as a nation, they are understood as being divine activities.[7] God as king delivers his people from Egypt. God as king gives the people his laws to live by. Later in Israel's history, the prophet Isaiah declares: 'the LORD is our judge, the LORD is our lawgiver, the LORD is our king, it is he who will save us' (Isa. 33:22).[8] Justice is God's.[9]

In biblical thought, God's actions in justice operate both as a condemnation of the wrongdoer and a vindication of the victim.[10] The wrongdoer therefore experiences God's verdict (*mishpat*) as an act of judgement, and the victim experiences it as an act of deliverance.[11] It is this quality of God's justice as deliverance which justifies the traditional attribution of the name 'Judges' to the sixth book of the Bible. The delivering nature of God's justice is demonstrated both by God's protection of the weak and vulnerable nation of Israel within the community of nations and his protection of the weak and vulnerable within the nation of Israel.[12]

Whereas some of the judges did exercise judicial and administrative functions,[13] others were cast more in the role of war leaders. What all of them had in common, however, was that they were used by God to bring about his deliverance for his people.[14]

[6] Cf. Exodus 12:12 where the Lord God declares that what is occurring is a judgement on the false gods of Egypt.

[7] O'Donovan, *Desire*, 35–46.

[8] O'Donovan, *Desire*, 35.

[9] O'Donovan, *Desire*, 60.

[10] Wright, *People of God*, 137. Cf. O'Donovan's analysis of the imagery in Psalm 97: *Desire*, 33.

[11] Wright, *People of God*, 138.

[12] O'Donovan, *Desire*, 32–3.

[13] E.g., Deborah in Judges 4:5.

[14] Wright, *People of God*, 144; A.E. Cundall, *Judges: An Introduction and Commentary*, 16 (Combined edition with L. Morris, *Ruth: An Introduction and Commentary*).

However, despite their individual successes, the views of the biblical commentators were that the time of the Judges was a period of lawlessness and lack of moral direction within Israel. The proposed solution was the adoption of the institution of monarchy.

The Vision for the King in the Old Testament

In the context of Israel, the Old Testament is ambivalent about the office of king. The editor of Judges bemoaned the social chaos caused by the absence of clear lines of authority, but God, through the prophet Samuel, seems to have been decidedly hostile to the idea initially.

The separation of powers within Israel

Even when God had agreed to the people's demands, the office of king in Israelite society was to be different from its status in the surrounding nations. Outside Israel, the king was regarded as the representative of the gods, if not a god himself.[15] In Israelite society, God was the true king[16] and the human king was only his vassal.[17]

Outside Israel, the king was an absolute ruler.[18] When Jezebel sought to introduce this model into the northern kingdom, Elijah among others, stoutly resisted it. Within Israel, right from the start it was made explicit that the kings were subject to God's laws.[19] The king was to read from the Torah on a daily basis 'so that he may learn to revere the Lord his God and follow carefully all the words of this law and these decrees and not consider himself better than his brothers and turn from the law to the right or to the left.'[20]

Although it was Lord Acton who first coined the phrase, 'Power tends to corrupt and absolute power corrupts absolutely',[21] this recognition appears to be built into the institutions of Israelite society. Samuel knew how kings tend to behave, and he warned the people that the king would put their sons into his army, and use others to plough his fields and reap his harvest.[22] He predicted that their daughters would become

[15] A phenomenon which the Jews would have experienced in Egypt: Lasor et al, *Old Testament Survey*, 173. See also de Coninck, *La justice et la puissance*, 37–9, 41, for examples of the same tendency in Mesopotamian civilisation.

[16] 1 Samuel 8:8. Cf. Judges 8:23.

[17] O'Donovan, *Desire*, 65.

[18] Lasor et al, *Old Testament Survey*, 172.

[19] 1 Samuel 12:14, also 1 Samuel 10:25. See Jackson, 'Letter and Spirit', 105; Wright, *People of God*, 112.

[20] Deuteronomy 17:19–20.

[21] Letter to Bishop Mandell Creighton, 3 April 1887, in L. Creighton, *Life and Letters of Mandell Creighton* Vol. 1, ch. 13.

[22] 1 Samuel 8:11–12.

perfumers, cooks and bakers to the royal court.[23] With a remarkable grasp of how the powers of political patronage have always been wielded, he announced that the king would 'take the best of your fields and vineyards and olive groves and give them to his attendants'.[24] And finally, the king's confiscations, expropriations and taxations would reduce the people to slavery.[25] Solomon's reign proved the truth of Samuel's predictions.

In Israel, the power of the king was to be circumscribed. As Saul discovered to his cost, the role of the king was distinct from that of the priests.[26] The priests and Levites had the great privilege of demonstrating God's character through their rituals and actions, and teaching God's requirements to the people. They were responsible for offering the sacrifices.

Jeroboam I also had difficulty grasping the separation between kingship and worship. Instead, he set up the golden calves at Bethel and Dan,[27] took upon himself the right to appoint priests 'from all sorts of people, even though they were not Levites'[28] and offered sacrifices.[29] For this, God condemned him through the mouth of the prophet Ahijah.[30] Even in Judah, kings, especially evil ones, intruded on the prerogatives of the priesthood and interfered with the worship of the Lord God. When Ezekiel had a vision of a new temple, built after the exile, he placed it in its own grounds, separate from the royal palace and the city, as the symbolic reassertion of the unique rights which *God* as king has over it (Ezek. 45:1–8).[31]

The failure of both the priesthood and the kingship to live up to their callings, led to God raising up prophets to speak out. Although there were sometimes schools of prophets, there was no succession;[32] instead God at times of particular crisis in the nation's history called them. They were there to call kings, priests and the people to account.

A significant part of the prophets' message was directed against the sacrificial system (the temple cultus), which the people were relying on as a cure for their failures to keep the law.[33] The prophets' point was not that the cultus per se was a positive evil, or even unnecessary, but that it was insufficient by itself without a desire for justice, mercy and

[23] 1 Samuel 8:13.
[24] 1 Samuel 8:15.
[25] 1 Samuel 8:15–17.
[26] 1 Samuel 13:8–14.
[27] 1 Kings 12:25–33.
[28] 1 Kings 12:31.
[29] 1 Kings 12:32–33; 13:34. The references to kings offering sacrifice are not consistently met with evidence of divine displeasure – see 2 Samuel 6:17 (David) and 1 Kings 8:62 (Solomon).
[30] 1 Kings 14:7–11.
[31] Lucas, *Ezekiel*, 211.
[32] With the exception of Elijah and Elisha.
[33] For example, Hosea 8:11–13; Isaiah 1:10–17.

humility.[34] Worship in the right forms was not acceptable to God without right behaviour.[35] The same went for the kings. Their failure to curb social injustice forms a major theme in the prophetic writings, which will be considered in chapter 5.

The role of the king

Although separated from the priesthood, the king's role was nonetheless an important one. The king was originally expected to be the nation's military leader.[36] Saul's first actions as king were military ones.[37] David's reputation was won on the battlefield[38] and his victories are listed in 2 Samuel 8. It was with a touch of bitter irony that the writer of 2 Samuel 11:1 began his description of David's affair with Bathsheba with the words: 'In the spring, at the time when kings go off to war, David sent Joab out ...'. The idea of the king in person as war leader was persistent, and we find records of Ahab,[39] Jehoshaphat,[40] Joram son of Ahab,[41] Jehoshaphat's son, Jehoram,[42] Jehoash and Amaziah of Judah[43] leading their armies in battle. Going to war was a vital part of the king's responsibility for delivering his people from their enemies.

The other key aspect of the king's role was that of dispensing justice,[44] and God's idea of justice at that.[45] David[46] and Solomon[47] are shown as doing so, while Absalom's bid for the kingship began by undermining his father's role in this regard.[48] With regard to Solomon, the people are specifically recorded as being in awe of the fact that Solomon 'had wisdom from God to administer justice'.[49]

[34] See Hosea 3:4, 8:11–13; Micah 6:6–8; See N.H. Snaith, *The Distinctive Ideas of the Old Testament*, 56–8.

[35] *The Lion Encyclopedia of the Bible*, 131. See 1 Samuel 15:22 and the comments thereon by J.G. Baldwin, *1 and 2 Samuel: An Introduction and Commentary*, 115.

[36] Baldwin, *1 and 2 Samuel*, 49. For an exploration of the theological challenges such a conception presented, cf. O'Donovan, *Desire*, 53–6.

[37] 1 Samuel 11, 13, 14.

[38] 1 Samuel 17, 18.

[39] 1 Kings 22.

[40] 1 Kings 22; 2 Kings 3:9.

[41] 2 Kings 3:9; 8:28–29.

[42] 2 Kings 8:21.

[43] 2 Kings 14:9–13.

[44] Baldwin, *1 and 2 Samuel*, 117; Wright, *People of God*, 38. Commenting on the position in English Law, Ben Wortley wrote in 'The Christian Tradition in English Law', *Law & Justice* 150 (2003), 10: 'justice is a matter of royal personal responsibility in our system: not the affair of an abstract entity called the State.'

[45] Wright, *People of God*, 119; O'Donovan, *Desire*, 56.

[46] 2 Samuel 8:15.

[47] 1 Kings 3.

[48] 2 Samuel 15:1–6.

[49] 1 Kings 3:28.

From God's perspective, kingship in Israel was covenantal in nature. In the southern kingdom, the covenantal nature of the kingship was clear from God's promises to David and meant that the king should always be one of his descendants.[50] And even in the northern kingdom, Jeroboam I was given the chance of establishing a dynasty as lasting as David's provided he was prepared to obey God's commands and statutes.[51]

In God's eyes, the king's primary responsibility was to uphold the covenant.[52] The king's covenant responsibilities were to keep the covenant personally,[53] to defend the covenant people, and to enforce the covenant among his people.[54] As part of that role, the organisation of military defence and the administration of justice were covenantal responsibilities, to be discharged faithfully towards God and towards the people.

In the books of Kings, the rulers are assessed in terms of their faithfulness to the Lord, and for the extent to which they led their people towards or away from faith in the true God. In the northern kingdom, the picture was invariably bleak.[55] In the southern kingdom, the record was more mixed. Judged according to whether they 'did what was right in the eyes of the LORD' and whether they did so to the same extent as their father David had done, there were twelve bad kings and one bad queen; four kings who were good, but not as good as David; and four who were recorded as good: Asa, Jehoshaphat, Hezekiah, and Josiah.[56] In the prophetic writings, the criteria against which the kings are judged is the extent to which they reigned according to justice or injustice, but the overall assessment is similarly negative.

---

[50] 1 Chronicles 17:11–14.

[51] 1 Kings 11:38.

[52] Deuteronomy 17:18–20.

[53] Wright, *People of God*, 118; O'Donovan, *Desire*, 62.

[54] 1 Samuel 12:14–15. Cf. Baldwin, *1 and 2 Samuel*, 101; Lasor et al, *Old Testament Survey*, 188; O'Donovan, *Desire*, 61–2.

[55] Even the reforming monarch, Jehu, is recorded in 2 Kings 10:31 as not having been 'careful to keep the law of the Lord'.

[56] The bad were Solomon, Rehoboam, Abijah (1 Kgs. 15:3), Jehoram (2 Kgs. 8:18), Ahaziah (2 Kgs. 8:27), Athaliah, Ahaz (2 Kgs. 16:2–3), Manasseh (2 Kgs. 21:2–6), Amon (2 Kgs. 19:20–22), Jehoahaz (2 Kgs. 23:32), Jehoiakim, Jehoiachin (2 Kgs. 24:9), and Zedekiah (2 Kgs. 24:18). Those who were who were good, but not as good as David were Joash, Amaziah (2 Kgs. 14:3), Azariah/Uzziah (2 Kgs. 15:4), Jotham (2 Kgs. 15:34–35); the good were Asa, Jehoshaphat (1 Kgs. 22:44), Hezekiah (2 Kgs. 18:3–5) and Josiah (2 Kgs. 22:2). Asa is singled out for special praise because 'Although he did not remove the high places, Asa's heart was fully committed to the Lord all his life' (1 Kgs. 15:14); Hezekiah and Josiah are both commended too, if anything in even more fulsome terms, Hezekiah for his faith (2 Kgs. 18:6) and Josiah for his obedience to the law (2 Kgs. 23:25).

Even in Judah, shortly after the death of Josiah, the king who was most faithful to the Law of Moses,[57] things were as bad as ever. The book of Jeremiah bears witness to the fact that the effects of the religious reforms of Josiah had entirely dissipated within four years of his death, with his son Jehoiakim sufficiently disrespectful of God's word to cut up and burn Jeremiah's prophecy of impending judgement.[58] Although the kingship could rise to heights under men of God like Hezekiah and Josiah, the Davidic kingship as a whole could not provide the godly leadership the nation required, and the second half of 2 Kings is a depressing testimony to that fact. In the end, Jeremiah prophesied and lived to see the day when, because of injustice and failure to uphold God's covenant, the Davidic kingship[59] and Zion, its capital city, fell.[60]

The perils of kingship

The paradox of the biblical vision of kingship is that the king who was meant to be its epitome became its antithesis. Righteous kingship would lead to shalom, a state of security, peace, justice and well-being. After the wars of his father David, Solomon, whose name comes from shalom, was meant to embody and to achieve shalom for his people.

The biblical aim of *shalom* among God's covenant people, 'a state of harmony, well-being and blessing ... can come about only when people live in accordance with God's laws'.[61] The kings were to exemplify and even embody this for the people.

> When the king gives the life of God's justice to the people, then the blessings of fertile land and far-reaching power follow. ... the word *shalom* ... brings together into a wholeness the political, economic, social, and spiritual dimensions of life – which is what *shalom* is all about. The integration encompassed in *shalom* extends into an integral unity between heaven and earth.[62]

Solomon, the man of *Shalom*, was to bring out this state of peace and harmony, by acting as his father David urged him from his deathbed. He was to 'be strong, show yourself a man, and observe what the LORD requires: Walk in his ways, and keep his decrees and commands, his laws and requirements, as written in the Law of Moses' (1 Kgs. 2:3). Tragically, from a promising beginning, his reign degenerated into injustice, oppression and religious compromise.

---

[57] 2 Kings 23:25: 'Neither before nor after Josiah was there a king like him who turned to the LORD as he did – with all his heart and with all his soul and with all his strength, in accordance with all the Law of Moses.'
[58] Jeremiah 36.
[59] Jeremiah 22:30.
[60] Jeremiah 17:3; 21:10, 13–14; 22:5–7.
[61] Lucas, *Ezekiel*, 74.
[62] M.E. Tate, *Psalms 51–100*, commenting on Psalm 72.

The book of Deuteronomy gives a set of guidelines for kingship, which can almost be read as a checklist of Solomon's failures to live up to his father's hope. For all his legendary wisdom, wealth and political power, it is striking how the commentary on Solomon's reign reads as a counter-example of the ideal king described in Deuteronomy 17:14–20.[63]

Deuteronomy 17:16 states that the king must not 'acquire great numbers of horses for himself', i.e. he must not trust in military strength for his nation's security. Horses were the military equivalent of tanks at that time. God's people were to rely on the Lord for their protection. Yet Solomon is recorded in 1 Kings 4:26 as having 'four thousand stalls for chariot horses, and twelve thousand horses.'[64]

Deuteronomy 17:17 warns that the king must not 'take many wives, or his heart will be led astray'. There are probably two thoughts here. One is that the king will become preoccupied with sexual pleasure or with family intrigues; the other is that marriage was often used as a political tactic. Marriage to foreign wives usually led to an importation of their gods. Not content with marrying the daughter of Pharaoh, king of Egypt (1 Kgs. 3:11), Solomon is recorded as 'loving many foreign women besides ... Moabites, Ammonites, Edomites, Sidonians and Hittites ... from nations about which the LORD had told the Israelites: "You must not intermarry with them, because they will surely turn your hearts after their gods" ' (1 Kgs. 11:1–2). It was this which, above all, led to Solomon's decline,[65] causing him to worship Ashtoreth, the goddess of the Sidonians, Molech the god of the Ammonites, and Chemosh the god of Moab, as well as the Lord God of Israel (1 Kgs. 11:5–8).

Deuteronomy 17:17 also warned that the king must not 'accumulate large amounts of silver and gold', yet 1 Kings 10:14 records that 'the weight of gold that Solomon received yearly was 666 talents (about 23 tons) not including the revenues from merchants and traders and from all the Arabian kings and the governors of the land'.

Although Solomon built a magnificent temple in seven years, he spent thirteen years on the construction of his own palace.[66] Perhaps that suggests where his priorities truly lay. In order to achieve these massive construction projects, he conscripted forced labour (1 Kgs. 5:13; 9:15, 20–23).[67]

The king as shepherd

Instead of using a position of authority for the purposes of self-aggrandisement, the biblical metaphor used in Scripture to describe

[63] D.J. Wiseman, *1 and 2 Kings: An Introduction and Commentary*, 26.
[64] See also 1 Kings 10:26.
[65] 1 Kings 11.
[66] 1 Kings 6:38–7:1.
[67] 1 Kings 9:21. Wright, *People of God*, 121.

the responsibilities of leadership is that of the sheep and the shepherd.[68] Even a pagan ruler like Cyrus could be described as a shepherd.[69] In respect of the greatest of all Israelite kings, the psalmist described how the Lord 'chose David his servant and took him from the sheep pens; from tending the sheep he brought him to be the shepherd of his people Jacob, of Israel his inheritance' (Ps. 78:70).[70] The idea behind the comparison between kings and shepherds is that of the servant leader, who gives special attention to the needs of the weak members of his flock.

Zechariah 11 contains an extended discussion of the failures, past and future, of the evil shepherds who did not care for the people they were supposed to be leading. Conversely, other biblical writers such as Ezekiel[71] and Micah[72] look forward to the day when God himself will gather his flock together and tend it.

Ezekiel condemns the 'shepherds of Israel' for looking only after their own interests, taking the wool and slaughtering the choice animals but failing to strengthen the weak, heal the sick or bind up the injured. They had not brought back the strays or searched for the lost, instead they had ruled harshly and brutally.[73] Such policies were not good shepherding, but rather a plundering of the shepherd's own flock.[74]

Instead of the bad shepherding displayed by the leaders of Israel, the Lord declares through Ezekiel:

> I myself will tend my sheep … I will search for the lost and bring back the strays. I will bind up the injured and strengthen the weak, but the sleek and the strong I will destroy. *I will shepherd the flock with justice* … I will judge between one sheep and another, and between rams and goats … I myself will judge between the fat sheep and the lean sheep … I will place over them one shepherd, my servant David, and he will tend them. (Ezek. 34:15–24)

In the New Testament, this culminates in Jesus' identification of himself as the Good Shepherd,[75] and with the promise in Revelation that, 'the Lamb at the centre of the throne will be their shepherd; he will lead them to springs of living water. And God will wipe away every tear from their eyes'.[76]

[68] Numbers 27:17; 2 Samuel 5:2; 7:7; 1 Kings 22:17; 1 Chronicles 11:2; 17:6; 2 Chronicles 18:16; Jeremiah 23:1; 50:6; Zechariah 10:2. See also 2 Samuel 24:17; 1 Chronicles 21:17. Lucas notes that the same imagery was common among other nations in the Ancient Near East, *Ezekiel*, 172.

[69] Isaiah 44:28.

[70] Jesus similarly asked Peter to 'take care of his sheep' in John 21.

[71] Ezekiel 34. See also Jeremiah 31:10.

[72] Micah 2:12; 5:4.

[73] Ezekiel 34:2–5; cf. Jeremiah 22:1–5; 23:1–4.

[74] Ezekiel 34:7–8.

[75] John 10:14. See also Hebrews 13:20; 1 Peter 2:25.

[76] Revelation 7:17.

The Exercise of Justice

When Old Testament leaders were appointed, they were commissioned to maintain justice (1 Kgs. 10:9; 2 Chr. 9:8; Ezra 7:25) and their failure to do that was regarded as acting in disobedience and rebellion to God.[77] Doing justice was a key part of the function of kingship and the failure to maintain justice amounted to a breach of covenant. It is no exaggeration for Joseph Blenkinsopp to say that, 'The administration of justice [was] the most important function of monarchy.'[78]

The book of Proverbs urges upon kings the importance of righteousness (*tsedeq(ah)*) and right judgements (*mishpat*) for the security of their rule:[79]

"To judge with *tsedeq*" is the usual phrase for "judging justly" … But the successful discharge of judicial duties, especially those of the monarch, is described … by a favourite combination of two nouns and a verb, as "doing judgment and justice" (2 Samuel 8:15; 1 Kings 10:9; Jeremiah 22:3, 15; 23:5; 33:15; Ezekiel 45:9).[80]

Tsedeq(ah) means 'straightness' or conformity to a norm. It is the word used in Deuteronomy 25:15 and Leviticus 19:36 to describe 'accurate' or 'honest' weights and measures. From that origin, 'it comes to mean righteous, that which ought to be so, that which matches up to the standard – "righteousness" in a very wide sense.'[81] Gerhard von Rad argues:

There is absolutely no concept in the Old Testament with so central a signifi-cance for all the relationships of human life as that of [*tsedeqah*]. It is the standard not only for man's relationship to God, but also for his relationship to his fellows, reaching right down to … the animals and to his natural environment … for it embraces the whole of Israelite life.[82]

As von Rad rightly notes, 'the Hebrew idea of righteousness is *compre-hensively relational*. … Righteousness is, at heart, the fulfilment of the demands of a relationship!'[83]

Mishpat is the noun associated with the verb *shaphat*. *Shaphat* 'can mean: to act as a lawgiver; to act as a judge by arbitrating between parties in a dispute; to pronounce judgement, declaring guilt and innocence respectively; [and] to execute judgement in carrying out the legal conse-quences of such a verdict'.[84] *Mishpat*

---

77 Cf. Proverbs 16:10.
78 Blenkinsopp, *Wisdom and Law*, 2.
79 Proverbs 16:12; 25:5; see also 29:4.
80 O'Donovan, *Desire*, 38.
81 Wright, *People of God*, 134; see also Jackson, 'Letter and Spirit', 103, footnote 10.
82 G. von Rad, *Old Testament Theology*, 2:370, 373.
83 Marshall, *Beyond Retribution*, 47.
84 Wright, *People of God*, 134.

can describe the whole process of litigation, or its end result of verdict and its execution; it can mean a legal ordinance, usually case law, based on past precedents ... [but] it can also be used in a more personal sense as one's legal right, the cause or case one is bringing as a plaintiff ... *Mishpat* is what needs to be done in a given situation if people and circumstances are to be restored to conformity with *tsedeq/tsedaqah*.[85]

The obligation, therefore, upon kings was to give judgements which were *tsedeq*, i.e. in accordance with God's standards, and which were *mishpat*, i.e. in accordance with people's legitimate expectations, in order to restore the *shalom* of the community. 'Socially and nationally ... peace is the fruit of righteousness.'[86]

The covenant and justice

Dunn and Suggate explore the biblical texts on justice and come to the conclusion:

> in Hebrew thought [justice] is a concept of relation ... People are righteous when they meet the claims which others have on them by virtue of their particular relationships. Thus, ... the king is righteous when he fulfils his responsibilities as king towards his people. The servant is righteous when he obeys his master.[87]

The Hebrew understanding of justice reflects the primacy of relationships within the moral order.[88]

In its Hebrew conception, justice is not so much a state of affairs to which actions must conform, that place is filled by the idea of *shalom*. Instead, justice is envisioned as an action.[89] Thus through the prophet Amos, God can call his people to 'let justice roll on like a river, righteousness like a never-failing stream' (Amos 5:24). Actions of delivering justice were to be as constant and ever flowing as a stream that would continue to flow even in the midst of a drought (a significant metaphor in the dry and dusty Near East). 'The similes also served to show how utterly essential justice and righteousness were to Israel's life and faith. A society in covenant with Yahweh could no more live without them than without an adequate and steady water supply.'[90]

In the Old Testament, there is a close connection between justice and deliverance. By giving judgement for the righteous claimant, the

---

[85] Wright, *People of God*, 134.

[86] Wright, *People of God*, 135.

[87] J.D.G. Dunn and A.M. Suggate, *The Justice of God: A Fresh Look at the Old Doctrine of Justification by Faith*, 32–7; see also Dumbrell, *Covenant and Creation*, 13, 91, 123, 155, 205; Wright, *People of God*, 135.

[88] Cf. Marshall, *Beyond Retribution*, 258–9.

[89] O'Donovan, *Desire*, 39.

[90] D.A. Hubbard, *Joel and Amos: An Introduction and Commentary*, 182–3.

king is seen as delivering him or her from the continued injustice of being deprived of their rights by the unrighteous defendant. In the contrary case, by giving judgement for the righteous defendant, the king is seen as delivering him or her from the unjust accusation brought by the unrighteous claimant. In particular, therefore, the king's justice would defend the afflicted, protect the children of the needy, and crush the oppressor (Ps. 72:4). 'The king is righteous when he acts to bring about justice and equity in the covenant community; by remitting debts, releasing lands, protecting the weak, and so on.'[91] This relational understanding of justice makes clear its covenant implications.

A concept of delivering justice also transforms the exercise of justice from a zero-sum game to a positive-sum game. Justice is not just a matter of preserving freedom but can confer freedom.[92] By maintaining peace, it can open new opportunities for human flourishing which were previously absent.

As Packer notes:

> The ... idea that a judge should be cold and dispassionate has no place in the Bible. The biblical judge is expected to love justice, play fair and loathe all ill-treatment of one person by another. An unjust judge, one who has no interest in seeing right triumph over wrong, is by biblical standards a monstrosity.[93]

The covenantal nature of kingship is expressed in Proverbs 20:28. The Hebrew concepts in this proverb are difficult to translate. The NASB renders it, 'Loyalty and truth preserve the king, and he upholds his throne by righteousness', while the NIV says, 'Love and faithfulness keep a king safe, through love his throne is made secure.' The word translated 'Love' by the NIV is the word *hesed*, which can be translated as 'mercy', 'loving kindness', 'loyal-love' or 'steadfastness'. It is a description of covenant commitment, of the attitude and actions of a stronger party who is committed to maintaining a relationship he knows the other party is in no position to enforce.

The word translated 'faithfulness' or 'truth' is the Hebrew word *emeth* and it carries connotations of reliability and constancy. Often found in conjunction with *hesed*,[94] it confirms the strength of the commitment.[95]

Therefore, says the Proverb, a king's authority is secure when he exercises it responsibly for the benefit of his people. Solomon's son,

---

[91] Marshall, *Beyond Retribution*, 50. Cf. 2 Samuel 8:15; 1 Kings 10:9; Psalm 72; Jeremiah 22:3, 15; 23:5; 33:15; Ezekiel 45:9; Isaiah 42.

[92] Cf. O'Donovan, *Desire*, 127.

[93] J.I. Packer, *Knowing God*, 159–60.

[94] Genesis 47:29; Exodus 34:6; Joshua 2:14; Psalms 25:10; 40:11–12; 57:4, 11; 61:8; 85:11; 89:15; 108:5; Proverbs 3:3; 16:6; 20:28; Isaiah 16:5; Hosea 4:1; Zechariah 7:9.

[95] Wright, *People of God*, 135.

Rehoboam, discovered that the reverse was also true. He rejected the advice of the elders: 'If today you will be a servant to these people and serve them … they will always be your servants' (1 Kgs. 12:7) and instead he chose the path of oppression and rule by force, and lost most of his kingdom when the people rejected him and his policies.[96]

> Isaiah makes clear the connection between justice and peace, even if his focus is not strictly forensic: "Then justice [*mishpat*] will dwell in the wilderness, and righteousness [*tsedeqah*] abide in the fruitful field. The effect of righteousness will be peace [*shalom*], and the result of righteousness, quietness and trust forever" (Isaiah 32:16–17; cf. Psalm 85:10).[97]

The prophets had much to say about the principles of justice to be observed by the kings, but the wisdom literature of the Old Testament also talks about the exercise of justice.

Wisdom and justice

In the Old Testament, justice is seen as a divine quality, to be discerned with the benefit of wisdom. Proverbs 28:5 expresses the conviction that 'Evil men do not understand justice, but those who seek the LORD understand it fully.'

When Solomon was given a choice of a gift from God, God was pleased that Solomon asked for wisdom, but what the text records him as asking for in fact was 'a discerning heart to govern your people and to distinguish between right and wrong'.[98]

The story of the two women fighting over the custody of the remaining live child, in which the famous 'judgement of Solomon' is displayed, is presented in Kings/Chronicles as the quintessential example of Solomon's wisdom. His apparent decision that the child should be cut in half provokes the disclosure of the true identity of the child's mother. Solomon's wisdom was judicial in its character, enabling him to make right decisions. It expressed itself in the ability to devise a solution that would identify the true mother of the child whose future he was asked to decide.

In Hebrew thought, wisdom was the essence of reaching right decisions. Therefore Moses proudly declared to the Israelites in his farewell speech that he had appointed as their judges 'wise, understanding and experienced men'.[99] Judges were expected to be people who walked closely with God and did his will.[100] Having these acknowledged character traits would enable the judges 'to apply a sense of justice tempered by the conventional norms of practical wisdom'.[101] Decisions that reflected

---

[96] Wright, *People of God*, 121.
[97] Marshall, *Beyond Retribution*, 49.
[98] 1 Kings 3:9.
[99] Deuteronomy 1:15.
[100] J. Burnside, 'Inspired Justice', *Justice Reflections* 1 (2002), JR-1, 3.
[101] Burnside, 'Inspired Justice', 3.

the spirit of the Torah were the aim, applying its guidance to the varied situations which confronted the judges. Wisdom is the prerequisite for just judgement.[102]

This close connection between wisdom and justice is evident from the wealth of references to justice contained in the book of Proverbs. Examining this material, Joseph Blenkinsopp writes:

> Together with traditional narrative or folktale, the corpus of proverbs in a traditional society serves to transmit its inherited values, thus helping to form the basis for an agreed pattern of behaviour against which the conduct of the individual can be measured and with reference to which social deviance can be discouraged. In many societies (e.g. tribal societies in Nigeria) proverbs also play an important role in the administration of justice. Since both proverbial lore and case or common law are based on precedent and draw their authority from the transmitted wisdom of the past, it is hardly surprising that in Israel the sapiental and legal traditions are so closely connected.[103]

The very opening of the book of Proverbs makes clear its purpose. It is expressed to contain: 'The proverbs of Solomon, son of David, king of Israel ... for acquiring a disciplined and prudent life, doing what is right and just and fair ...'.[104] The emphasis on wisdom leading to an understanding of what is *right (tsedeq) and just (mishpat) and fair (meyshar)* is repeated in Proverbs 2:6, 9.[105]

The implications for a king of possessing wisdom are spelt out in Proverbs 8:12–21:

> I, wisdom, dwell together with prudence; I possess knowledge and discretion. To fear the LORD is to hate evil; I hate pride and arrogance, evil behaviour and perverse speech. *Counsel and sound judgement are mine*; I have understanding and power. *By me kings reign and rulers make laws that are just; by me princes govern, and all nobles who rule on earth.* I love those who love me, and those who seek me find me. With me are riches and honour, enduring wealth and prosperity. My fruit is better than fine gold; what I yield surpasses choice silver. I walk in the ways of righteousness, along the paths of justice, bestowing wealth on those who love me and making their treasuries full.

A king who fears the Lord will be wise, able to govern and make laws that are just, and enjoys the expectation of the 'reward' of a full treasury, and a long life.[106] However, if the choice is between wealth and righteousness, the biblical writers are unequivocal as to which path must be chosen.[107] It

---

[102] See Ezra 7:25.
[103] Blenkinsopp, *Wisdom and Law*, 20–1.
[104] Proverbs 1:1, 3.
[105] The same trilogy of ideas is to be found in Psalm 99:4. See O'Donovan, *Resurrection*, 189–90.
[106] Proverbs 28:16; 21:21; Psalm 106:3.
[107] Proverbs 15:16: 'Better a little with the fear of the Lord than great wealth with turmoil.' See also Proverbs 16:8; 10:9.

is only the path of justice that leads to the greatest of all blessings, a close relationship with God.[108]

Judgements must be just

If righteousness/justice is a relational concept, then for a king to be righteous/just in his judicial capacity means, first and foremost, that he must give just judgements.[109] His judgements must be right and straight. In other words, they must not be bent or crooked.

In words which urge judges to strike a balance which is seemingly impossible to find in human legal systems, Proverbs 17:15 says: 'Acquitting the guilty and condemning the innocent – the LORD detests them both.'

A king sitting on his throne to judge must winnow out all evil with his eyes.[110] Wickedness must be addressed; it must not be allowed to flourish.[111] Partiality in judgement is condemned,[112] and punishment of the innocent and righteous denounced.[113] Upright officials are to be praised and promoted not flogged.[114]

Gary Haugen's description of justice – 'Justice occurs when power and authority is exercised in conformity with God's standards'[115] – is a good account of the view of justice demanded of the kings of Israel and Judah. Haugen's approach to justice is also consonant with a relational understanding of justice, to which feminist theologians have made a helpful contribution. Karen Lebacqz sees justice as 'power-in-relation',[116] and it is therefore possible to understand justice as 'the existence of justice where there is no exploitation, and all parties exercise appropriate power'.[117] Haugen's concern is with injustice, with situations in which power is abused, and people are exploited and oppressed.

Impartial judgements

The Torah, the prophets and the wisdom literature of the Old Testament all lay stress on treatment of the poor. 'The righteous care about justice for the poor, but the wicked have no such concern' (Prov. 29:7).

In the courtroom, there are specific injunctions to 'Speak up for those who cannot speak for themselves, for the rights of all who are destitute.

[108] Psalm 11:7.
[109] Cf. O'Donovan, *Resurrection*, 129.
[110] Proverbs 20:8.
[111] Proverbs 20:26.
[112] Proverbs 18:5; 24:23–25; 28:21.
[113] Proverbs 17:26.
[114] Proverbs 17:26.
[115] Haugen, *Good News*, 71–2.
[116] K. Lebacqz, 'Justice', in L.M. Russell and J.S. Clarkson (eds.), *Dictionary of Feminist Theologies*, 159. See also A.M. Isasi-Diaz, 'Justice and Social Change', at 159–62 in the same work.
[117] Marshall, *Beyond Retribution*, 28.

Speak up and judge fairly; defend the rights of the poor and needy'[118] and not to deny justice to poor people in their lawsuits.[119] Those who are socially as well as economically disadvantaged are singled out as deserving of special protection: the foreigner, the orphan and the widow.[120]

For a judge to be just, to be righteous in his relationships with the litigants, he must deliver justice impartially. Central to Proverbs' argument that judges must dispense justice impartially is the assertion that rich and poor alike have an equal right to expect it because 'The Lord is the Maker of them all.'[121] Oppression or mockery of the poor is abominable, because it amounts to contempt for their divine Maker.[122]

When Moses appointed judges, he commissioned them to:

> Hear the disputes between your brothers and judge fairly, whether the case is between brother Israelites or between one of them and an alien. Do not show partiality in judging; hear both small and great alike. Do not be afraid of any man, for judgement belongs to God. (Deut. 1:16–17)

The Bible is not so naïve as to be mono-causal in its approach to poverty.[123] However, the biblical writers recognise that it is sometimes (perhaps often) the result of injustice and oppression by the haves of the have-nots.[124] Proverbs 13:23 says, in words which could be a direct condemnation of contemporary Western food subsidies and tariff barriers, 'A poor man's field may produce abundant food, but injustice sweeps it away'.[125]

Whatever the origins of their respective states, it remains the case that, 'The rich rule over the poor, and the borrower is servant to the lender' (Prov. 22:7).[126] Their financial inequality creates an imbalance of power that is capable of being abused. Therefore, the writers of Proverbs recognise that in order to achieve impartial justice the judges must pay special attention to the claims of the poor.[127]

In contrast to the just king who administers justice impartially, the prophet Isaiah pronounces judgement on 'those who make unjust laws … who issue oppressive decrees, to deprive the poor of their rights and withhold justice from the oppressed of my people, making widows their prey and robbing the fatherless'.[128] King Lemuel is urged in Proverbs

---

[118] Proverbs 31:8–9.

[119] Exodus 23:6.

[120] Deuteronomy 24:17; 27:19.

[121] Proverbs 22:2; 29:13.

[122] Proverbs 14:31; 17:5.

[123] Griffiths distinguishes three major causes of poverty identified in the Bible: oppression and exploitation, misfortune, and laziness: *Morality and the Marketplace*, 96.

[124] Proverbs 22:16.

[125] See Wright, *People of God*, 73.

[126] Proverbs 22:7.

[127] Proverbs 21:13.

[128] Isaiah 10:1–2.

31:4–5 not to get drunk on wine or beer lest he 'forget[s] what the law decrees and deprive[s] the oppressed of all their rights.'[129] Proverbs 28:3 says: 'A ruler who oppresses the poor is like a driving rain that leaves no crops.'

The poor are vulnerable simply because they are poor. They are vulnerable to having their stake in the nation's economic and social life eroded or taken away from them.[130] Rather than conniving in the oppression of the poor by the rich, the courts should act as a counter-balance to it.[131]

However, the poor woman is entitled to judgement in her favour not simply because she is poor; that would not be true justice; it would be bias.[132] So Leviticus 19:15 warns, 'Do not pervert justice; do not show partiality to the poor or favouritism to the great, but judge your neighbour fairly.'[133]

The poor woman is entitled to judgement in her favour when and because she has been wronged. The king must take care that the financial inducements (bribes) and clever arguments of the rich do not blind him to his duty in such circumstances. Because keeping faith with those who have the least to offer in return is the true test of character and demonstration of *hesed*, Proverbs promises: 'If a king judges the poor with fairness his throne will always be secure.'[134]

The writers of the Proverbs are particularly vituperative about two vices that afflict legal systems: bribery and false testimony. Of course, the first makes the second more palatable to a judge.

False witness

For litigants to be righteous, they must not bring unfounded claims against their neighbours, nor must they make false allegations or give false testimony against them. The gravity of this offence is such that it was included in the Ten Commandments. The writers of Proverbs are insistent about it.[135]

Proverbs 3:29, 30 says, 'Do not plot harm against your neighbour, who lives trustfully near you. Do not accuse a man for no reason – when he has done you no harm.' In Proverbs 6:16–19, sins of this type are singled out for a litany of condemnation. 'There are six things the LORD hates, seven that are detestable to him: haughty eyes, a lying tongue, hands that shed innocent blood, a heart that devises wicked schemes, feet that are quick

---

[129] See also Isaiah 5:22–23.

[130] See Proverbs 22:28; 23:10–11. To move an ancient boundary stone was to reduce the size of the poor man's fields, and therefore ultimately to deprive him of his livelihood.

[131] Proverbs 22:22–23. See also Proverbs 18:23.

[132] Wright, *People of God*, 147.

[133] See also Exodus 23:3.

[134] Proverbs 29:14.

[135] Proverbs 12:17; 14:5, 25; 19:5, 9, 28; 25:18.

to rush into evil, a false witness who pours out lies and a man who stirs up dissension among brothers.'[136]

The importance of this injunction is:

> in the legal processes described in the Old Testament, the accuser is not a neutral policeman but the personal enemy of the accused, who might be acting with malicious intent. The judge is expected not simply to apply the law but to vindicate the righteous. If he gives a verdict in favour of the defendant, he would be considered to have rescued the innocent person from oppression'.[137]

The utter seriousness with which false testimony was treated is spelt out in Deuteronomy 19:16–21:

> If a malicious witness takes the stand to accuse a man of a crime, the … judges must make a thorough investigation, and if the witness proves to be a liar, giving false testimony against his brother, then do to him as he intended to do to his brother. You must purge the evil from among you … Show no pity: life for life, eye for eye, tooth for tooth, hand for hand, foot for foot.

Lying about someone else's involvement in a crime was to be treated as morally equivalent to committing the crime oneself.[138]

Kings are warned in Proverbs 21:28 that, 'A false witness will perish, and whoever listens to him will be destroyed for ever.' The choice for kings is a stark one: 'If a ruler listens to lies, all his officials become wicked … If a king judges the poor with fairness, his throne will always be secure.'[139]

Bribes

The writers of Proverbs were quite sanguine about the reasons why a judge might listen to false testimony; they were aware of the real dangers of bribery and acknowledged its potential to 'pervert the course of justice'.[140] Despite the temptation, however, accepting bribes was nothing other than greedy[141] and wicked.[142]

In order to counter this temptation, Moses' father-in-law, Jethro, advised him in Exodus 18 to appoint as judges, 'able men … such as fear God … men who are trustworthy and who hate a bribe' (Exod. 18:21).

The Deuteronomist similarly cautioned:

> Appoint judges and officials for each of your tribes in every town the Lord your God is giving you, and they shall judge the people fairly. Do not pervert justice or show partiality. Do not accept a bribe, for a bribe blinds the eyes of

---

[136] See also Isaiah 29:20–21.
[137] Marshall, *Beyond Retribution*, 48.
[138] Marshall, *Beyond Retribution*, 82.
[139] Proverbs 29:12, 14. See also Proverbs 16:13.
[140] Proverbs 17:23. See also Proverbs 17:8 and 21:14.
[141] Proverbs 15:27.
[142] Proverbs 17:23.

the wise and twists the words of the righteous. Follow justice and justice alone, so that you may live and possess the land the Lord your God is giving you. (Deut. 16:18–20)

The writers of Proverbs do not pretend that bribes are not effective; on the contrary, their objection is that bribes are apt to 'blind the eyes of the wise,' so that instead of giving straight judgements, the judgements they pronounce are bent. For a judge to accept bribes is a betrayal of his office.

Ultimately, says Proverbs 29:4, 'By justice a king gives a country stability, but one who is greedy for bribes tears it down.' Time and time again, from a number of different angles, the biblical writers make the point that there can be no lasting peace, no state of *shalom*, without justice. Bribery and corruption will, in the end, destroy the societies that are built upon them.[143] The only durable social order is a righteous social order.

Procedures matter too

However, although the substance of justice is the main thing, procedures matter too. After all, churches have split or denominations been formed over procedural questions such as the way decisions are taken, and by whom.

Proverbs 18:17 warns judges not to jump to conclusions, on the basis that: 'The first to present his case seems right, till another comes forward and questions him.' Biblical law also contains rules of evidence, requiring corroboration before someone could be convicted of a capital crime (Num. 35:30; Deut. 17:6) and in Deuteronomy 19:15 it is said: 'One witness is not enough to convict a man accused of any crime or offence he may have committed. A matter must be established by the testimony of two or three witnesses.'[144] The Old Testament contains, therefore, rules of procedural or so-called *natural* justice, allowing both parties to put forward their case and requiring sufficient evidence to discharge the burden of proof before criminal guilt could be established.

Conclusion

The Old Testament therefore, contains a clear vision of the king as (1) the upholder of the covenant; (2) the administrator of justice and (3) defender of the rights of the weak and the poor. In general, however, the kings of both Israel and Judah failed to live up to this vision and had to be warned and called to account by the prophets.

[143] Deuteronomy 16:20.
[144] Although again, this follows immediately after a passage dealing with the question of murder.

'[It] is the duty of the king as the *most* powerful to champion the cause of the *least* powerful.'[145] In doing this, the king is following the example of the Great King, the Lord God,[146] who exercised his power to deliver his people from slavery in Egypt. *Justice occurs when power is used in the service of the powerless.*[147]

[145] Wright, *People of God*, 145.
[146] de Coninck, *La justice et la puissance*, 13.
[147] Cf. O'Donovan, *Resurrection*, 128.

5

The Prophetic Call to Justice

The Importance of Justice in the Prophetic Message

This is the heart of this book, because justice is close to the heart of God. As we have seen in chapter 2, the creation narratives contain within them the elements of a vision of a just society, and can be used to identify the endowments which God has graciously given to human beings. In chapter 3, we looked at the Mosaic Law, and put it into the context of God's gracious covenant with the nation of Israel, and discovered how the principles of fairness, equity and social justice reflected Israel's understanding of herself as a people redeemed from slavery. In chapter 4, we considered the role of the king and saw how he was to uphold the covenant by keeping the covenant personally, defending the covenant people, and enforcing the covenant among his people. We saw how the administration of justice was central to his role, and how this was viewed in covenantal terms; how for a king to be righteous was to be just in his relations with his subjects.

The sad reality of the kingship was that the kings were not often righteous in their dealings with their subjects. Bribery, oppression and favouritism were more often characteristic of their reigns than generosity, justice and even-handedness. Ultimately, it was the economic and social injustice fostered, fomented and tolerated by the kings which distorted to the point of disintegration the distinctive social shape of Israel.[1]

Into such a context, God sent his prophets. Nathan confronted David over his adultery with Bathsheba and murder of her husband.[2] Jeroboam I was faced down by an anonymous man of God,[3] and condemned by Ahijah.[4] Ahab was challenged by an anonymous prophet,[5] by Elijah[6] and by Micaiah.[7] Elijah pronounced God's judgement on Ahaziah.[8]

Some prophets saw it as their role to monitor the king's obedience to the covenant and to remind the king that he ruled subject to God's designation and was accountable to God for his actions.[9] Elijah's condemnation of Ahab over Nabaoth's vineyard is an important illustration of the way in

---

[1] Wright, *People of God*, 61.
[2] 2 Samuel 12:1–14.
[3] 1 Kings 13.
[4] 1 Kings 14:6–16.
[5] 1 Kings 20:35–43.
[6] 1 Kings 21:1–29.
[7] 1 Kings 22.
[8] 2 Kings 1:3–17.
[9] Birch et al, *Theological Introduction*, 231–3.

which the prophets reinforced the importance of the covenant and of a king observing the Law. Ahab desired to take possession of Nabaoth's vineyard, to use as a vegetable garden for his palace. Nabaoth refused because the land was his ancestral inheritance and, in fact, selling the land would have broken the Mosaic Law[10] which forbade the alienation of such property. Ahab complained to his wife, Jezebel, about Nabaoth's refusal and she arranged for trumped-up charges that he had cursed both God and the king to be brought against Nabaoth before a kangaroo court. Nabaoth was convicted as Jezebel had planned, and was stoned to death. With him out of the way, Ahab took possession of Nabaoth's vineyard.[11] It was as flagrant an abuse of power as you are ever likely to see.

Other prophets – particularly Elisha,[12] Isaiah[13] and Jeremiah[14] – acted as advisers to the king. These prophets indicated the godly course of action in given situations, and the consequences of disobedience.

As well as addressing the kings, the eighth-century prophets also spoke to the people, condemning them, and especially the rich, for their sins.[15] Amos' focus was social injustice; Hosea's was Israel's unfaithfulness to God; Micah's the sins of the nobles; Jeremiah's the false gods and unchecked corruption in Judah.[16] But in all of them, social injustice is part of the reason why God will bring judgement on the kingdoms of Israel and Judah. 'The prophets simply would not allow Israel to get away with claiming the blessing and protection of the covenant relationship for their society while trampling on the socio-economic demands of that relationship.'[17]

Although we tend to focus on their predictions about the future, the primary responsibility of all the prophets was to speak God's word for now to the rulers and to the people.[18] The role of the prophets was to call people back to the covenant and to challenge the kings, priests and other leaders to obey God's law.[19] The prophets pronounced God's judgement in the hope that it would lead to repentance.[20] When the kings heeded the warnings, even kings as wicked as Ahab,[21] the judgement was postponed or even averted.

---

[10] Leviticus 25:23–31.

[11] 1 Kings 21:1–16. See Wright, *People of God*, 55.

[12] 2 Kings 3:11–19; 6:8–10, 21–23; 6:33–7:2; 8:7–15; 9:1–10; 13:14–19.

[13] Isaiah 37:1–7.

[14] Jeremiah 27:12–15; 34:1–7; 36:1–24; 37:1–21; 38:14–26.

[15] LaSor et al, *Old Testament Survey*, 226; N.H. Snaith, *The Distinctive Ideas of the Old Testament*, 59.

[16] *The Lion Encyclopedia of the Bible*, 142–3; LaSor et al, *Old Testament Survey*, 229.

[17] Wright, *People of God*, 62.

[18] Birch et al, *Theological Introduction*, 293–4; *The Lion Encyclopedia of the Bible* 142; Knight, *Christian Theology*, 315; Wiseman *1 and 2 Kings*, 24.

[19] Wright, *People of* God, 146.

[20] *The Lion Encyclopedia of the Bible* 131, 143; Birch et al, *Theological Introduction*, 294.

[21] 1 Kings 21:17–28.

Prophets were sent at points where the kings, the priests and or the people were failing to live up to their covenant responsibilities, to warn that God was displeased by their actions and to call them to account. God had already warned in Deuteronomy that the people and their judges should 'follow justice and justice alone, so that [they might] live and possess the land the Lord [their] God was giving [them]'.[22] 'Biblical prophecy is precisely a preaching of the blessing and curse already known from biblical covenant arrangements.'[23] Time and again in the books of the prophets, God warns his people and their leaders about the consequences of their unjust behaviour.

Amos

The whole of the book of the prophet Amos is about justice. Scholars are agreed that Amos exercised his ministry between 760 and 753 BC.[24] He has left us a book that is an exquisitely crafted, clearly structured, gem,[25] whose central message is about God's concern for justice.

The book, in the form that it has come down to us, consists of five broad sections: an introduction (1–2); judgement speeches against the nations (1:3–2:16); judgement speeches against Israel (3:1–6:14), five visions (7:1–9:10), and salvation promises (9:11–15).[26]

1. The setting of Amos in the overall history of Israel

Harold Macmillan famously said, 'You've never had it so good',[27] and it was at a time like that that Amos came and spoke to the northern kingdom. Jeroboam II had just extended the borders of Israel.[28] Outwardly, Israel was as well off and powerful as it had ever been.[29] The elites felt secure and invulnerable in their mansions.[30]

---

[22] Deuteronomy 16:20.

[23] J.G. McConville, *Judgment and Promise*, 157. Cf. Deuteronomy 28.

[24] H.E. Freeman, *An Introduction to the Old Testament Prophets*, 187; Hubbard, *Joel and Amos*, 89–90; LaSor et al, *Old Testament Survey*, 244.

[25] Hubbard, *Joel and Amos*, 101: 'How much of the book is the words or writing of the prophet Amos himself is, [however,] a sharply debated question.'

[26] Hubbard, *Joel and Amos*, 118; Freeman, *Old Testament Prophets*, 184.

[27] Or at least, that is what he is thought to have said. In fact, in a speech in Bedford on 20 July 1957, reported in *The Times* on 22 July 1957, he said, 'Let us be frank about it: most of our people have never had it so good.'

[28] 2 Kings 14:25, 28; LaSor et al, *Old Testament Survey*, 245.

[29] Freeman, *Old Testament Prophets*, 188; H.L. Ellison, *The Prophets of Israel: From Ahijah to Hosea*, 62.

[30] Amos 6:1–3, 13. Freeman, *Old Testament Prophets*, 185, 188.

But underneath the prosperous surface lay deep social divisions.[31] The rich seemed blissfully unaware of the misery that their lavish lifestyle and business practices were causing to the poor.[32] In contravention of the principles underlying the Mosaic Law, in Israel the distribution of wealth was becoming ever more unequal.[33] 'The rich were living in luxury, while the poor could scarcely afford a pair of shoes or a covering to keep them warm at night; their overcoats had gone to the pawnbroker!'[34] '[T]he prosperity of Israel was merely a thin veneer over a mass of poverty and misery.'[35]

Although Jeroboam I had erected calf-idols at Bethel and Dan, Amos' criticism of Israel's religious practices was not based on their dubious elements or their non-Levitical priesthood, but on the fact that they were not accompanied by a righteous lifestyle.[36] It was because of a lack of justice in the nation that judgement was coming, and in less than forty years, it had come: Israel had collapsed politically[37] and Samaria had fallen. As Amos had prophesied, most of those led into captivity were the elite, the rich whom Amos had condemned for their contempt of the poor.[38]

2. Judgement against the other nations

However, Amos begins his oracles by condemning the nations surrounding Israel: Damascus, Gaza, Tyre, Edom, Ammon and Moab (Amos 1:1–2:5), before turning his focus in on Judah and then finally the northern kingdom. Perhaps this was a way of grabbing his audience's attention, but Amos also uses this approach to make two important theological points.

The first is that Israel's God is the Lord: he is sovereign over all the nations, and all the nations are accountable to him. While the nations initially appear to be judged for how they have behaved towards Israel, and those who have attacked Gilead come in for special criticism,[39] a closer reading shows that God was also holding them accountable for the way in which they had treated one another.[40]

The second is that God's own people will be subject to his judgement like all the other nations if the way in which they live is no different from that of all the other nations. Amos was making the telling criticism that,

---

[31] Amos 3:9.
[32] Amos 6:1–7; Ellison, *Prophets of Israel*, 64.
[33] Ellison, *Prophets of Israel*, 64.
[34] H. Young, *Major Themes from Minor Prophets*, 28.
[35] Ellison, *Prophets of Israel*, 64.
[36] Ellison, *Prophets of Israel*, 82.
[37] With six kings in twenty-five years: Birch et al, *Theological Introduction*, 285; LaSor et al, *Old Testament Survey*, 209–10.
[38] Ellison, *Prophets of Israel*, 81.
[39] Amos 1:3, 13.
[40] See especially Amos 2:1.

despite all that God had done for them, Israel and its rulers were just as bad as all the other nations.

Amos' understanding of universal judgement stands in line with that of the New Testament, and his particular emphasis on the fact that God's people are not exempt from that judgement accords with the teaching of 1 Peter 4:17 that this is in fact where judgement begins.[41]

3. Judgement against Israel

In the book of Amos, Israel is judged for its lack of social justice. The poor and needy are oppressed, denied justice in the courts[42] and forced into slavery.[43] The goods of the poor are confiscated,[44] and their garments taken in pledge, in direct violation of Exodus 22:25–27.[45] Trade is dishonest, with prices inflated and dishonest weights and measures used.[46]

> This is what the LORD says: 'For three sins of Israel, even for four, I will not turn back my wrath. They sell the righteous for silver, and the needy for a pair of sandals. They trample on the heads of the poor as upon the dust of the ground and deny justice to the oppressed?'
> (Amos 2:6–7)

The prophet Amos announced judgement on Judah on two counts: rejection of the law of the Lord, and following false gods.[47] Then turning to Israel, Amos poured scorn on the religious observances at Bethel and Gilgal.[48] Much good it will do you to make your sacrifices there, if you persist in your sin. Going to Bethel and Gilgal is of no value, what is required is to seek the Lord.[49] Amos says to the people: 'Seek good, not evil, that you may live. Then the Lord God Almighty will be with you, just as you say he is.'[50] Without justice, their worship, feasting, and sacrifices were unacceptable to God.[51] Amos would agree with William Temple that, 'It is a mistake to say that God is only interested in religion.'[52] 'God ... considers worship, divorced from right conduct, an abomination.'[53]

---

[41] The AV's translation 'the house of God', and the RSV and NRSV translation 'the household of God' are to be preferred to the NIV's 'the family of God'.
[42] Amos 5:7, 10, 12, 15.
[43] Amos 2:6–7; 8:6.
[44] Amos 5:11.
[45] Amos 2:8.
[46] Amos 8:5.
[47] Amos 2:4.
[48] Amos 4:4–5; Freeman, *Old Testament Prophets*, 185.
[49] Amos 5:4–6.
[50] Amos 5:14–15.
[51] Amos 5:21–24; O'Donovan, *Desire*, 63; Lucas, *Ezekiel*, 205.
[52] Quoted in Young, *Major Themes*, 33.
[53] Freeman, *Old Testament Prophets*, 185.

Although they are never explicitly quoted, Amos was clearly calling Israel back to God's covenant standards of righteousness.[54] They are the criteria against which Israel's conduct is judged to have fallen short.

God's fury against Israel is all the greater because of what he has done for them: rescuing them from Egypt,[55] destroying the Amorites,[56] giving them prophets and Nazirites[57] to remind them of the need for holiness, and choosing them as his people.[58] Amos' uncomfortable message is that 'Israel's election did not give her a monopoly on divine favor, but called her to special moral responsibility; she was called to be "a holy people unto Yahweh …"'.[59]

Nothing God had done has woken Israel up to the realities of the situation. When he sent famine, they ignored it:[60] when he sent drought, they did not turn to him for water:[61] when pests devoured their crops or plagues afflicted the people, that made no difference to their attitudes;[62] even military defeat and the loss of territory had not brought them to their senses.[63]

4. The five visions

The failure of Israel to respond to the warnings of the past led to a threat of further punishments in the future: a plague of locusts that would devour every green thing,[64] a drought causing fire which would scorch the land,[65] and then in the vision of the plumb line, God's judgement of the city walls of Israel as out of true, prone to collapse at any moment because they were built on rotten foundations.[66]

The last two visions 'mark the nearness and completeness of the coming judgement'.[67] The basket of summer fruit shows that the time is ripe for judgement;[68] the vision of the Lord above the altar indicates that the time has come for the destruction of the northern kingdom's shrines.[69]

[54] Birch et al, *Theological Introduction*, 302–3; Hubbard, *Joel and Amos*, 112–14; Lasor et al, *Old Testament Survey*, 249, 252.
[55] Amos 2:10; 3:1.
[56] Amos 2:9.
[57] Amos 2:11.
[58] Amos 3:1.
[59] Freeman, *Old Testament Prophets*, 186; LaSor et al, *Old Testament Survey*, 252.
[60] Amos 4:6.
[61] Amos 4:7–8.
[62] Amos 4:9–10.
[63] Amos 4:10b–11.
[64] Amos 7:1–3.
[65] Amos 7:4–6.
[66] Amos 7:7–9; Young, *Major Themes*, 31; Ellison, *Prophets of Israel*, 66–7.
[67] Ellison, *Prophets of Israel*, 67.
[68] Amos 8:1–14; Ellison, *Prophets of Israel*, 67–8.
[69] Amos 9:1–10; Ellison, *Prophets of Israel*, 68.

5. Amos' teaching about God's character

The God of Amos is unquestionably the God of the poor. Ellison goes so far as to say that 'For Amos the fundamental characteristic of God was justice.'[70] This 'righteousness' means that he could not let oppression go unpunished indefinitely.[71] To the rich, 'who hoard plunder and loot in their fortresses',[72] the warning was that 'An enemy will overrun the land; he will pull down your strongholds and plunder your fortresses.'[73] Their beautiful mansions and palaces would be demolished.[74] Rich women, whom Amos describes as 'fat cows', will be led away as captives with hooks through their nose.[75]

The people had ignored all the previous warning signs, and now Amos thunders 'prepare to meet your God, O Israel'.[76] Israel will be crushed as a nation. Only a remnant will be left.[77] The popular hope of the Day of the Lord when Israel would be vindicated and its enemies defeated is stood on its head.[78] Amos warns that it will be a day of darkness not light,[79] of judgement and exile.[80]

But in amongst the prophecies of judgement are the shoots of hope. There was still time to 'seek the Lord and live'.[81] Even if judgement came, a remnant would be spared.[82] There was the promise that one day 'I will bring back my exiled people Israel; they will rebuild the ruined cities and live in them. ... I will plant Israel in their own land, never again to be uprooted from the land I have given them.'[83] God's character is not only to be just, but also to be merciful.

6. The salvation promises

The salvation promises of Amos 9:11–15 are such a contrast to the prophecies of doom in the earlier chapters that some scholars feel they come from a different hand.[84] Yet those verses pick up on themes identified

---

[70] H.L. Ellison, *The Message of the Old Testament*, 56.
[71] Amos 8:2; Ellison, *Prophets of Israel*, 67.
[72] Amos 3:10.
[73] Amos 3:11.
[74] Amos 3:14–15; 5:11; 6:8, 11.
[75] Amos 4:1–2.
[76] Amos 4:12.
[77] Amos 5:3.
[78] Ellison, *Prophets of Israel*, 86.
[79] Amos 5:18, 20.
[80] Amos 5:26–27; 6:14; 7:17.
[81] Amos 5:4, 6, 14–15.
[82] Amos 5:3, 15; 9:8–10.
[83] Amos 9:11–15.
[84] For a brief discussion of this issue, see Hubbard, *Joel and Amos*, 100–1; Ellison, *Prophets of Israel*, 70, sees this passage as 'an appendix added by [Amos] after he had returned to Judah'.

earlier in the book – the remnant spared (v. 14), the idea of God's lord-ship over the nations (v. 12), and the images of rebuilding the ruins, replanting the vineyards, drinking wine and eating fruit, are so precisely the inverse of what was foretold earlier that the whole passage functions as a clear counterpoint, or epilogue, to what has gone before. It develops a prophetic theme of mercy beyond judgement, which comes to a crescendo in the writings of Jeremiah and Ezekiel, who saw the Exile as inexorable judgement, and yet the promise of a restoration of God's people beyond it.

Justice in the Other Prophets

Amos was not a lone voice, out of tune with his prophetic brethren.[85] Although they each have their distinct emphases, the other eighth-century prophets Hosea, Micah and Isaiah all affirm the same truth: judgement is coming, because of 'the injustice and inhumanity of the great and the powerful towards the weak, poor and helpless'.[86]

1. Hosea

In chapter 12, Hosea condemns Israel for its lies and violence (v. 1), its dishonest scales and fraud (v. 7), as well as its idolatry and unfaithfulness to God which form the main theme of the book. Hosea 12:6 urges: 'But you must return to your God; maintain love and justice, and wait for your God always.'

2. Micah

Micah denounced the rulers for their disregard for justice and their oppression of the people: 'Listen, you leaders of Jacob, you rulers of the house of Israel. Should you not know justice, you who hate good and love evil, who tear the skin from my people and the flesh from their bones' (Mic. 3:1–2).

Micah 3:8–12 declares:

> But as for me, I am filled with power, with the Spirit of the Lord, and with justice and might, to declare to Jacob his transgression, to Israel his sin. Hear this, you leaders of the house of Jacob, you rulers of the house of Israel, who despise justice and distort all that is right; who build Zion with bloodshed and Jerusalem with wickedness. Her leaders judge for a bribe, her priests tell for a price, and her prophets tell fortunes for money.

One of God's complaints about his people was that bribery and corruption were commonplace. Money was more important than truth. The economic had absolute priority over reality. Another of his complaints was about the 'bloodshed' that was taking place in the city. In biblical

---

[85] In addition to the prophets quoted below, see also Joel 3:3; Job 24:2–4, 9–10.
[86] Ellison, *Message of the Old Testament*, 55–6.

thought and prophetic language, this word 'bloodshed' is used to refer to social injustice and violence.[87]

In Micah's day, the establishment had become sophisticated in their extortion and injustice, and their behaviour was mutually reinforcing. 'Both hands are skilled in doing evil; the *ruler* demands gifts, the *judge* accepts bribes, the *powerful* dictate what they desire – they all conspire together' (Mic. 7:3).[88]

Instead of injustice, bribery, violence and oppression, Micah 6:8 asks: 'What does the LORD require of you? To act justly and to love mercy and to walk humbly with your God.'

3. Isaiah

The book of Isaiah begins with a condemnation of Judah that is identical in tone to the prophecies of Amos. In it, God addresses the nation and its leaders as the 'people of Gomorrah' and the 'rulers of Sodom'.[89] Again, God declares the people's sacrifices, worship and offerings to be unacceptable because the people are ignoring his Law, and because 'Your hands are full of blood ... Stop doing wrong, learn to do right! Seek justice, encourage the oppressed. Defend the cause of the fatherless, plead the case of the widow' (Isa. 1:15b–17).[90]

Jerusalem, the faithful city, which once was full of justice and righteousness, has now become a harlot, inhabited by murderers (Isa. 1:21). Its rulers are described as 'rebels, companions of thieves [who] all love bribes and chase after gifts' (Isa. 1:23a). God condemns them because 'they do not defend the cause of the fatherless' or deal with the case of the widow (Isa. 1:23b), because they 'acquit the guilty for a bribe, but deny justice to the innocent' (Isa. 5:23). In Isaiah 5:7, the prophet describes how the Lord 'looked for justice, but saw bloodshed; for righteousness, but heard cries of distress.'

4. Jeremiah

Jeremiah prophesied at a time when Judah was about to be invaded and Jerusalem was about to fall. What was God's message to his people, at this time?

> Say to the royal house of Judah, 'Hear the word of the LORD; O house of David, this is what the LORD says: "Administer justice every morning; rescue from the hand of his oppressor the one who has been robbed, or my wrath will break out and burn like fire because of the evil you have done – burn with no-one to quench it"'.
> (Jer. 21:12)

---

[87] Lucas, *Ezekiel*, 131; de Coninck, *La justice et l'abondance*, 18.
[88] Haugen, *Good News*, 131.
[89] Isaiah 1:11.
[90] Cf. O'Donovan, *Desire*, 39.

"Their evil deeds have no limit; they do not plead the case of the fatherless to win it, they do not defend the rights of the poor. Should I not punish them for this?" declares the LORD. "Should I not avenge myself on such a nation as this?"
(Jer. 5:28–29)

Jeremiah made plain just how highly God rates justice. He compared the sons of Josiah, Shallum (Jehoahaz) and Jehoiakim with their father. In blunt terms, at the palace, Jeremiah declared:

"Hear the word of the LORD, O king of Judah, you who sit on David's throne – you, your officials and your people who come through these gates. This is what the LORD says: Do what is just and right. Rescue from the hand of his oppressor the one who has been robbed. Do no wrong or violence to the alien, the fatherless or the widow, and do not shed innocent blood in this place. For if you are careful to carry out these commands, then kings who sit on David's throne will come through the gates of this palace, riding in chariots and on horses, accompanied by their officials and their people. But if you do not obey these commands, declares the Lord, I swear by myself that this palace will become a ruin."
(Jer. 22:2–5)

The survival of the royal dynasty was, God declared, dependent on the justice or injustice of the king's reign. Maintaining justice was a key part of the king's covenant obligations, and failing to uphold justice was a sin on a par with idolatry.[91]

Lest there be any doubt about this, Jeremiah pushed the comparison further:

Woe to him who builds his palace by unrighteousness, his upper rooms by injustice, making his countrymen work for nothing, not paying them for their labour. He says, "I will build myself a great palace with spacious upper rooms." So he makes large windows in it, panels it with cedar and decorates it in red. "Does it make you a king to have more and more cedar? Did not your father have food and drink? *He did what was right and just, so all went well with him. He defended the cause of the poor and needy, and so all went well. Is that not what it means to know me?*" declares the LORD. "But your eyes and your heart are set only on dishonest gain, on shedding innocent blood and on oppression and extortion."
(Jer. 22:13–17)

For all Josiah's religious, reforming zeal, what he is commended for in this passage is doing what is right and just, and defending the cause of the poor and needy. That, says the Lord, is what it means to know me.[92] As Jesus

---

[91] Jeremiah 22:9.

[92] See also Proverbs 21:3: 'To do what is right and just is more acceptable to the LORD than sacrifice' and Micah 6:8.

would later show, the two great commandments: 'Love the Lord your God with all your heart, soul, mind and strength', and 'Love your neighbour as yourself', are inextricably linked. And for a king, to love his people is to act justly towards them.

But Jeremiah's condemnation of injustice was not just reserved for their leaders. He stood at the Temple Gate and announced that instead of acting justly, the people were guilty of theft and murder, adultery, perjury and idolatry (Jer. 7:9). The Ten Commandments are directly in view here, and it is clear from Jeremiah's message that he regards them as having been totally desecrated.[93] How could the people imagine that they could do such things, and then come and offer their offerings at the Temple, secure in the knowledge that God would never do anything about it?[94]

The temple sermon recorded in Jeremiah 7 is a devastating exposé of this behaviour.[95] Underlying Jeremiah's denunciation is the message '"But I have been watching!" declares the LORD' (Jer. 7:11, 17). God was aware that the people's worship was as two-faced as the rest of their conduct.[96] Despite their offerings, the eyes and heart of the people were really 'set only on dishonest gain, on shedding innocent blood and on oppression and extortion'.[97] What God required was not sacrifices, but rather moral obedience.[98]

Instead of the evil they were practising, Jeremiah called the people to obey God's law.[99] In chapter 7:5–6, he urges them to 'really change your ways and your actions and [to] deal with each other justly', and he expressly mentions the paradigm cases in the Old Testament of those at the fringes of society to whom a duty to act justly was owed: the alien, the fatherless and the widow.

5. Ezekiel

In Ezekiel 22:1–16, the prophet presents the Lord's prosecution case against his people for violation of his covenant. First, they are condemned for their violence and idolatry,[100] and then the detailed allegations are highlighted. 'They cover the family, social justice, the temple cult, pagan worship, sexual matters, abuse of the legal system and

---

[93] R.K. Harrison, *Jeremiah and Lamentations: An Introduction and Commentary*, 86. See also D. Kidner, *The Message of Jeremiah*, 49; and R. Mason, *Jeremiah: The People's Bible Commentary*, 48.

[94] Jeremiah 7:9–10.

[95] Especially Jeremiah 7:9–11.

[96] Jeremiah 9:8; 3:22a.

[97] Jeremiah 22:17.

[98] Jeremiah 7:21–23.

[99] Jeremiah 26:4. Because of the arrangement of Jeremiah, chapters 7 and 26:1–6 almost certainly describe the same event.

[100] Ezekiel 22:3–5.

economic justice.'[101] The prophet condemns 'the princes of Israel' because each of them 'uses his power to shed blood' (v. 6), treats his mother and father with contempt (v. 7a), oppresses the alien and mistreats the fatherless and the widow (v. 7b). He hints at false testimony in the courts (v. 9a). He then lists a catalogue of sexual sins (v. 9b–11) before condemning them for bribery, usury and extortion (v. 12). In all these areas, which cover the whole of social, economic and religious life, the people had violated the covenant and had forgotten the Lord.[102]

The behaviour of the princes is like 'a roaring lion tearing its prey; they devour people, take treasures and precious things and make widows within [Israel]' (v. 25). The officials are 'like wolves tearing their prey; they shed blood and kill people to make unjust gain' (v. 27). Greed has ousted all sense of duty and respect for the weak. Everywhere 'the people of the land practise extortion and commit robbery; they oppress the poor and the needy and the alien, denying them justice' (v. 29).

All of this is evidence that the people had forgotten the Lord their God, and for which God would 'pour out my wrath upon them and consume them with my fiery anger, bringing down on their own heads all they have done' (v. 31). Because of their 'unjust gain' and 'the blood you have shed in your midst' Israel would be scattered among the nations (v. 13).

Injustice has consequences, and the ultimate consequence is the collapse of the civilisation. Like a creeping parasite such as ivy, in the end it will strangle its host to death.

6. Isaiah again

Towards the end of Isaiah, the theme of injustice is re-examined at length in chapters 58 and 59. Whether written by the same or a different hand, it is clear that the prophet is describing the situation in Israel after the return from exile.[103] What is startling is that he paints a picture of hypocritical religion and social injustice that is little different from that which pertained in Jerusalem in the years before the exile.

The people perform their religious duties, attending the temple 'as if they were a nation that does what is right and has not forsaken the commands of its God' (Isa. 58:2a). They wondered why God was not answering their prayers. The prophet's explanation was that the people's fasting was undermined by their exploitation of the workers (Isa. 58:3b) and used to degenerate into fighting and arguing (Isa. 58:4a):

> Rather than one day's humility, this, declares the LORD, is "the king of fasting I have chosen:
> To loose the chains of injustice and untie the cords of the yoke,
> To set the oppressed and break every yoke?

---

[101] Lucas, *Ezekiel*, 118.
[102] Ezekiel 22:12; cf. Deuteronomy 8:11, 19.
[103] J.A. Motyer, *Isaiah: An Introduction and Commentary*, 348.

... To share your food with the hungry
and to provide the poor wanderer with shelter –
when you see the naked, to clothe him,
and not to turn away from your own flesh and blood.
... Then you will call, and the Lord will answer;
you will cry for help, and he will say: Here am I."
(Isa. 58:6–7, 9)

Love for one's neighbour would be a far better demonstration of devotion to God than participation in religious rituals. True holiness was not a matter of ritual cleanliness, but a clean heart that opposed oppression, avoided unjust accusations and gossip (Isa. 58:9); which worked to feed the hungry and satisfy the needs of the oppressed (Isa. 58:10a): 'the ultimate measure of a leader's greatness lies in the extent to which he gives himself to and for the very needy of his people.'[104]

If God's people exhibited such qualities of holiness, *then* they could expect to experience his blessing (Isa. 58:11–12). Instead, however, the people's hands are stained with blood and their fingers with guilt (Isa. 59:3). Their society would descend into violence and anarchy (Isa. 59:6b–7) because of deception and lies (Isa. 59:3b). Litigants were no longer pursuing honest claims; it was a free-for-all in the courts (Isa. 59:4). The inevitable fruit of violence, deception and dishonesty was that:

> The way of peace they do not know; there is no justice in their paths ... So justice is far from us, and righteousness does not reach us. We look for light, but all is darkness ... Like the blind we grope along the wall, feeling our way like men without eyes ... We look for justice, but find none; for deliverance, but it is far away.
> (Isa. 59:8–11)

Shalom, justice and deliverance are nowhere to be found. What is required is a decisive act of delivering justice, an intervention in favour of righteousness and shalom which is so drastic in its effect that it merits the description 'salvation'.[105]

Isaiah's predictions proved all too accurate. In the time of Nehemiah, a combination of famine and heavy Persian taxation had forced the poor to mortgage their fields, their vineyards and even their homes in order to buy grain (Neh. 5:3). Others had had to sell their sons and daughters into slavery to make ends meet (Neh. 5:4). It was a point of honour for Nehemiah that, unlike his predecessors as governor, he did not tax them heavily (Neh. 5:15) and instead provided food for 150 people at his own table every day (Neh. 5:17–18). Furthermore, he persuaded the nobles and officials to return the fields, vineyards, olive groves and houses they had taken from the people, and to stop charging them usury.

---

[104] J.D.W. Watts, *Isaiah 34–66*, 275.
[105] Motyer, *Isaiah*, 367.

Isaiah criticises the religious rituals performed by the rich whilst on the same day they are exploiting their workers.[106] While the rich were worshipping, they were forcing the poor to continue working. He was not alone in making the connection: 'economic exploitation is linked to violation of the sabbath day for greedy motives, by Amos (8:5f.), Isaiah (58:3–14) and Jeremiah (17:19–27; cf. 7:5–11).'[107]

The people's behaviour was offensive to God. It amounted to 'rebellion and treachery against the LORD' (Isa. 59:13a). Although claiming to seek him, in fact, the people had turned their backs on God, 'fomenting oppression and revolt, uttering lies [their] hearts have conceived' (Isa. 59:13). The result of such a disregard of God and of his standards was that 'justice is driven back, and righteousness stands at a distance; truth has stumbled in the streets, [and] honesty cannot enter. Truth is nowhere to be found, and whoever shuns evil becomes a prey' (Isa. 59:14f.).

A society built on violence, deception and dishonesty is one in which justice, righteousness, truth and honesty are endangered species, and where the upright man is more likely to be victimised than honoured.[108] Ultimately, such societies come under God's judgement:

> The LORD looked and was displeased that there was no justice. He saw that there was no-one, he was appalled that there was no-one to intervene; so his own arm worked salvation for him, and his own righteousness sustained him. He put on righteousness as his breastplate, and the helmet of salvation on his head; he put on the garments of vengeance and wrapped himself in zeal as in a cloak. According to what they have done, so will he repay wrath to his enemies and retribution to his foes … "The Redeemer will come to Zion, to those in Jacob who repent of their sins", declares the LORD.
> (Isa. 59:15b–18, 20)

The significance of Isaiah 58–59 is that they lead up to a picture of the Redeemer, 'a third messianic figure, completing the portrayals of King (chapters 1 to 37) and Servant (chapters 38 to 55). The King reigns, the Servant saves and the [Redeemer] consummates salvation and vengeance.'[109] In the end, it is not the cycle of exile and restoration which will lead to the establishment of a just society. Ultimately, what will be required is the intervention of God himself.

7. Zechariah

Looking back from beyond the exile, the prophet Zechariah sought to remind the generation returning to Israel why it had occurred:

> This is what the LORD Almighty says: "Administer true justice; show mercy and compassion to one another. Do not oppress the widow or the fatherless, the alien

---

106 Wright, *People of God*, 79.
107 Wright, *People of God*, 79.
108 Motyer, *Isaiah*, 368.
109 Motyer, *Isaiah*, 371.

or the poor ..." But they refused to pay attention ... So the LORD Almighty was very angry ... [and] scattered them with a whirlwind among all the nations. (Zech. 7:8–12)

8. Malachi

Even at the end of the Old Testament period, the last of the prophets, Malachi had to write:

> "So I will come near to you for judgement. I will be quick to testify against sorcerers, adulterers and perjurers, against those who defraud labourers of their wages, who oppress the widows and the fatherless, and deprive aliens of justice, but do not fear me," says the LORD Almighty. (Mal. 3:5)

Calvin's conclusion from his study of the Old Testament was that, 'It is righteousness (justice) to take charge of the innocent, to defend and avenge them, and set them free: it is judgement to withstand the audacity of the wicked, to repress their violence and punish their faults.'[110] The force of the prophets' message about justice is inescapable.

Equally inescapable was the prophets' explanation for the people's alienation from God, from the land and from each other. It was because of Israel's covenant breaking, because of her unfaithfulness, because of her unrighteousness and her injustice that the Second Temple was a shadow of the glory of the First Temple, and Israel had lost its sovereignty over the Promised Land. Even at the time of Jesus, at least some Jews understood this state of affairs to be a continuation of the exile from the land which the Deuteronomist and the prophets had foretold, or at least a continuation of the curse of Deuteronomy 29.[111]

9. Justice in the New Testament

The cross of Christ as the epochal justice-making event dominates the New Testament vision of justice. Jesus Christ, the Saviour of the world, died a criminal's death on behalf of sinful human beings and the result of his conquest of sin and death was that the way was opened for renewed fellowship between God and man.[112] The implications of that event are, literally, infinite. Controversy surrounds its interpretation. Nonetheless, whether it is seen in terms of a substitution,[113] a sacrifice,[114] a representa-

---

[110] Calvin, *Institutes* Book IV, ch. 20, para. 9.

[111] N.T. Wright, *The Climax of the Covenant: Christ and the Law in Pauline Theology*, 141; *The New Testament and the People of God*, 270; M.A. Knibb, *The Qumran Community*, 20.

[112] Romans 4:25: 'He was delivered over to death for our sins and was raised to life for our justification.' See also Romans 5:1, 11; Ephesians 2:18.

[113] 2 Corinthians 5:14, 21; 8:9.

[114] 1 Corinthians 5:7; Romans 8:32; Hebrews 1:3; 7:26–28; 9:14, 23–28; 10:12, 14.

tive action or punishment,[115] a propitiation,[116] an expiation, a ransom,[117] a redemption,[118] all are agreed that through the atonement, God's justice was satisfied.[119]

On the cross, Jesus Christ was 'made sin'[120] and suffered the curse of the law.[121] Yet, he exhausted the curse. He overcame sin and death.[122] God, who raised him from the dead, vindicated him.

The resurrection of Jesus declared him with power to be the Son of God.[123] It established him as the one with the right to judge justly, the one with authority to declare the final judgement,[124] the implications of which are explored in chapter 9.

The declaration of Jesus as the Son of God also means that he is Lord over the law of God, with authority to interpret it, amend it, abrogate it and fulfil it. The ways in which he exercised that authority are examined in chapter six, and some of the implications of his teaching for the shape of human laws are explored in chapters 6, 7 and 8.

However, what can be stated unequivocally is that Jesus reaffirmed the importance of the call to justice that the prophets had declared. Jesus saved his harshest words for the Pharisees who claimed great knowledge of God but neglected 'the more important matters of God's law: justice, mercy and faithfulness' (Mt. 23:23). He condemned them because their meticulous religious observances were not matched by a concern about the things which actually matter most to God: 'Woe to you Pharisees, because you give God a tenth of your mint, rue and all other kinds of garden herbs, but you neglect justice and the love of God. You should have practised the latter without leaving the former undone' (Lk. 11:42). Jesus therefore affirmed the primacy of justice over the technicalities of obedience to the minutiae of the Torah.

Neither did Jesus' followers neglect the importance of justice. The concerns of Amos are reflected in the book of James, although whether this is a result of direct influence or merely a shared understanding of biblical ethics is an open question.[125] James knew that under the new covenant, justice remained as important to God as it

---

[115] Galatians 3:13.
[116] Romans 3:25.
[117] 1 Timothy 2:16; Hebrews 9:15.
[118] Romans 3:24; Galatians 4:5.
[119] Further development of this topic is not pursued here not because it is not important but because, on the contrary, to address the issues properly requires a book of its own!
[120] 2 Corinthians 5:21.
[121] Galatians 3:13.
[122] Cf. Romans 6:9–10.
[123] Romans 1:4.
[124] Cf. Romans 2:16; 1 Corinthians 15:20–28.
[125] Hubbard, *Joel and Amos*, 117; Young, *Major Themes*, 32.

had been under the old covenant. He wrote: 'Religion that God our Father accepts as pure and faultless is this: to look after orphans and widows in their distress and to keep oneself from being polluted by the world' (Jas. 1:27).

The prophetic call to justice is as applicable to Christians today as it was to the original audience of the prophets' words.

Justice and the Nations

The Old Testament prophets confirmed that the Lord God was sovereign not only over the affairs of Israel but also over all the nations of the earth. This divine sovereignty is expressed through their writings in an understanding of God's ability to use even pagan kings as instruments of his purposes, but also in the proclamation of divine judgement against the nations for their sins.

1. Pagan kings as instruments for God's purposes

The prophets' teaching on the sovereignty of the Lord God over the nations is exemplified by their portrayal of the Babylonian Empire. In around 702 BC, shortly after the Assyrian army had withdrawn from the gates of Jerusalem, Isaiah prophesied to King Hezekiah that 'the time will surely come when everything in your palace, and all that your fathers have stored up until this day, will be carried off to Babylon' (Isa. 39:6). A hundred years later, as Babylonian invaders marched upon Jerusalem for the third and final time, Jeremiah confirmed the inevitability of their victory, but looked beyond it to a return from exile in Babylon after seventy years (Jer. 29:10). Isaiah then picks up the theme again and announces judgement on Babylon and the overthrowing of its empire by the Persian ruler Cyrus.

The first inclination of the secular, modern world would be to regard the dominance of the Babylonian Empire simply as might being right.[126] Instead, Jeremiah saw Israel's God as 'the key character and [the] decisive agent in the public processes of history'[127], not only in and for the nation of Israel, but also for all the nations of the world. In Jeremiah 27:4–5, the point is made plainly: 'This is what the LORD Almighty, the God of Israel, says: "Tell this to your masters: With my great might and out-stretched arm I made the earth and its people and the animals that are on it, and *I give it to anyone I please*."'

From the first, Jeremiah prophesied that Judah would fall to Babylon.[128] He understood clearly that Judah was in breach of her covenant promises and obligations to her God, and that she was therefore the subject of

---

[126] Birch et al, *Theological Introduction*, 323.
[127] Birch et al, *Theological Introduction*, 324.
[128] Jeremiah 25:9.

God's wrath.[129] He saw Babylon as the chosen agent by which that judgement would come, just as Assyria had been the divine agent used to execute God's judgement on the northern kingdom of Israel.[130]

It was God's will that Nebuchadnezzar's enemies should be 'handed over' to him.[131] Having nominated Nebuchadnezzar as his servant, disobedience to him would only bring further punishment and destruction.[132]

The prophet Jeremiah announced to his generation that, contrary to popular expectation, God was *with* the murderous, Babylonian invader Nebuchadnezzar and against Jerusalem, its temple and its rulers. The message of Jeremiah destroys any facile 'God-is-on-our-side' theology. Jeremiah was crystal clear in affirming the teaching of Deuteronomy that God's blessing was conditional upon righteous living.[133] God could no longer tolerate the injustice/unrighteousness of the people and their leaders, which had been challenged and condemned by the prophets.

Jeremiah plainly shows how God's people, those who claim to be identified with him, whether as the worshippers at his temple, or the Christians who claim to be his Son's disciples, are potentially the subjects of God's wrath if their deeds do not match their words. "'… what else can I do because of the sin of my people? … Should I not punish them for this?" declares the LORD. "Should I not avenge myself on such a nation as this?"'[134] Faith is to be matched by faithfulness.

Jeremiah deliberately chose to give his message about the inevitability of the Babylonian yoke not only to the Judaean king Zedekiah but also to the ambassadors from the surrounding nations who had come to form an alliance against Nebuchadnezzar.[135] But in addition to his message of judgement on the surrounding nations, Jeremiah also contains promises of salvation for Judah's neighbours, somehow mediated by Israel.[136] The fundamental point is that it is the Lord God, and not the individual national deities, who is in charge of all their fates.[137] Israel's God laid claim to universal lordship and in the exercise of that lordship was going to use the sinful nation of Babylon in order to punish other sinful nations in the Middle East for their sins. Nebuchadnezzar's victory was certain, because it was divinely ordained. Jeremiah's message is that Nebuchadnezzar and his armies may be murderous thugs, but he has been

---

[129] Jeremiah 40:3: 'All this happened because you people sinned against the Lord and did not obey him.' Cf. Deuteronomy 28:15, 58–68; 30:17–19.

[130] Mason, *Jeremiah*, 73.

[131] Jeremiah 20:4–6; 21:7; 27:6; 32:25, 28: 34:2, 21–22; 38:3; 46:24.

[132] Jeremiah 27:8–11; 28; 29:32; 32:5.

[133] Mason, *Jeremiah*, 48.

[134] Jeremiah 9:9. See also Jeremiah 10:17–18; 15:14.

[135] Jeremiah 27:3.

[136] Jeremiah 3:17; 12:14–17; 16:19; 46:26; 48:47; 49:6, 39. McConville, *Judgment and Promise*, 47.

[137] Mason, *Jeremiah*, 137.

chosen by Yahweh as his appointed agent to execute judgement on Israel.[138] Fighting against Nebuchadnezzar will be as futile as fighting against God himself.[139]

The Lord God could even describe the Babylonian king Nebuchadnezzar as 'my servant'.[140] God would 'summon' him and his armies, and bring them against Judah[141] and later against Egypt.[142] Time and again three possible judgements are mentioned in tandem – sword, famine and plague.[143] God is seen by Jeremiah as just as much in charge of the sword as of the other two 'natural' disasters.

For Jeremiah, 'Events in Judah, Egypt, and Babylon resulted much more from divine sovereignty than from human politics. Human politics could succeed only when they agreed with God's will.'[144] Jeremiah's view of history and of God's power to achieve his purposes therefore stands in contradiction to that of the process theologians, who think God is somehow limited to using only persuasive means to achieve his purposes.[145]

But even those who are used by God as instruments to execute his judgement do not thereby gain immunity or impunity from it. Jeremiah prophesies not only against Judah but also against the surrounding nations[146] and, lastly, against Babylon herself.[147] The Lord is sovereign. He is ultimately in control.[148] Because of her brutality, because of her pride, because of failure to recognise that her victories were dependent on the actions of Israel's God, Babylon herself will be judged.[149]

The message of Jeremiah is that all the nations, and God's people among them, stand under God's judgement if they persist in their sinfulness. God is not above using one sinful human regime after another to achieve his purposes of blessing[150] or judgement.[151] The Lord sees injustice and will not let it continue forever.

---

[138] Jeremiah 25:8–11.
[139] Jeremiah 12:12; 21:3–7.
[140] Jeremiah 25:9; 27:6; 43:10.
[141] Jeremiah 25:9–11. See also Daniel 1:2.
[142] Jeremiah 43:8–13.
[143] Jeremiah 14:11; 29:17–18; 27:12; 32:24, 36; 34:17; 38:2; 42:17, 22.
[144] Lasor et al, *Old Testament Survey*, 349.
[145] C.H. Pinnock, *Most Moved Mover: A Theology of God's Openness*, 146–7.
[146] Jeremiah 25:15–26; 46:1–49:39.
[147] Jeremiah 25:12–14, 26b; 50:1–51:64.
[148] Jeremiah 27:4–7; 32:27; 51:15–16.
[149] Greater insight into the nature of this judgement is given through Daniel – see Daniel 2:31–45; 7.
[150] As Cyrus was used – Isaiah 45:1–7.
[151] As Nebuchadnezzar was used, and then as Cyrus was used against Babylon – see Jeremiah 51 and Isaiah 46–47.

Writing at around the same time as Jeremiah, the prophet Habbakuk delivered the same message. Habbakuk complained directly to God about the continuing injustices which he saw in the nation of Judah. He went to God and said:

> How long, O Lord, must I call for help, but you do not listen? Or cry out to you, 'Violence!' but you do not save? Why do you make me look at injustice? Why do you tolerate wrong? Destruction and violence are before me; there is strife and conflict abounds. Therefore the law is paralysed, and justice never prevails. The wicked hem in the righteous, so that justice is perverted. (Hab. 1:2–4)[152]

God's answer was that he would use the Babylonians, the cruel, militaristic Babylonians, to execute his judgement on the rulers of the land. Habbakuk found this hard to stomach. The prescribed cure for the godlessness and oppression practised by Israel's leaders seemed worse than the disease. So God went on to reveal to Habbakuk how the day would eventually come for Babylon herself to be judged, and to fall and be plundered (Hab. 2:2–17).

2. The Lord of the nations (Isa. 40:15–17, 22–24)

In Isaiah, the announcement in chapter 39 that one day Jerusalem would be conquered by Babylon is followed by a call to a change of perspective. Isaiah 40 says look beyond those human leaders who seem powerful to you, and think instead about the God who made the universe. Compared with God's achievements in creation, what are the nations and their leaders? They are insignificant, as insignificant as withered grass or faded flowers (Isa. 40:6–8). Who were Sennacherib and Nebuchadnezzar? In their time, they were as powerful and invincible as Napoleon, Hitler or Stalin; but now they have been and gone, and the world hardly remembers them at all.

It is God who raises up and strikes down the rulers. As Isaiah 40:24 says: 'Scarcely have they been planted, scarcely have they been sown, scarcely has their stock taken root in the earth, But he merely blows on them and they wither' (NASB).

Although Babylon had been God's chosen agent of judgement, she was also responsible for her own actions. She was the devourer.[153] Neither Isaiah nor Jeremiah saw anything incongruent in declaring Babylon in one breath to be summoned by God to bring judgement on Judah, and then in the next breath announcing that she is subject to God's punishment because of her guilt.[154] Just as Babylon's victory was inevitable because she was being used as God's servant, so her ultimate collapse was assured because she was under God's judgement.[155]

---

[152] See also Malachi 2:17.
[153] Jeremiah 5:16–17.
[154] Jeremiah 25:9–12.
[155] Jeremiah 25:12–14.

Babylon would be judged according to the way she had dealt with others, and treated in exactly the same way she had treated them.[156] In particular, she would be judged for her massacres of Judah: 'Babylon must fall for the slain of Israel, as the slain of all the earth have fallen because of Babylon' (Jer. 51:24, 49; NRSV).[157] The prophet Isaiah does not mince his words. In Isaiah 47 he announces that as Babylon had murdered, raped and pillaged her way across the Middle East, killing children and leaving widows, so she would experience the same (Isa. 47:8–9). Isaiah 47:1 describes a pampered princess, tender and delicate; who will be taken from her throne and forced to sit in the dust. She will be treated as a slave, given millstones to use to grind flour (Isa. 47:2a), and then taken as a naked captive into exile, there to be raped and abused (Isa. 47:3a).

In Isaiah 47:7, Babylon is condemned for failing to learn the lessons of history. The fact that *even* God's special people do not escape his judgement ought to have taught the Babylonians a lesson – they too would fall under his wrath if they did not change their ways (v. 7). Instead, they believed their own publicity (Isa. 47:5, 7–8) and attributed their success to their own wisdom and know-how (Isa. 47:9–15). For their pride, cruelty and self-satisfaction, they would be judged.

In October 539 BC, King Cyrus of Persia marched out of Iran into Southern Iraq. Leaving Babylon (near the site where one day Baghdad would be built) until last, he conquered and occupied the surrounding territory. Seeing which way the wind was blowing, King Nabonidus of Babylon deserted the city, leaving it in the charge of his son, Belshazzar. While Belshazzar held a final, wild party,[158] Cyrus and his army crept into the city, either via the river or because the gates had been opened to them from the inside. The next morning, Babylon had fallen. Then, as Isaiah had prophesied, Cyrus allowed the Israelite exiles to return home.

Today, we have an intellectual difficulty with the idea of divine judgement. But the message of the Old Testament, as of the New, is that God's wrath is not a hasty reaction to people's momentary lapses into sin. On the contrary, both the Old and New Testaments affirm that the Lord is 'slow to anger and abounding in love' (Jonah 4:2). Jonah's explanation as to why he did not want to prophesy to Nineveh was that he feared that the people would repent and God would not bring the promised disaster upon them.[159]

In the Old Testament there are repeated references to God's judgement against a people awaiting its appointed time.[160] The whole tenor

---

[156] Jeremiah 50:15.

[157] Harrison, *Jeremiah*, 189 suggests possible alternative translations for Jeremiah 51:49.

[158] Daniel 5.

[159] See chapter 1.

[160] Jeremiah 27:7; 50:31; 51:11; Genesis 15:16. See also Jeremiah 44:22 where the same principle is applied to Judah herself!

of the biblical message is that God withholds judgement for as long as possible. This can be seen from the deferment of the sentence of death on Adam and Eve, through to the teaching of 2 Peter 3:9 that 'The Lord is not slow in keeping his promise, as some understand slowness. He is patient with you, not wanting anyone to perish, but everyone to come to repentance.' Through the active working of God's common grace, the full and awful consequences of sin are restrained. When God's judgement is administered, it is not that people are suddenly struck by a punishment they could not have seen coming, but rather that having hardened themselves in their ways, and become immune to the call to repentance,[161] God's protection is withdrawn and they experience the consequences of the path of rebellion that they have chosen for themselves.

3. Judgement against the nations

The judgement on Babylon was not peculiar; rather it was the culmination of God's judgement against the nations. All the surrounding nations were to be judged.[162] In Jeremiah 25:15–38, the cup of God's wrath is passed around from nation to nation, with Babylon the last to drink.

Despite their focus on God's judgement against his own people, the biblical prophets are also notable for their oracles against the nations. These can be found in Amos,[163] Isaiah,[164] Jeremiah,[165] Ezekiel,[166] Nahum and Obadiah, Zephaniah[167] and Zechariah.[168] In the oracles against the nations, 'God shows his sovereignty in history by judging nations directly' with no mention made of the human agent responsible.[169]

The oracles against the nations are 'testimony to the belief that God is Sovereign Lord of the whole world and not just the domestic deity of Israel.'[170] Nahum is uncompromising about the Lord's actions, declaring that, 'The LORD is a jealous and avenging God; the LORD takes vengeance and is filled with wrath. The LORD takes vengeance on his foes and maintains his wrath against his enemies' (Nah. 1:2). Although, 'the LORD is slow to anger', he is 'great in power' and 'will not leave the guilty unpunished' (Nah. 1:3).

---

[161] Cf. the references to Pharaoh hardening his heart in Exodus (Exod. 7:13–14, 22; 8:15, 19, 32; 9:7, 12, 35) and to the people of Judah in Jeremiah (Jer. 16:12; 18:12; 22:17).

[162] Jeremiah 48–51.

[163] Amos 1–2.

[164] Isaiah 13–23.

[165] Jeremiah 46–51.

[166] Ezekiel 25–32 and 35.

[167] Zephaniah 2:4–15.

[168] Zechariah 9:1–8.

[169] LaSor et al, *Old Testament Survey*, 350.

[170] Mason, *Jeremiah*, 210, 227; de Coninck, *La justice et la puissance*, 88.

The main reason for judgement against the nations expressed in Ezekiel,[171] Jeremiah[172] and Isaiah[173] is their pride, self-confidence and worship of false gods. It is their failure to acknowledge the Lord which was identified as their prime error.

But alongside this, emerge other themes. In Ezekiel, the prophet condemns the king of Tyre for his pride and wealth gained by dishonest trade.[174] He offers another explanation, alongside that of sexual perversity,[175] for the destruction of Sodom: 'arrogant, overfed and unconcerned; they did not help the poor and needy. They were haughty and did detestable things before me. Therefore I did away with them' (Ezek. 16:49).[176] Isaiah prophesies against Babylon for the oppressive and aggressive nature of its empire.[177] Nahum condemns Nineveh as 'the city of blood, full of lies, full of plunder, never without victims!' (Nah. 3:1).[178] Violence, dishonesty, extortion and oppression are among its crimes. The Assyrian wars of conquest are condemned as having been driven by 'the wanton lust of a harlot' (Nah. 3:4). Obadiah denounces Edom for its 'violence against your brother Jacob' (Obad. 10, 13–14).

In the New Testament, in Revelation chapter 18, Ezekiel's condemnation of Tyre is updated and revised and applied as a denunciation of Rome, and of the unjust trade system that sustains the luxurious lifestyle of the Roman elite.[179]

Amos, probably the first prophet whose oracles against the nations have been recorded, announces judgement on the surrounding nations not only because of treatment of God's people and their rape of God's land, but also for the way in which they have behaved towards one another, in violation of the common basic norms applicable to all humanity. Thus Damascus is condemned because 'she threshed Gilead with sledges having iron teeth' (Amos 1:3), Gaza and Tyre for taking captive whole communities and selling them as slaves,[180] Tyre for disregarding its

---

[171] Ezekiel 27:3; 28:2, 5–6; 29:3, 9.

[172] Jeremiah 48:7, 29–30, 42; 49:4, 16; 50:31–2. The worship of false gods is a particular focus of the oracles against the nations in Jeremiah, and in many cases judgement is declared explicitly to be a punishment against the nation's god(s): Jeremiah 46:25; 48:13; 49:3; 50:2b; 51:47.

[173] Isaiah 10:12–19; 13:11b, 19; 14:13; 16:6; 23:9. See also Zephaniah 2:10, 15.

[174] Ezekiel 28:16, 18.

[175] Genesis 19:24–25; Jude 7.

[176] See also Isaiah 1:9f. and Amos 4:11 were similar prophetic comparisons are drawn between the state of oppression and injustice in Judah and Israel, and Sodom. See Wright, *People of God*, 107.

[177] Isaiah 14:2, 4–6.

[178] O'Donovan, *Desire*, 68.

[179] de Coninck, *La justice et la puissance*, 88–9.

[180] Amos 1:6, 9.

treaty obligations,[181] Ammon for ripping open the pregnant women of Gilead,[182] and Moab for defiling the bones of Edom's king.[183] The 'gods' of the nations would be judged for their violence and injustices. The angelic forces, the political structures, and the human rulers of the nation would be accountable to God for their actions. They were called to the same vocation to exercise justice as Israel was,[184] and would be judged for their favouritism towards the unjust and the wicked, and their failure to defend the cause of the weak, the fatherless, the poor, the needy and the oppressed (Ps. 82:1–4).

Worship of false gods, social injustice, greed, violence and pride are all interlinked. Failure to acknowledge the nature of the true God (and the true nature of God), failure to acknowledge the nature of our obligations to others, and disregard for what God has revealed to us about morality all lead to a perverted scale of values in which 'might is right'. Against such a state of affairs, wherever it occurs, God will act. Right from the beginning of the prophetic Oracles Against the Nations, Amos had preached that: 'If it is true that YHWH's *tsedeq* is his vindication of the righteous against their adversaries, it is also true that it is his vindication of the *righteous*, and that a faithless nation, though chosen of God, cannot escape God's judgment of its ways.'[185]

Conclusion: The Contrast Between Current Injustice and Divine Justice

There are common themes in the writings of the prophets. All are agreed that God hates oppression. He is angered by the powerful throwing their weight around, abusing their power and influence. God is angry when the rights of the powerless are not protected, when there is no one to plead their case or to help them enforce their entitlements. Abuse of power and unequal access to justice anger him. He is furious when money, when economics, is given priority over people, when things matter more than individuals, when oppression takes the place of compassion.

God's love of justice and hatred of injustice are a recurrent theme. 'For I, the LORD, love justice; I hate robbery and iniquity' (Isa. 61:8). '"[L]et him who boasts boast about this: that he understands and knows me, that I am the LORD, who exercises kindness, justice and righteousness on earth, for in these I delight," declares the LORD' (Jer. 9:24). Many of the prophets made their point by drawing a contrast between current injustice and divine justice. The Psalmist proclaimed: 'The LORD

---

181 Amos 1:9.
182 Amos 1:13.
183 Amos 2:1.
184 O'Donovan, *Desire*, 68.
185 O'Donovan, *Desire*, 38.

is a refuge for the oppressed ... He does not ignore the cry of the afflicted' (Ps. 9:9, 12).[186] Isaiah 58–59 describes a whole catalogue of injustices. The situation is both desperate and shocking.

> But your iniquities have separated you from your God; your sins have hidden his face from you, so that he will not hear. For your hands are stained with blood, your fingers with guilt ... The LORD looked and was displeased that there was no justice. He saw that there was no one, he was appalled that there was no one to intervene.
> (Isa. 59:2, 16)

What did the Lord do about it?

> so his own arm worked salvation for him, and his own righteousness sustained him ... According to what they have done, so he will repay wrath to his enemies and retribution to his foes ... The Redeemer will come to Zion, to those in Jacob who repent of their sins.
> (Isa. 59:16, 18, 20)

The contrast between current injustice and divine justice led to an expectation of a 'Day of the Lord' when wrongs would be righted, and justice upheld[187] and of a righteous ruler who would rule with perfect justice.

The later prophets foresaw that the only proper solution to human injustice is divine intervention, a ruler who will come to rule in justice, who will redeem and rescue his people and execute judgement on all the enemies of God, whose justice and laws will be displayed among the nations (Isa. 51:4–5).

In fact, the testimony of the New Testament is that the Lord will come to earth twice. Jesus came to earth as Christ, as Messiah, as Redeemer, as Saviour. He will come again as Judge (Rev. 19:11). Until then, we have to live with the frustration of knowing that in Christ the kingdom of God is already come but that until he returns again the kingdom of God will not come in its fullness.

In prophetic thought the God who will one day act definitively, at the end of history, in order to bring justice to his people is also the God who acts in history to bring justice for his people.[188] When Jesus, the instrument of God's deliverance, came to earth he responded to human sickness with healing; to human hunger with food; and to human fears with protection. He calls his followers to do likewise.[189]

---

[186] See also Psalm 11; 12:5; Exodus 23:7; Deuteronomy 20:10; Proverbs 6:16–17; 1 Kings 20:31; 2 Kings 6:22; 24:4; Isaiah 59:7; James 5:4. Cf. O'Donovan, *Desire*, 74.

[187] Malachi 4; Zechariah 14; Zephaniah 1:14–18.

[188] Haugen, *Good News*, 94.

[189] Haugen, *Good News*, 95.

6

Christ and Caesar

Jesus is King

There can be no doubt that Jesus saw himself as a king and that others did too. When he was born, the wise men came from the East looking for the king whose star had been seen in the heavens.[1] King Herod in Jerusalem, who was prepared to go to the most drastic and despicable lengths to eliminate his rival, saw Jesus' birth as a threat. The proclamation of the angels in the heavens in Luke 2:14 was a divine re-appropriation of terms of praise which obsequious courtiers had been offering to the Emperor Augustus.[2]

When Jesus grew up, he was continually preaching and teaching about the kingdom. That was his message. Everywhere he went, he announced, 'The kingdom of God is coming' (Mt. 4:17; Mk. 1:14–15). The prayer Jesus taught his followers begins, 'Our Father in heaven, hallowed be your name, *your kingdom come* ...'.[3]

On Palm Sunday, Jesus entered Jerusalem in triumph, like a conquering general, a king claiming the city in victory. The manner of his entry was a conscious fulfilment of Zechariah 9, the entry into the capital city of the righteous and saving king, who would proclaim peace to the nations and whose rule would extend from sea to sea (Zech. 9:9–10).[4] The people shouted and screamed, 'Hosanna to the Son of David', which was the equivalent of saying: 'All Hail the King', or 'Jesus rules'. The people were declaring Jesus to be the heir to the long lost throne, just like Aragorn in *The Lord of the Rings*. And King Jesus acknowledged their praises.[5]

A week later, when he was executed they put above his head, in three languages, for the entire world to see, 'The King of the Jews'. He was executed by the political authorities, on the basis that he was a dangerous pretender to the throne of David, the greatest of all the Jewish kings.

Jesus was born a king, he proclaimed a kingdom, and he died as a king. His resurrection was the proof of his kingship. He is the one who will one day 'judge the world with justice' (Acts 17:31). There can be no doubt that the Christian church should be proclaiming him as the 'King of Kings'.

---

[1] Matthew 2:1–2.

[2] de Coninck, *La justice et la puissance*, 17–18.

[3] Matthew 6:10.

[4] O'Donovan, *Desire*, 24.

[5] See also Nathanael's declaration, 'Rabbi, you are the Son of God; you are the King of Israel' (Jn. 1:49).

When Jesus was taken before Pilate, the Roman governor, who had to decide what to do with Jesus, three of the Gospels record simply that Pilate asked him, 'Are you the king of the Jews?' and Jesus replied, 'Yes, it is as you say.'

John's Gospel expands on that conversation in John 18:33–40. John records that Jesus told Pilate, 'I am a king', but 'my kingdom is not of this world'. And herein lies the difficult question: how does the kingship of Jesus relate to the kingdoms of this world?

There is an immediate tension for the Christian believer between Jesus' declaration of a kingdom (of which he was, implicitly, the king) and his pronouncement that his kingdom was not of this world. His opponents grasped the implications of his first assertion, even if his subsequent followers have not. He was crucified, as Yoder points out, as a political as well as a religious threat.

Jesus himself came to preach of a kingdom, a kingdom not of this world, but one which, as George Beasley-Murray has painstakingly demonstrated, was characterised in the present era by the already-but-not-yet dynamic, which is the constant of Christian eschatological thought.[6]

What Manner of King?

In the New Testament, the Apostle Paul continually refers to Jesus in his letters as 'Christ Jesus' or 'Jesus Christ'. He uses the term as a title, just as we would refer to our ruler as 'Queen Elizabeth'.[7]

But what was meant by the term 'Christ', which is the Greek translation of the Hebrew word 'Messiah'? 'Messiah' was originally a descriptive word meaning 'the Anointed One'. Although the word 'Messiah' as a proper noun only appears twice in the Old Testament, in two neighbouring verses in Daniel 9,[8] the 'anointed' is referred to a further thirty-seven times, sometimes referring to a priest or king and sometimes to a future figure sent by God.

F.F. Bruce identifies five main features of Old Testament messianism:

1. God chooses the anointed one.
2. He is chosen to accomplish a redemptive purpose towards God's people.
3. He is to bring judgement on God's foes.
4. He is given dominion over the nations.
5. In all of his activities the Lord is the one ultimately at work.[9]

---

[6] G.R. Beasley-Murray, *Jesus and the Kingdom of God*.
[7] Wright, *What Saint Paul Really Said*, 51.
[8] Daniel 9:25–26.
[9] 'Messiah', in *The New Bible Dictionary*, 811.

By the time of Jesus, there were multiple messianic expectations, as different people looked forward to this or that sort of Messiah – but all focussed around common themes: political triumph, vindication for the Jews, judgement on the nations, the end of history and the inauguration of a golden age, and the victory over evil.[10]

In Jesus' day, most popular among the visions of the Messiah was that of 'a glorious and triumphant prince of David's line, who would restore the kingdom to Israel'.[11] Given the political context, where the Romans were the latest in an almost unbroken line of foreign occupying powers stretching back to the Babylonians,[12] it is hardly surprising that the hope of a national liberator was an extremely attractive one. Advocates of the political Messiah could point with confidence to Jeremiah 23:5–8, 30 and Ezekiel 34:20–31 as promises of a political ruler who would bring peace for the nation. The Zealots longed for a military general who would lead them to victory in battle against the Romans.[13]

But Jesus was not the political Messiah the people hoped for. He turned down the kingdoms of the world when Satan offered them to him (Mt. 4:8–10; Lk. 4:5–6), he walked through the crowd when he thought that they would proclaim him king (Jn. 6:15) and he told Pilate that his kingdom was not of this world (Jn. 18:36).

Nonetheless, he accepted the adulation of the crowds on Palm Sunday (Mt. 21:9–10; Mk. 11:8–10; Lk. 19:37–40; Jn. 12:12–13) and he was crucified under the citation 'THE KING OF THE JEWS' (Mk. 15:26). While the Jews' motivation for executing Jesus was that he was a blasphemer (Mk. 14:61–64),[14] the formal charge presented to Pilate was one of rebellion (Lk. 23:1).[15]

To both onlookers and his followers, what was puzzling about Jesus was that at times he seemed to be on the verge of embracing the ideal of being the longed-for political Messiah, only then to reject it decisively. It is highly significant that immediately after Peter's confession of Jesus as the Messiah (Mt. 16:16), Jesus began the slow process of explaining to his disciples that his mission would end in suffering and death not the establishment of the messianic kingdom by force (Mt. 16:17–21; Mk. 8:27–33; Lk. 9:18–22).

---

[10] A. Richardson, *The Political Christ*, 44–5.

[11] Richardson, *Political Christ*, 36; Drane argues that variations on this idea were held by the Zealots, the Pharisees and the Essenes. See J. Drane, *Jesus and the Four Gospels*, 19, 41.

[12] The Hasmoneans (165 BC to 37 BC) being the exceptions to the rule.

[13] J.H. Yoder, *The Politics of Jesus: Vicit Agnus Noster*, 42, 56–8.

[14] A charge which they found proved on Jesus' confession that he was the 'Christ', i.e. the Messiah, and 'the Son of the Blessed One', i.e. the Son of God.

[15] Richardson, *Political Christ*, 28, 40; Yoder, *Politics of Jesus*, 50.

When he entered Jerusalem in triumph, Jesus did not do so in a tank, or a limousine, or on the equivalent of his time, a beautiful, tall, black stallion. Instead, he entered Jerusalem in humility, on a donkey.

In fact, for those with ears to hear, the nature of Jesus' messiahship and the characteristics of his kingdom had been set out by him much earlier in his ministry.

The nature of Jesus' messiahship

In Luke 4, Jesus went to the synagogue in Nazareth, and announced there his manifesto. If Jesus were going around today, seeking to establish his kingdom by getting elected as a politician, this would have been the moment at which he announced his political programme.

Jesus stood up in the synagogue, turned to the book of the prophet Isaiah, and read from it:

> The Spirit of the Lord is on me,
> Because he has anointed me to preach good news to the poor.
> He has sent me to proclaim freedom for the prisoners[16]
> And recovery of sight for the blind,
> To release the oppressed,
> To proclaim the year of the Lord's favour.
> (Lk. 4:18–19)

And Luke says that when he had finished, Jesus rolled up the scroll, gave it back to the attendant and sat down, before adding, 'Today this Scripture is fulfilled in your hearing' (Lk. 4:17–21). In so doing, Jesus had attributed to himself the kingly role of the Servant of the Lord set out in Isaiah 42:1–9.[17]

Matthew 4:23–24 describes the fulfilment of that manifesto. Matthew tells us:

> Jesus went throughout Galilee, teaching in their synagogues, preaching the good news of the kingdom, and healing every disease and sickness among the people. News about him spread all over Syria, and people brought to him all who were ill with various diseases, those suffering severe pain, the demon-possessed, those having seizures, and the paralysed and he healed them.

When John the Baptist had doubts about whether Jesus really was the Anointed One sent to bring in God's kingdom, Jesus told John's disciples, 'Go back and report to John what you hear and see: The blind receive sight, the lame walk, those who have leprosy are cured, the deaf hear, the dead are raised, and the good news is preached to the poor' (Mt. 11:4). In

[16] de Coninck points out that, as in Victorian England, the majority of prisoners at the time of Christ were poor peasants or artisans who had been imprisoned because of their inability to pay their debts: *La justice et la puissance*, 18.
[17] O'Donovan, *Desire*, 84.

testing the credibility of his promises, Jesus had no fear of being judged upon his record.[18]

The Jews dreamed of the Messiah who would be a person of great power and authority, with the ability to restore sight, bring about healing, grant longevity and end poverty (Isa. 9:3; 11:9; 61:1). They looked forward to the realisation of the vision of a time of material prosperity when the Messiah would satisfy all physical needs.[19]

But despite his provision of food for the multitudes, Jesus rejected the role of the economic Messiah, producing prosperity for his people through the supernatural provision of food in the desert when the devil presented him with this temptation (Mt. 4:3). Despite his miracles, Jesus rejected the role of spiritual superstar, maintaining cult status by wonder working stage-shows (Mt. 4:6).

Healings, miracles, the defeat of demons, the rescuing of those who are as good as dead, good news to the poor, release for the prisoners – the prisoners of bad habits, of alcohol, of drugs, of prostitution, of greed, of injustice and of racism, all these were characteristics of the kingdom of God that Jesus was announcing. But it was the deliverance that they accomplished rather than the power that they displayed which was the focus of Jesus' ministry.

Matthew saw in Jesus the fulfilment of the prophecies of Isaiah 42:1–4 about a Servant-King who would bring about justice among the nations:

> Here is my servant whom I have chosen, the one I love, in whom I delight; I will put my Spirit on him, and he will proclaim justice to the nations. He will not quarrel or cry out; no-one will hear his voice in the streets. A bruised reed he will not break, and a smouldering wick he will not snuff out, till he leads justice to victory. In his name the nations will put their hope.
> (Mt. 12:18–20)

Here was a gentle king who would nonetheless 'lead justice to victory', who would achieve through his actions God's intended deliverance, not just for the people of Israel but also for the nations of the world.

Jesus did defeat his enemies, but they were not the Romans. He took on the 'real' enemies of God's purposes in the world: sickness, sin, demons, and death. The stories he told were about what the kingdom is like; the actions he took demonstrated the nature of his kingdom – he healed the sick; he raised the dead; he expelled demons; he forgave sins. His was a kingdom at war with its enemies – sickness, sin and death. Jesus knew that these, rather than external human allegiances, were the true causes of our rebellion and he dealt with them.[20]

---

[18] O'Donovan, *Desire*, 89.

[19] Drane, *Jesus and the Four Gospels*, 40.

[20] O'Donovan, *Desire*, 130.

The characteristics of Jesus' kingdom

In his Gospel, Matthew places 'The Sermon on the Mount', Jesus' exposition of the characteristics of his kingdom (Mt. 5:1 – 7:29), immediately after the passage in Matthew 4 which records the nature of Jesus' messiahship and his victory over sickness and demons. 'The Kingdom is the theme of the beatitudes ... It is the comprehensive idea that holds them all together.'[21]

It is a kingdom whose citizens will be characterised by a thirst for righteousness, by mercy, purity and peace making. It is a kingdom whose citizens will be persecuted, because they take their cue from the prophets (Mt. 5:12). It is a kingdom that will reflect God's emphasis on justice and mercy being shown to the weak, the poor and the needy (Mt. 25:31–46).

Servant leadership

In the New Testament, Jesus adopted the metaphor of shepherd leadership and applied it to himself.[22] He declared, 'I am the good shepherd, who lays down his life for his sheep' (Jn. 10:11). He then passed it on to his followers, asking Peter to feed his lambs and tend his sheep (Jn. 21:15–17). The writer of 1 Peter urged church elders to 'Be shepherds of God's flock that is under your care ... not greedy for money, but eager to serve; not lording it over those entrusted to you, but being examples to the flock' (1 Pet. 5:2–3). This is to be done because they are answerable to Jesus who is 'the Chief Shepherd' (1 Pet. 5:4).

When Jesus' disciples were arguing among themselves about who was the greatest, Jesus said, 'The kings of the Gentiles lord it over them; and those who exercise authority over them call themselves Benefactors. But you are not to be like that. Instead, the greatest among you should be like the youngest, and the one who rules like the one who serves' (Lk. 22:25–26). By reference to his own example (Lk. 22:27), Jesus issues a challenge for a new style of authority to be exhibited, one which does not enjoy power for the purposes of self-glorification, but instead uses it for the service of others.

This is part of the challenge the Christian church ought to be presenting to the governing authorities in our time:

> telling them, in the name of Jesus, that there is a different way of being human, a way characterised by self-giving love, by justice, by honesty, and by the breaking down of the traditional barriers that reinforce the divisions which keep human beings separate from, and ... at odds with, one another... This is not a matter, as is sometimes said, of 'bringing religion into politics'. It is bringing the whole world under the lordship of Christ. The gospel message leaves us no choice.[23]

---

[21] Forster, *Kingdom of Jesus*, 80.
[22] See also Matthew 2:6.
[23] Wright, *What Saint Paul Really Said*, 153–4.

The rule of the Messiah over the nations

As a people who had suffered a miserable history of oppression, the Jews longed for the establishment of a new world order, in which the vicious cycle of history would be at an end. The most obvious reading of the Old Testament prophecies was that the Messiah would usher in a golden age (Isa. 9:7; 11:1–10, Ps. 45:2–6; 72:1–19; Ezek. 37:24–28). In inter-testamental times there had been an obsession among the Jews with predictions of the 'end times', which gave rise to a whole genre of literature known as 'apocalypses'.[24]

The Jews of Jesus' day expected the Messiah to vindicate them as God's chosen people. Was that not the promise of Jeremiah 33:6–9? The Pharisees looked forward to the restoration of the kingdom to Israel and the other blessings of the Messianic age being bestowed on the Jews once they were worthy of them through strict obedience to the Law.[25]

But far from vindicating the Jews, Jesus scandalised them by declaring that they were not children of Abraham but of the devil (Jn. 8:37–44). He reserved his most scathing attacks for the Pharisees, those who were most confidently expecting to be pronounced by God to be worthy of his approval (Mt. 15:7–9; 23:1–36; Lk. 11:37–52; 18:9–14, Jn. 5:45–47).

The Jews not only expected the Messiah to come and liberate Israel, but to lead them on in triumph over the nations. The Jews believed that 'some day [led by the Messiah] they would rule the world'.[26] The Jews understood the reign of the Messiah over the nations – as foretold in Isaiah 11:10–16; 49:22–26 and Jeremiah 30:8–11, among other passages – as being achieved by the Messiah conquering the foreign nations and subjecting them to Israelite rule. In the light of Isaiah 63:1–6 where the Messiah is described as 'coming from Edom … with his garments stained crimson', treading the winepress of God's wrath and 'trampling the nations in … anger', such an interpretation was the one that would first come to mind.

Yet Jesus taught that the world would be saved not condemned through him (Jn. 3:14–17). His cross would become the banner to which the nations would rally (Isa. 11:10–12) and he would bring God's salvation to the ends of the earth (Isa. 49:6; Lk. 24:46–47).

Jesus drove a wedge between the messianic prophecies about salvation and the prophecies about judgement. Luke's record of the Nazareth Manifesto (Lk. 4:16–21), where Jesus read the opening verses of Isaiah 61 in the synagogue, stops mid-sentence. Jesus announced that he had come 'to proclaim the year of the Lord's favour' but did not carry on to say 'and the day of vengeance of our God'. The New Testament teaches us that he came as saviour and that it is at his second coming that he will return to

---

[24] Drane, *Jesus and the Four Gospels*, 20–1; Richardson, *Political Christ*, 45.
[25] Richardson, *Political Christ*, 18.
[26] Drane, *Jesus and the Four Gospels*, 14.

judge the earth (Jn. 5:24–30; 12:47–48; Acts 10:42; 17:31; Rom. 2:16; 1 Cor. 4:5; 2 Tim. 4:1).

Until his return, the reign of Jesus as the Christ of God is guaranteed by the resurrection, and the return of Jesus as the Christ of God is guaranteed by the ascension.

Conclusions

Jesus stood the expectations of his contemporaries on their heads. He rejected the facile interpretations of the Old Testament prophecies in favour of a more costly, more profound, more holistic mission of redemption. And yet, he was the non-political Messiah who died a traitor's death; he was the Messiah whose primary aim was never to demonstrate his credentials by miracle working, yet whose legacy of signs and wonders was unparalleled; he was the Messiah whose mission ended with the failure of a criminal's execution, yet who made a public spectacle of his real enemies at his own execution (Col. 2:15). He was the Messiah whose coming did not bring about the end of history immediately, and yet he promised to return again to wrap up time.

The problem with the messianic expectations of Jesus' day, as with many heresies, was not what they affirmed so much as what they denied. The visions in Isaiah of the Davidic prince who would reign forever had to be taken in conjunction with the Servant Songs of Isaiah 42:1–4; 50:4–9; 52:13 – 53:12. Jesus took hold of the Old Testament prophecies as Lord over them, and fulfilled and combined them in a way that was wonderful beyond any of the guesses of the people of his time as to the true nature and extent of the Messiah's mission.

The Kingship of Jesus and the Law of Moses

Jesus' attitude to the Law of Moses showed that he regarded himself as master over it. He quoted it – at the devil. He discussed and debated it with his opponents. He challenged traditional interpretations – 'you have heard it said' … 'but I say to you'.[27] But above all, *he pointed to the heart of law*. 'Fulfilment' is the key word to describe what Jesus did to the Law of Moses.

In the Sermon on the Mount, Jesus gave an exposition of those of the Ten Commandments that his generation had particularly misunderstood.[28] Before exploring the true meaning and depth of the sixth commandment against murder (Mt. 5:21–26), the seventh commandment against adultery (Mt. 5:27–32), and the ninth commandment against bearing false witness (Mt. 5:33–37), he made his position plain:

---

[27] Forster, *Kingdom of Jesus*, 2.
[28] Chantry, *God's Righteous Kingdom*, 95.

'Do not think that I have come to abolish the Law or the Prophets; *I have not come to abolish them but to fulfil them.* I tell you the truth, until heaven and earth disappear, not the smallest letter, not the least stroke of a pen, will by any means disappear from the Law until everything is accomplished. Anyone who breaks one of the least of these commandments and teaches others to do the same will be called least in the kingdom of heaven, but whoever practises and teaches these commands will be called great in the kingdom of heaven. For I tell you that unless your righteousness surpasses that of the Pharisees and teachers of the law, you will certainly not enter the kingdom of heaven.' (Mt. 5:17–20)

The word 'fulfil' is an interesting one in this context. In English, it carries with it the idea of filling up to the brim. For New Testament scholars, there has been much debate about the precise nuances to be attached to the Greek word *plerosai*. Perhaps here it has a double meaning 'to complete and to transcend', for Jesus understood himself to be giving the final revelation of God's will to which the Old Testament pointed forward, and yet to be transcending the Old Testament's approach to God.[29] What Jesus then goes on to do, in Matthew 5:21ff., is to go behind the scribal traditions and the Old Testament text, and to draw out the powerful ethical principles which lay at the heart of the Old Testament injunctions. Jesus expounded the reasons behind the rules.

It is clear that Jesus regarded himself as having come to fulfil the law. But how did he do that? Here the distinction between the three types of law – moral, ceremonial and judicial (civil) – is a helpful exegetical tool. All three aspects of the Old Testament Law were fulfilled in Christ but in different ways.[30] He kept every requirement of the moral law and expounded its true application in the Sermon on the Mount. He is the High Priest, who offered the perfect, eternal sacrifice of which all the Old Testament sacrifices were only shadows (Heb. 10:1, 3–14, 18).[31] He is the King, who will one day usher in the perfect theocracy.[32] Just as Israel the nation was descended from the one man Jacob, whom God renamed,[33] so Israel's destiny was fulfilled in Jesus. He was 'the embodiment of what Israel was supposed to have been but had failed to be, namely a manifestation of God himself.'[34]

---

[29] France, *Matthew*, 113–14, 119.
[30] Nothing, not even 'the least stroke of a pen' can 'drop out of the Law' without its fulfilment in 'the good news of the kingdom of God': Anderson, *Freedom under Law*, 122; see also Chantry, *God's Righteous Kingdom*, 123; Reisinger, *Law and the Gospel*, 115–17.
[31] *Letters of John Newton*, 43.
[32] Until then, he declared to Pilate (Jn. 18:36), his kingdom is not of this world.
[33] Genesis 32:28.
[34] Wright, *People of God*, 41–3; Wright, *Climax of the Covenant*, 146.

The superseding of the ceremonial rules in the Mosaic Law

The ceremonial rules in the Mosaic Law were demonstrations of God's holiness and his requirements for purity.[35] So all the sacrifices were simply shadows of the great sacrifice which Jesus would make on the cross.[36] Once he had died, the meaning of the sacrifices had been fulfilled. There was no longer any need for them. They were completed.[37] This much is abundantly clear from the letter to the Hebrews.

However, that is not the end of a consideration of the ceremonial law, if Wright is correct to place the 'ceremonial' law rendered obsolete by Christ's priestly work within a broader category of 'cultic law', which included matters such as dietary and hygiene regulations, Sabbaths and other festivals, and the rules on offerings, tithes, first fruits and gleanings which had practical benefits attached to them.[38]

There is a powerful contrast between the concerns of the Jewish purity laws and the attitude of Jesus. Whereas the holiness codes of the Old Testament exhibited a fear that uncleanness would contaminate the purity of the people of God, Jesus ate with the tax collectors and sinners, touched the lepers and healed them. Jesus turned the Law's concern for purity inside out. Whereas Torah observance focussed on external purity, Jesus made it clear that it was not what was on the outside that made a man pure, but rather what was in his heart.[39] Jesus taught that at the heart of the commands 'Do not murder' and 'Do not commit adultery' was an obligation not to cherish anger and lust in our hearts.[40]

In fact, one of the first questions that the early church had to address was the validity of the Mosaic Law, and in particular its ceremonial aspects, for Gentile converts to Christianity. 'Then some of the believers who belonged to the party of the Pharisees stood up and said, "The Gentiles must be circumcised and required to obey the law of Moses"' (Acts 15:5). A church council was called to resolve the issue. The Apostle Peter made an impassioned plea against the imposition of the Mosaic Law on the Gentiles:

> God, who knows the heart, showed that he accepted [the Gentiles] by giving the Holy Spirit to them, just as he did to us. He made no distinction between us and them, for he purified their hearts by faith. Now then, why do you try

---

[35] Anderson, *Freedom under Law*, 111; Chantry, *God's Righteous Kingdom*, 115.

[36] Reisinger, *Law and the Gospel*, 52, 55; the technical theological word for these 'shadows' is 'types'.

[37] Chantry, *God's Righteous Kingdom*, 115–16; Reisinger, *Law and the Gospel*, 53–4.

[38] Wright, *People of God*, 156. Although as Paul argues in Colossians 2:16–17, the ceremonial usefulness of such things is at an end, now that Christ has come.

[39] Matthew 15:11, 16–20.

[40] Cf. Matthew 5:21–22 and 27–28, respectively.

to test God by putting on the necks of the disciples a yoke which neither we nor our fathers have been able to bear? No! We believe that it is through the grace of our Lord Jesus that we are saved, just as they are.
(Acts 15:8–11)

The council determined the issue in accordance with a proposal put forward by James:

It is my judgement, therefore, that we should not make it difficult for the Gentiles who are turning to God. Instead, we should write to them, telling them to abstain from food polluted by idols, from sexual immorality, from the meat of strangled animals and from blood.
(Acts 15:19–20)

The church council resolved to refrain from imposing on the Gentiles the ceremonial requirements of the Jewish Law. The early church's discovery that what God wanted was circumcision of heart not circumcision of foreskin[41] was in line with Jesus' teaching that what mattered to God was not (or was no longer) external ritual purity but rather inward purity of heart.

It would be extraordinary, however, given the clear stance on morality which Paul[42] and others present take in their letters, if what was meant by that council was that none of the Mosaic Law, not even the moral imperatives of the Ten Commandments, needed to be obeyed by the Gentiles.[43]

The non-applicability of the judicial (civil) aspects of the Mosaic Law

In Galatians 3:24–25, Paul writes: 'So the law was put in charge to lead us to Christ that we might be justified by faith. Now that faith has come, we are no longer under the supervision of the law.' Part of the difficulty of discerning what Paul's approach to the Law is, is that what is meant by 'law' or 'the Law' in the New Testament differs from place to place.[44] Walter Chantry argues: 'Paul's meaning [in Galatians 3:24–25] is that the Mosaic order (covenant administration, economy, dispensation) was a schoolmaster to bring men to the New Covenant in Christ.'[45] He asks:

[41] Acts 15.
[42] For example, for Paul see Romans 1:29–32; 6:15–16; 1 Corinthians 5:1–2; 6:18; Galatians 5:19–21; Ephesians 4:25–31; Colossians 3:5–10; 1 Thessalonians 4:3–8. For other New Testament writers, see James 2:9–11; 1 Peter 2:1; 4:3; 1 John 2:9; 3:4; Jude 4–8, 16.
[43] Reisinger, *Law and the Gospel*, 134–5.
[44] Chantry, *God's Righteous Kingdom*, 101; Reisinger, *Law and the Gospel*, 47–57. Although how much is a matter of fierce scholarly debate and N.T. Wright, in particular, has championed the reading of *nomos* as Torah as often as possible in the writings of Paul.
[45] Chantry, *God's Righteous Kingdom*, 101–2.

what purpose did the law (the Mosaic covenant administration) serve? ... Was the Mosaic system presented as God's model for all world governments? Was it introduced as the perfect ideal for social management in all ages? Was this dispensation God's blueprint for social reconstruction which, when vigorously executed, would usher in millennial victory? Was it a pattern of social and political philosophy for all ages? "It was added ... till the seed should come" (Gal. 3:19) ... the Mosaic economy is no longer appropriate to us. Its usefulness passed away with the coming of Jesus Christ.[46]

The judicial aspects of the Mosaic Law were rules specifically given to the Israelites 'to follow in the land that you are crossing the Jordan to possess' (Deut. 4:14). Under the new covenant, not only was the early church not in a political position where it could re-establish the Old Testament theocracy of Israel, but also Jesus had himself said, 'My kingdom is not of this world'.[47] In the new covenant era, the Promised Land which the people of God were to take possession of was no longer a geographical entity on the face of the earth, but instead the new heaven and the new earth of the age to come.[48]

So, if the ceremonial aspects of the Mosaic Law were no longer binding, and the judicial aspects of the Mosaic Law were no longer applicable, what about the moral aspects of the Mosaic Law?

The enduring validity of the moral teaching of the Mosaic Law

The New Testament provides us with no indications that Jesus ever had anything other than the highest regard for the Mosaic Law and for its moral teaching. Jesus himself set out the Ten Commandments in Mark 10:19 to the rich young man: 'You know the commandments: "Do not murder, do not commit adultery, do not steal, do not give false testimony, do not defraud,[49] honour your father and mother."'

But did Jesus not also summarise the law as 'Love God' and 'Love your neighbour' (Mk. 12:29–31)? Isn't love alone enough? Can we not say with Augustine, 'Love God and do what you like'?[50] But that immediately

---

[46] Chantry, *God's Righteous Kingdom*, 104, 106; France, *Matthew*, 115, writes 'The [Mosaic] law is unalterable, but that does not justify its application beyond the purpose for which it was intended' – see also 117.

[47] John 18:36.

[48] Wright, *People of God*, 90–100.

[49] Jesus gave a narrow definition of this commandment to the rich young man, then challenged him 'to give all his possessions to the poor', thereby extending the tenth commandment to its logical extreme. In so doing, he exposed the rich young man's inner lust for possessions Wright. *God's People in God's Land*, 138–9.

[50] W. Temple explains Augustine's remark in *Christianity and Social Order*, 76, on the basis that: 'of course, if he loved God he would like and could do the right thing, and if he did not love God he could not do it however much he tried'.

begs the question: What will we like to do if we love God? '[W]hat constitutes a devout person? Someone who is seeking to do the will of God,
someone who is instructed in sanctified behaviour. And ... in what does
that behaviour consist? In doing the will of God as summarised in the Ten
Commandments.'[51] As Reisinger puts it, 'The law is love's eyes, without
which love is blind.'[52]

Cranfield argues:

> since Paul was apparently well aware that Christians can very easily persuade
> themselves that they are loving when they are not ... it seems most unlikely
> that he would have countenanced the idea that Christians should forget the
> particular commandments and rely on the commandment of love as a suffi-
> cient guide. Is it not more likely that he recognised that, while Christians cer-
> tainly need the summary to save them from missing the wood for the trees and
> from understanding the particular commandments in a rigid, literalistic, un-
> imaginative or loveless way, they also need the particular commandments to
> save them from resting content with vague and often hypocritical sentiments
> which ... we are all of us prone to mistake for Christian love?[53]

'[H]ow is love to God and neighbour to express itself? ... To answer this
the apostles always return to the Ten Commandments.'[54] In case there
was any doubt on this point, Paul says in Romans 13:8–9: '... he who
loves his fellowman has fulfilled the law. The commandments, "Do not
commit adultery", "Do not murder", "Do not steal", "Do not covet"
and whatever other commandments there may be, are summed up in this
one rule: "Love your neighbour as yourself".'[55] Augustine could say
what he did because he understood that the person who loved God
would desire to please God and that desire to please God would lead to
obedience to God's commandments.[56] Both the Apostles John and Paul
knew and explored in their writings the close relationship that necessarily
exists between love for God and obedience to God. They expressed
themselves in similar terms. John wrote, 'This is the love for God: to obey
his commands' (1 Jn. 5:3), while Paul said, 'Love does no harm to its
neighbour. *Therefore love is the fulfilment of the law*' (Rom. 13:10).

---

51 Reisinger, *Law and the Gospel*, xix.
52 Reisinger, *Law and the Gospel*, 95; see also Wright, *God's People in God's Land*,
    264–5; and I.H. Marshall, 'Using the Bible in Ethics', in D.F. Wright (ed.),
    Essays in Evangelical Social Ethics, 52; O'Donovan, *Resurrection*, 199–201.
    John Warwick Montgomery debated Joseph Fletcher on this issue – *Situa-
    tion Ethics*.
53 C.E.B. Cranfield, *On Romans and Other New Testament Essays*, 111–12.
54 Chantry, *God's Righteous Kingdom*, 96–7; Reisinger, *Law and the Gospel*,
    91–6.
55 Chantry, *God's Righteous Kingdom*, 85.
56 Reisinger, *Law and the Gospel*, 89–90.

There is no hint anywhere in the New Testament that the Law has lost its validity in the slightest degree, nor is there any suggestion of its repeal. On the contrary, the New Testament teaches unambiguously that the Ten Commandments are still binding upon all men.[57]

But what about Jesus' own ethical teaching? Jesus was radical in his treatment of the Mosaic Law, both in the sense of bringing a new and a fresh approach to it, and in the sense of returning to its roots. In his exposition of the sixth, seventh and ninth commandments in the Sermon on the Mount, he expands on those commandments, and points to the importance before God, who sees the heart, of internal conformity to the requirements of God (Mt. 5:21–37). However, he then goes on to propose a new ethic in place of the *lex talionis*, urging his disciples to turn the other cheek rather than insisting on an eye-for-an-eye (Mt. 5:39–48).

To the woman caught in adultery, Jesus did not demand the penalty prescribed in the Mosaic Law, but invited any one of the woman's accusers who was without sin to be the first to stone her. When the others had, one by one, walked away, Jesus, who alone was qualified to cast the stone, declared 'neither do I condemn you. Go now and leave your life of sin' (Jn. 8:11). There was something more powerful than the rigours of the Mosaic Law at work in the saving actions of Christ, the grace of God reconciling the world to himself in Christ (Col. 1:20).[58]

Christopher Marshall writes:

> in Matthew's account of the teaching of Jesus, mercy and love serve as the hermeneutical keys for accessing the true meaning of the fulfilled law … It is the primacy of love and compassion over the letter of the law that also explains Jesus' own conduct with respect to the law – his preparedness to eat with sinners, to neglect external purity stipulations, to heal and harvest on the Sabbath, and so on. Mercy is the true meaning of the law; mercy is at the heart of God's justice; mercy "fulfills all righteousness" (Mt. 3:15).[59]

What Jesus does is not render the moral guidance of the Torah redundant for his followers; instead he provides his followers with the hermeneutical keys and with the Holy Spirit as an interpreter, in order to assist them to understand it aright and fulfil its intentions.

There is a clear relationship between Jesus' ethical teaching and the Mosaic Law. Towards the end of the discourse of the Sermon on the Mount, Jesus states the golden rule: 'So in everything, do to others what you would have them do to you, for this sums up the Law and the Prophets' (Mt. 7:12). That is Jesus' authoritative interpretation of the Old Testament in its fullness.[60] Later on in the Gospel, when asked which was

---

[57] Ernest F. Kevan in the Tyndale Biblical Theology Lecture of 4 July 1955, quoted by J.W. Montgomery in J. Fletcher and J.W. Montgomery, *Situation Ethics*, 37.

[58] Marshall, *Beyond Retribution*, 230–4.

[59] Marshall, *Beyond Retribution*, 229.

[60] France, *Matthew*, 145.

the greatest commandment in the Law, he replied, '"Love the Lord your God with all your heart and with all your soul and with all your mind." This is the first and greatest commandment. And the second is like it, "Love your neighbour as yourself."[61] All the Law and the Prophets hang on these two commandments' (Mt. 22:37–40). Both of those formulations were drawn from the Old Testament text itself.[62]

When Jesus went beyond those formulations, it was by reference to his own example. At the Last Supper, Jesus told his disciples: 'A new command I give you: Love one another. *As I have loved you, so you must love one another.* By this all men will know that you are my disciples, if you love one another' (Jn. 13:34; cf. 15:12). In going beyond the Old Testament revelation, Jesus completed it by his self-revelation of God and God's standards. His own life and death provide a new motivation for ethical excellence. Because God has loved us so much that Jesus came to earth, lived as a man, and died on a cross, because God has loved us that much, we must love one another. Because God has forgiven us because of what Jesus has done, so we must forgive one another. Following Jesus, 'love your neighbour as you love yourself' becomes 'love your neighbour as you yourself have been loved'.[63]

This in no way weakens the ethical validity of the Mosaic Law. Jesus' own example provides both an additional motivation for moral behaviour, and beyond the natural ethic of do as you would be done by, a supernatural ethic of self-sacrifice for others.[64] He establishes a standard of ethical excellence that in no way detracts from the obligatory force of the moral law within the Old Testament. To adapt Jesus' own illustration in the Sermon on the Mount, to 'love your neighbour as yourself' is to go the first mile; to 'love your neighbour as Jesus has loved you' is to go the second mile. You cannot walk the second mile without having travelled the first. The divine command to love one another is drawn out to its infinite extent by the teaching of Jesus.[65]

---

[61] 'Love your neighbour as yourself' is also identified as the heart of the law in Matthew 19:19, Luke 10:27, Romans 13:9, Galatians 5:14 and James 2.8.

[62] From Deuteronomy 6:5 and Leviticus 19:18, respectively.

[63] See Yoder, *Politics of Jesus*, 119.

[64] de Blois, 'Foundation of Human Rights', 11, writes: 'All human beings are responsible to their creator for the way they comply with God's commandments (Rom. 1:18–32). This being said on the moral responsibility of all human beings, it is at the same time clear from the New Testament that of the disciples of Christ a more excellent life is required than the life to be expected from other human beings.' This ethic of self-sacrifice which Jesus urges on his followers can be seen as the inward sacrifice of the Body of Christ which is itself a fulfilment of the heart of the Law, just as inward obedience to the Law by the Body of Christ is a fulfilment of the heart of the Law. See also P. Ricoeur, 'The Golden Rule: Exegetical and Theological Perplexities', *New Testament Studies* 36 (1990), 392–7.

[65] Wright, *People of God*, 158.

Conclusions on the lordship of Christ over the Mosaic Law

Jesus Christ is Lord over both the Old Testament as well as the New Testament, and because Christ's own interpretation of the Old Testament was radical and surprising, any adequate Christian interpretation of the Old Testament law must see it through the prism of the New Testament. Such must be the appropriate theological methodology for approaching the Old Testament law.

Adopting such a methodology, Christopher Wright's distinctive contribution to the debate has been his clear assertion that the Mosaic theocracy is not intended to be regarded as a blueprint but rather as a paradigm.[66] Explaining his choice of term, he says:

> A paradigm is something used as a model or example for other cases where a basic principle remains unchanged, though details differ ... A paradigm is not so much imitated as applied. It is assumed that cases will differ but, when necessary adjustments have been made, they will conform to the observable pattern of the paradigm ... We cannot simply transpose the social laws of an ancient people into the modern world and try to make them work as written. That would be tantamount to taking the paradigms of a grammar book as the only words one could use in that particular language. The paradigms are there, not to be the sum of possible communication ever after, but to be applied to the infinite complexities of the rest of the language.[67]

The Kingship of Jesus and the Kings of this World

The relationship between the early church and the Roman Empire was a nuanced one. The *Pax Romana* and the widespread adoption of Greek and Latin as languages of trade and learning enabled the rapid spread of the Christian gospel. Roman law provided a theoretical system of legal

[66] Wright, *People of God*, 88, where he in fact argues that the Old Testament law is relevant for the Christian in three ways: as a type, as a paradigm and as an eschatological vision; although he concedes that not all of the Mosaic Law is relevant in all three ways. See also O'Donovan, *Desire*, 23.

[67] Wright, *People of God*, 40–5, esp 43, see also 89, 162. At 101 he offers an illustration of how the idea of paradigm might be applied to the institution of the jubilee. He offers the necessary corrective to a focus on the Old Testament, 44: 'Israel's social shape and characteristics, her institutions, laws and ideals ... are not, of course, the exclusive paradigm for social ethics; the Christian brings this, as he does every other aspect of the Old Testament, into the light of the new age of fulfilment and the Kingdom of God inaugurated by Christ. He therefore sets his Old Testament social paradigm alongside the paradigm of the social life of the early church as well as the explicit social teaching of Jesus and the apostles. Only then is he beginning to formulate a wholly biblical social ethic.'

protection and Roman soldiers a practical force for maintaining law and order which created social stability in many of the regions under the Empire's control.

And yet, the Roman *imperium* tended towards blasphemy, as emperors regarded themselves as gods. And the Roman system of taxation has been described by one commentator as 'the baksheesh elevated to the heights of an institution.'[68] Political and economic power was concentrated in the Roman Empire in a manner very different from the way it was distributed in the ideal of Israel.

For the early church, therefore, there were important questions to be resolved regarding its relationship to the Roman authorities. The most pressing issue, however, was not about the extent to which the church could claim moral or executive authority in temporal matters but rather about the manner of its resistance to imperial claims of divinity.

> In the pagan world of [the early church], particularly in the Eastern empire but increasingly in Rome itself, it was natural for emperors to be treated with divine honour. Already in the time of Tiberius, his predecessor, Augustus, was regarded as divine, so that the emperor became first the son of a god and then, in turn, a god himself. *Kyrios Kaisar* was the formula which said it all: Caesar is Lord.
>
> Most pagans within the Roman world were quite happy to acknowledge Caesar as Lord; they did it politically, and doing it religiously was all part of the same overarching package. And Paul said: no, *Kyrios Iesous Christos*: Jesus Christ is Lord. In particular, he said this when addressing [the Philippians] a community for whom, based in a Roman colony, the lordship of Caesar was a very live issue. In addition to the wealth of Jewish theology which lies behind the Christology of Philippians, particularly chapter 2, there is a clear sense of confrontation with one of paganism's treasured heartlands, the imperial ideology.[69]

The same tendency repeats itself in history again and again. The Egyptian pharaohs were regarded as divine. So too the Babylonian kings. In recent times, the cult of personality in the Soviet Union, with statues of Lenin and Stalin, set them up as modern day gods for the atheistic state!

As we have seen in chapters 3 and 4, in sharp distinction from the nations around them, the Israelites thought exactly the opposite: instead of their king being a god, *God was their king*.

But somehow, along the way, the Israelites had lost their focus and chosen to be ruled by human kings. Those kings, almost without exception, let the people down and ruled unjustly; so the prophets increasingly looked forward to 'the Day of the Lord' when the Lord God himself would appoint a just king to rule. They awaited the day when the true

---

[68] P. Veyne, *Le Pain et le Cirque, Sociologie historique d'un pluralisme politique*, 15.
[69] Wright, *What Saint Paul Really Said*, 88; see also de Blois, 'Foundation of Human Rights', at 166.

God would become king, and all the false gods would find themselves de-
throned. They looked forward to the moment when 'The powers of the
world are confronted with the one who is the true Lord of all.'[70]

What was strange about Jesus' coming was the way in which he transcended the pretensions of human politics. When the devil offered to put
Jesus in the place of the human rulers of the world, to give him their
power and their splendour (Mt. 4:8–9), Jesus rejected it. For him, the issues regarding the kingship of God were higher and deeper than who you
acknowledged as your political master. The issue of the kingship of God
is about who you worship.

What did Jesus teach about the relationship between his king-dom and the kingdoms of this world?

When Jesus was challenged over the issue of paying taxes to Rome, he
asked whose head was on the coin. The response was Caesar's. So Jesus
said, 'Render to Caesar the things that are Caesar's, and to God the things
that are God's' (Lk. 20:25; NASB).

Within the context of the biblical assertion of divine sovereignty, Jesus' words cannot mean that there are two equal obligations upon human
beings: one to our earthly lords and the other to our divine Lord. After all,
did he not say (when talking about money), 'No servant can serve two
masters. Either he will hate the one and love the other, or he will be devoted to the one and despise the other' (Mt. 6:24).

Also, Jesus commanded his followers to seek first the kingdom of God
and his [justice] (Mt. 6:33). The word I have translated 'justice' is usually
translated into English as 'righteousness', but in French the same word
'justice' covers both ideas and in Hebrew and Greek thought the two
ideas were far more closely related and intertwined than we habitually
think today.

Given the primacy of God's kingdom, what Jesus must mean is that out
of everything which is under the sovereignty of God, there are some
things authority over which has been temporarily placed into the hands of
human rulers.[71] In the new covenant era, such a conclusion may also be
implied in Jesus' declaration to his disciples after his resurrection, at the
moment he gave them the great commission: 'All authority in heaven
and on earth has been given to me' (Mt. 28:18). He did not then go on
and tell his disciples to conquer kingdoms and seize political power, but
rather to 'go and make disciples of all nations' (Mt. 28:19).

Before his death, in the Garden of Gethsemane, Jesus predicted the
persecution his disciples would face. They replied to him, 'See, Lord,
here are two swords.' Jesus said: 'That is enough' (Lk. 22:31–38). This
verse has been used as a proof-text to justify two swords theory. There
may be nothing wrong with the theory but is not immediately apparent
that this verse has got anything to do with it.

[70] Wright, *What Saint Paul Really Said*, 88.
[71] Cranfield, *On Romans*, 172.

Two swords theory has taken a number of different forms. In mediaeval Western Europe, the Pope asserted that as God's vice-regent on earth all authority, whether temporal or spiritual, was vested in him and he then conferred temporal authority on the Holy Roman Emperor.[72] This assertion, and symbolic transferral of power, was demonstrated each time the Pope crowned the Holy Roman Emperor.[73] In Eastern Europe, the Byzantine emperors took their cue from Constantine. Just as Constantine had convened church councils in order to resolve matters of doctrine, so the Eastern Emperor was seen as the ultimate authority, whether temporal or spiritual. It was he who ordained the Patriarch of Constantinople.[74]

In Luther's version of the two swords theory, 'Luther argued that the authority of the Church ("the sword of doctrine") extended only to "spiritual" matters and that the Church should never interfere with the running of the state ("the sword of the princes").'[75] The two swords are therefore seen as wholly separate, each deriving its authority independently from God. John Witte argues that Luther's theory is more properly characterised as a two kingdoms theory (*Zweireichelehre*),[76] and that Luther's distinctive innovation was to turn the mediaeval hierarchy of being on its side, so that instead of the secular being inferior to the spiritual, instead of the secular prince being inferior to the spiritual prince (i.e. the bishop), instead of the laity being inferior to the clergy, 'before God, all persons and all institutions ... were equal'.[77] There was now an earthly kingdom and a heavenly kingdom, and Christians were citizens of both. But crucially, there was now an invisible heavenly church and a visible

[72] The doctrine originates from the letter of Pope Gelasius I to the Emperor Anastasius in AD 494 in which he wrote: 'There are two powers, august Emperor, by which this world is chiefly ruled, namely, the sacred authority of the priests and the royal power. Of these that of the priests is the more weighty, since they have to render an account for even the kings of men in the divine judgement. You are also aware, dear son, that while you are permitted honourably to rule over human kind, yet in things divine you bow your head humbly before the leaders of the clergy and await from their hands the means of your salvation. In the reception and proper disposition of the heavenly mysteries you recognise that you should be subordinate rather than superior to the religious order, and that in these matters you depend on their judgement rather than wish to force them to follow your will.' Translated in J.H. Robinson, *Readings in European History*, 72–3. On the development of this doctrine, cf. O'Donovan, *Desire*, 203ff.

[73] The first emperor to be so crowned was Charlemagne, in \\ad// 800.

[74] Forster, *Kingdom of Jesus*, 5.

[75] Witte, *Law and Protestantism*, 57; A.C. Sippo, 'Totalitarianism: the Effects of Martin Luther', *St Catherine Review* Nov/Dec 1996.

[76] Witte, *Law and Protestantism*, 88, 89ff.

[77] Witte, *Law and Protestantism*, 106–12.

earthly one.[78] The visible church was no longer, in the person of the Pope, the plenipotentiary of God, but instead a limited social institution alongside the family and the state.[79]

Luther's theological concern was to reject mediaeval canon law, which had, founded upon a theory of seven sacraments, accomplished what seemed to him to be a takeover of many areas in which secular law ought properly to be sovereign.[80] Henceforth, the church was to be deprived of formal legal authority in order that it might concentrate on its God-given tasks of 'preaching and teaching the law of God to magistrates and subjects alike, and ... pronouncing prophetically against injustice, abuse and tyranny'.[81]

Luther's radical challenge to both the church hierarchy and the church's jurisdiction undercut its authority. The implications of his doctrine of the priesthood of all believers seemed obvious to others, if not to him. Equality was a God-given right and individual interpretation of the Bible now a duty. These new doctrines, years of discontent about the state of Germany and economic collapse was an explosive combination.[82] With the church unable to restore order, it was left to the princes to do so.

Luther came to see the prince and the magistrate, not the pope, as the vicegerent of God and the father of the community.[83] The magistrate was 'to elaborate and enforce God's word and will, to reflect God's justice and judgment on earthly citizens'.[84] This obligation meant that the prince was justified in determining which form of the Christian religion would be observed upon his territory.[85] It also meant, so Luther's critics argue, that Luther provided a theological justification for the use by princes of whatever means necessary to maintain their authority, or at least that Luther left such an option open to his inheritors.[86]

The Lutheran separation of the two kingdoms was accompanied by a bifurcation of ethical obligations:

> In the Lutheran tradition, every Christian belongs simultaneously to two realms. In the private, spiritual realm, he or she is accountable to the gospel's

[78] Witte, *Law and Protestantism*, 97–8.
[79] Witte, *Law and Protestantism*, 109.
[80] Witte, *Law and Protestantism*, 53–8.
[81] Witte, *Law and Protestantism*, 110.
[82] R. Bainton, *Here I Stand*, 268–85.
[83] Witte, *Law and Protestantism*, 112.
[84] Witte, *Law and Protestantism*, 111.
[85] K. Tan, *Lost Heritage: The Heroic Story of Radical Christianity*, 155, notes that like Luther, Zwingli had a 'territorial concept' of the church, under which the Christian magistrates of a city had the right to determine the external forms of the church's worship and life and to govern the 'Christian commonwealth' in co-operation with the prophet who expounded the Scriptures.
[86] Sippo, 'Totalitarianism'; J.H. Yoder, *Karl Barth and the Problem of War*, 96.

demand of radical love. In the public, temporal realm, though still under divine command, he or she operates according to natural law and civil justice, which will sometimes require the exercise of punitive – even lethal – judgment.[87]

The accusation is therefore that the Lutheran approach of 'station-ethics' tends towards the privatisation of morality that has been the elephant-trap into which much of evangelical Christianity has fallen in its haste to avoid offering a 'social gospel' without Christ.

Many, including Karl Barth, have discerned in Luther's thinking, and in the sharp distinction which he draws, the origins of a view in which the church could have nothing to say to the state, thereby accounting for its silence in the face of Nazism in Germany.[88] John Witte argues that this charge is exaggerated, and singles Luther out for unwarranted vilification.[89]

In Calvin's account, the two swords of church and state are separate and distinct, but not antithetical, because it is part of the function of civil government 'to foster and maintain the external worship of God, [and] to defend sound doctrine and the condition of the Church ...'.[90] Luther would have agreed.[91]

To critical eyes, such as those of Nobbs, the Calvinist version of the 'two swords' polity involves a fundamental contradiction between the desire of the church to have full powers to govern herself outside of state interference, and the insistence that the state was to uphold both tables of the Decalogue and ensure that the true religion was established and furthered while the false was rooted out.[92]

Calvin's position therefore involves the assumption that although it is the responsibility of the church to determine its doctrine and its order free from governmental interference, government ought then to preserve the purity of the church and of the nation through the enforcement of biblical morality and Christian truth. Rightly ordered polities, such as Calvin's Geneva or Interregnum England, are therefore capable of becoming for the rest of the world what Israel was intended to be in her day, 'a light to the nations', a shining example of a just society under the rule of God.

Calvin was right in realising that the Torah was given to Israel because Israel was meant to be a holy nation. However, he was mistaken in that he failed to recognise that no other nation has ever been given such a vocation before God.[93]

---

[87] Marshall, *Beyond Retribution*, 19; Colwell, *Living the Christian Story*, 233–6.
[88] Colwell, *Living the Christian Story*, 234–6.
[89] Witte, *Law and Protestantism*, 297–8.
[90] Calvin, *Institutes* Book IV, ch. 20, para. 2.
[91] Witte, *Law and Protestantism*, 11.
[92] D. Nobbs, *Theocracy and Toleration: A Study of the Disputes in Dutch Calvinism from 1600–50*, 202.
[93] de Blois, 'Foundation of Human Rights', 169–70.

There is also something ironic in Calvin's doctrines of the elect and of justification by faith alone being held in conjunction with an ordering of civil society which imposes 'Christian morality' upon society as a whole.[94] The only way to square the circle is to determine that the external action produces earthly results, while the internal intention (when present) leads to heavenly rewards.

The alternative theories available in early modern Europe were those of the radical Anabaptists, for whom the state was an evil with whom true Christians should avoid contamination at all costs,[95] or the contrary view, which was that kings ruled by divine right. Exponents of the theory of the divine right of kings argued that monarchy (or human forms of government in general) derived from creation, and had existed long before there was a church. Within the created order, therefore, the king has been appointed directly by God and rules by divine right. The church belongs to the order of redemption, which is wholly separate.

The revolutions of Europe did for the divine right of kings, and the wars of religion in Europe demolished the viability of Calvin's view of the two swords. The diversity of religious belief within each society in Europe rendered it impractical, in the long run, to seek to enforce religious conformity. From the view that social cohesion was best maintained by religious uniformity, rulers increasingly realised that social stability was most likely to be preserved by divorcing the concerns of the state and the church(es), a principle which was taken to its logical conclusion in the French and American Revolutions.

After those revolutions the doctrine of the kingship of Jesus went into eclipse. The public, social and political implications of the declaration 'Jesus is Lord' were lost as 'the lordship of Christ' came to be seen as related to private, personal, pietistic morality. Today, the comprehensive nature of Jesus' kingship is once again being reaffirmed.[96]

But in the reaffirmation and the public proclamation of the kingship of Jesus there is a danger that the primary truth that doctrine expresses will be lost. To the rulers of the world, the declaration is, 'Jesus is King; and you are not.' It is God and his Christ whom the Bible declares to be the rightful ruler of the world. His rule and his rule *alone* is absolute in nature. The major effect of the announcement of the kingship of Jesus is the relativisation of all human power and power structures.[97] *The key element*

[94] C. Hill, *Puritanism and Revolution*, 224–5; de Blois, 'Foundation of Human Rights', 172.

[95] As to their ideas, see Hill, *Puritanism and Revolution*, 312; Colwell, *Living the Christian Story*, 231–2. As to the more moderate views held by those who came to be known as 'Baptists', see de Blois, 'Foundation of Human Rights', at 168ff.

[96] By groups as diverse as the Christian Reconstructionists and the Restorationists, and by influential thinkers like N.T. Wright and Oliver O'Donovan.

[97] O'Donovan, *Desire*, 146.

of the recognition by earthly powers of the lordship of Christ is the acknowledgement of their own limitations.[98] British coins pay lip service to this truth, they say on them 'Elizabeth D.G. Reg', which is an abbreviation for 'Elizabeth *Deo Gracia Regina*', 'Elizabeth, by the grace of God, Queen'. In their coinage at least, the nominal rulers of our nation acknowledge that they hold power by the grace of the sovereign Lord.

Where such an acknowledgement is not made, or where Christ is nominally recognised as Lord but in practice the king usurps absolute authority for himself, the spiritual reality is not altered: Christ remains Lord, but his rule is hidden. The rule of Christ is as disguised today as it was during his lifetime (although that is primarily because of the church's failure to proclaim it as it should).

Jesus himself said relatively little about the Christian view of government. But in his actions he did not resist either the authority of the Roman rulers over him or of the Jewish religious leaders. He paid the Roman taxes and encouraged his followers to do likewise.

Jesus' subversion of political power was demonstrated in oblique fashion. Rather than overthrowing the political structures of his day, Jesus challenged them by his actions to a new attitude towards power. Jesus did not grasp at power, but instead recognised its temptations. In his use of power, he acted justly. His power was deployed in the service of the poor, the weak and the needy.

Jesus' power was used in the service of *delivering justice*. Jesus' message of the in-breaking of God's kingdom is a declaration of 'the radical restoration of God's justice, setting things right but bringing judgement and destruction to those who resist God's will'.[99]

Jesus is justice embodied. He is *Tsedeqah*-Incarnate. The focus of Jesus' mission was not on denouncing injustice (although he did that) but on demonstrating justice. As the wielder of the ultimate power he used it in service of the powerless, deliberately identifying with, dignifying and offering release to those who were the most marginalised by their society.

Jesus also displayed a revolutionary attitude to the power of leadership, using it in the service of others rather than for purposes of self-aggrandisement. He demonstrated that the essence of justice is power used in service of the powerless.

Jesus' power was not exercised in coercive fashion, except against his implacable enemies: sickness and demons. The controversial incident(s) in the Temple (Mt. 21:12–17; Mk. 11:12–19; Lk. 19:45–48; Jn. 2:13–17) was a symbolic demonstration of the moral bankruptcy of the Temple authorities, the proclamation that the Jewish religious establishment had aligned itself with the forces of darkness, and had become a place of worship for the spirit of Mammon.

---

[98] O'Donovan, *Desire*, 219; *Resurrection*, 72.
[99] Marshall, *Beyond Retribution*, 71.

Jesus himself rejected the pretensions of theocracy. He did not seek to recreate an independent, sovereign state of Israel.[100] His concerns were both bigger and deeper. Jesus eschewed political power because it was too limited in its nature and scope to achieve the redemptive purposes of God.

The lordship of Christ and the gospel of Christ

That Jesus is King was proclaimed by the title put above his head when they crucified him. He was, truly, 'The King of the Jews'. That Jesus is King was demonstrated at the cross when he disarmed the powers and authorities and made a public spectacle of them (Col. 2:15). That Jesus is King was proclaimed at the resurrection, when God raised him again to life.

Instead of wresting the kingships of the world from their human authorities, or accepting them from the hand of Satan, Jesus founded a new kingdom, a new society, whose citizens would be sealed with the mark of the Holy Spirit, and whose leaders would be commissioned not to reign over nations in the present age but instead to make disciples of all nations.[101]

The message of the Jesus event and of the nature of his kingship is that the fundamental problems of human existence: our alienation from God and from one another are the result of sin, and that these problems are not susceptible of resolution by political means.

The incarnation, death and resurrection of Jesus Christ demonstrate that legislation is not God's final answer to the problem of human sinfulness. There are limits to what human law, even if guided by Christian principles, can be expected to achieve in restraining human sinfulness.

Through the cross, Jesus extends the call to repentance and the offer of amnesty to all human beings. '*Christ's lordship is only truly understood in the light of the cross.*'[102] It was the failure to reflect sufficiently on this central fact, or the subversion of its remembering by the human will-to-power which led to the errors of Christendom. As John Colwell puts it:

> If the phenomenon of Christendom was vitiated by the Church's adoption of the coercive and violent strategies of the nations this was not an inevitable outcome of its proclamation of Jesus' kingship, nor an inevitable outcome of its confession of Christ as the source and goal of the universe and its history; it was rather the consequence of a failure to remember the unique manner of his kingship.[103]

There are limits on the extent to which Christian law makers ought to be seeking to enforce Christian behaviour and Christian belief, because of

---

[100] de Coninck, *La justice et la puissance*, 52.
[101] O'Donovan, *Desire*, 217.
[102] Cranfield, *On Romans*, 172.
[103] Colwell, *Living the Christian Story*, 246.

the important distinction between the role of government and the calling of the visible church. Ensuring that people have a genuinely *free* opportunity to accept the lordship of Christ has to be paramount over the enforcement of Christian morals.[104]

The implications of the nature of Christ's kingship on the Old Testament prophecies of the 'prince' to come (Isa. 9:6; Ezek. 34:24; 37:25)

Jesus' adoption of the 'Suffering Servant' paradigm in Isaiah 42:1–7; 52:13 – 53:12 for his life's work necessitated a radical reinterpretation of the traditional messianic hope of a revival of the Davidic kingdom. In fact, Jesus totally exploded the idea of a national, ethnic, religiously conservative Jewish state. The purification of Israel that Jesus exemplified was not to be purification from foreign influences but from indwelling sin.

Although it became a more prominent theme towards the end of his time on earth, and especially after his resurrection, Jesus made it clear that his kingdom was to be non-national, non-ethnic, multi-cultural.[105] The traditional hope that Jesus would revive the nation-state of Israel was transcended. Even at the moment of his ascension, Jesus' disciples were *still* asking, 'Lord, are you at this time going to restore the kingdom to Israel?' (Acts 1:6). Jesus informed them God alone knew the divine timetable (Acts 1:7). Instead of inaugurating an earthly kingdom, he commanded his disciples to be his witnesses 'in Jerusalem, and in all Judea and Samaria, and to the ends of the earth' (Acts 1:8).

Right to the end of his time on earth, Jesus made it clear that his kingdom was 'not of this world'. Amongst the things that this rich phrase means, it meant that Jesus' kingdom was not focussed around an earthly territory. The Promised Land that he offers to his followers is not historical Palestine, but heaven. His capital city is not earthly Jerusalem, but heavenly Zion.

By eschewing violence as the means by which his kingdom was to be established, and by pointedly refuting the accusation that he was plotting an armed rebellion, Jesus demonstrated that his kingdom was to be non-coercive in its nature.

All of these factors explain why government has only a limited role to play in God's purposes under the new covenant. The ideas of territory and shared heritage (be it nationality, *ethnos*, culture or even history) by which governmental authorities sustain themselves run at cross-purposes to the nature of the new people of God made up of Jesus' followers. The coercive power of government is simply not capable of leading to the voluntary swearing of allegiance and heartfelt obedience which Jesus seeks. The weapons of government are not apt to bring about the

---

[104] See P. Beaumont's Introduction to *Christian Perspectives on the Limits of Law*, 7–8, also 6.

[105] Matthew 8:5–12; 28:16–20; Mark 16:15–18; Luke 2:28–32; 13:29.

kingdom of God on earth; they are designed to achieve a different, more limited, goal.

What did Paul and the other apostles teach about the relationship between Jesus' kingdom and the kingdoms of this world?

In stark comparison with Jesus' teaching, references to the 'kingdom of God' are limited in Paul's letters.[106] Yet, N.T. Wright has convincingly demonstrated that the kingship (lordship) of Jesus the Christ was at the heart of Paul's proclamation of the gospel.[107] Paul wrote about the Christ, a term he uses over 160 times in his letters. For Paul, the Christ, the Anointed One was God's chosen King.[108]

Paul realised the centrality of the kingship of Jesus. At the heart of Paul's mission was his understanding of the kingship of Jesus, and of himself as the herald of the king.[109]

Paul begins his greatest letter, to the Romans, by declaring himself to be a servant of Christ Jesus, who was as to his human nature a descendant of king David and therefore the rightful heir to the Jewish throne. But Paul also says that Jesus was declared by the Holy Spirit to be the Son of God (and therefore the rightful heir to the divine throne, to the throne of God himself!). What was Paul's job for this great king: 'to call people from among all the non-believers to the obedience that comes from faith' (Rom. 1:3–5).

In one sense, the proclamation of the lordship of Christ by the apostles and particularly by Paul was nothing new. It was the assertion of the rule of the Lord over all the kingdoms of the world in just the same way as the Old Testament prophets had declared.[110] The rule of God would be established on earth through the Anointed One he had chosen.

But what was radical was its emphasis within their preaching and its implications. The rule of God was announced at the level of universal truth *and* of personal challenge. The Lord God was declared to be the sovereign of the universe and Jesus Christ to be his appointed regent. Individuals and households were challenged to acknowledge and submit to his lordship. Even kings and governors were presented with the message.[111]

Of course, Jesus is a different sort of king to Caesar. That is part of the point. Paul is not simply setting up a new empire of the same variety, another

---

[106]   Forster notes 13 references: *Kingdom of Jesus*, 2.

[107]   Wright, *What Saint Paul Really Said*.

[108]   Forster, *Kingdom of Jesus*, 2.

[109]   N.T. Wright has pointed out what has somehow got lost in centuries of debate about what Paul *really* said.

[110]   Cf. e.g., Psalm 89:19–20, 26–27; Wright, *What Saint Paul Really Said*, 55, 58, 148–9.

[111]   Paul presented his case before the Roman governors Felix (Acts 24:2–25) and Festus (Acts 25:1–12) and to king Agrippa II (Acts 25:23 – 26:32).

oppressive human regime. But it will not do to suppose that the differences between Christ and Caesar, for Paul, are that the one is 'spiritual' and the other 'temporal', so that they become locked in two separate compartments with no relation between them. The whole point of 'confessing Jesus Christ as Lord' is that at his name every knee shall bow. Caesar has a role (Romans 13), but a strictly limited one. He is to be obeyed because his office and his authority are derived from the creator, who intends his human creatures to live in order, safety and stability, rather than in chaos or anarchy. As soon as Caesar acts as though he were a god – as of course in Paul's day most Caesars did – Paul would be the first to call a spade a spade. If the early Christian community saw the death of Herod Agrippa as divine judgement on a monarch who gave himself divine honours (Acts 12:20–23), there is no doubt what Paul would have said about pagan worship of the Roman emperor. There was only one God; this God had exalted his Son, Jesus, as the true Lord of the world; his empire was the reality, Caesar's the parody.[112]

The New Testament writers saw this parody taken to its extreme in the imperial cult, which they identified as 'Antichrist', the assertion by human authorities of a fusion between earthly political rule and divine rule.[113] Such a claim usurped the role belonging to Christ alone.

---

[112] Wright, *What Saint Paul Really Said*, 148; see also O'Donovan, *Desire*, 152.
[113] O'Donovan, *Desire*, 214–15.

7

Law and the Spirit

Law and the Holy Spirit

Christian perspectives on law in the past have often been insufficiently trinitarian. Those which have drawn a sharp distinction between creation ethics and kingdom ethics, and between the revelation of God's will in the Old Testament and the revelation of God's will in Christ Jesus have drawn too acute a division between God the Father and God the Son. By locating the work of the Son of God exclusively in the incarnation, they have excluded him from the work of creation and failed to recognise his lordship over it.[1] Conversely, those who have insisted on 'the perfection of Christ' as the sole applicable standard have collapsed the Trinity into the person of Christ without remainder. What both tendencies have in common is a neglect of the third person of the Trinity, the Holy Spirit.

The Holy Spirit is an indispensable part of Christian theology. Among the functions which the recognition of his personality fulfils is the confirmation that God's activity in the world always has been and continues to be personal, even after the ascension of Jesus to the right hand of God the Father.

The Holy Spirit is, in the words of the Nicene Creed, 'The Lord and giver of life'.[2] He is the revealer of Christ (Jn. 16:13–14). His participation in both the creative purposes of God and in the redemptive purposes of God, together with God the Father and God the Son is the assurance of 'the coherence of creation and redemption'.[3] One of the tragedies of the great schism between the Eastern and Western churches, which is formally over the interrelationship between the three persons of the Trinity, is that it has left the Eastern Orthodox Church to emphasise the Holy Spirit's activity in the created order, while the Western churches (whether Catholic or Protestant) have focussed almost exclusively on his work within the church. Neither focus is complete without the other.

Jesus declared in John 16:8–11 three of the important tasks which the Holy Spirit would perform: (1) convicting the world of its sin and calling it to repentance (vv. 8–9); (2) revealing the standards of God's righteousness (v. 10); and (3) demonstrating Christ's judgement on

---

[1] John 1:1; 1 Corinthians 8:6; Colossians 1:16–17; Hebrews 1:2–3. Cf. O'Donovan, *Desire*, 246; Gunton, *Revelation*, 43, 59.

[2] Cf. Psalm 104:30.

[3] Colwell, *Living the Christian Story*, 240.

Satan (v. 11).[4] The Holy Spirit therefore has an important role to play *in the world*. Indeed, he must perform such a role of necessity because it is in the world that he finds human hearts to convict of sin and into which to breathe faith.

Therefore, it is not so much that the Holy Spirit is wholly *absent* from the world, but rather that his activities are *hidden* and his presence is not acknowledged. He only indwells believers. 'The world cannot accept him, because it neither sees him nor knows him' (Jn. 14:15–17). In the new covenant era, the church is the *polis* of the Holy Spirit; his activities in the world go unrecognised by the world.

Central among the Holy Spirit's activities in the world is the revelation of God.[5] Hence, he is the interpreter of God's self-revelation in nature and he is the interpreter of God's self-revelation in Christ.[6] It is the Holy Spirit who reveals Christ to be none other than the Logos, the Son of God through whom all things were made (Jn. 1:1–3; 1 Cor. 8:6; Heb. 1:2–3, 10–13).[7] It is the Spirit who 'reveals Jesus as the truth: as the revelation of God the Father.'[8] It is the Holy Spirit who discloses that 'the Christ who is the source and goal of redemption is beforehand the source and goal of creation'.[9]

It is through the inspiration of the Holy Spirit that Paul is able to write the Christological hymn of Colossians 1:15–23 in which he describes the majesty of Jesus as Lord over all, and the one in whom all things hold together. In this passage, Paul grasps the awesome truth that the creation of God finds its coherence in the Christ of God:[10]

> He is the image of the invisible God, the firstborn over all creation. For by him all things were created: things in heaven and on earth, visible and invisible, whether thrones or powers or rulers or authorities; all things

---

[4] A. McGrath, '*I Believe*': *Exploring the Apostle's Creed*, 97.

[5] Gunton, *Revelation*,119–20.

[6] As with all things trinitarian, the matter is more complicated and nuanced than that, because as the Spirit reveals Jesus so Jesus reveals the Father: Gunton, *Revelation*, 76.

[7] O'Donovan, *Resurrection*, 53.

[8] Gunton, *Revelation*, 121, see also 122; V-M. Kärkkäinen, *Pneumatology: The Holy Spirit in Ecumenical, International and Contextual Perspective*, 18, 32, 34–5. See John 1:18.

[9] Colwell, *Living the Christian Story*, 243; O'Donovan, *Resurrection*, 54–5. Colwell describes this approach to questions of revelation and knowledge as Pneumatological epistemology and traces it back to Jonathan Edwards and beyond him to Irenaeus. See also Gunton, *Revelation*. O'Donovan stresses the Christological foundations of epistemology, and insists that true knowledge is to be found in the incarnate Logos: *Resurrection*, 85, 87.

[10] See also 1 Corinthians 8:6. Gunton finds the same line of thinking in the Gospel of John: Gunton, *Revelation*, 124–5.

were created by him and for him. He is before all things, and in him all things hold together.

In Christ all things hold together. Any ideology taken on its own becomes an idol, and idols have demons behind them. So free-market capitalism, if taken to extremes, will destroy the poor. Communism will destroy freedom. Education will destroy creativity and innocence. Materialism will crush simplicity. Liberalism will lead to anarchy. Egalitarianism will lead to greyness and blandness. Workaholism will destroy rest.

Christianity is, in fact, a whole lot more relativistic than people give it credit for being. That is to say, because all things hold together in Christ, the demands of freedom and justice, of mercy and punishment, of form and spontaneity, can only be reconciled in him. Ultimately, everything must give way to and acknowledge the claims of the Christ of God.

The Torah and the Holy Spirit

In Romans 7:14, Paul describes the Mosaic Law as *ho nomos pneumatikos estin*. The Torah is *pneumatikos*, spiritual. In Paul's usage of the word, *pneumatikos* functions as an adjective for the Holy Spirit, referring to that which belongs to, or pertains to, the Spirit.[11] What Paul is saying is that the Torah belongs to and was given by the Spirit! It is his Law.[12]

This insight is also to be found in the Old Testament. In Nehemiah 9:13, the writer praises the Lord God because 'You came down on Mount Sinai; you spoke to [your people] from heaven. You gave them regulations and laws that are just and right, and decrees and commands that are good ...'. 'You gave your good Spirit to instruct them. You did not withhold your manna from their mouths, and you gave them water for their thirst ...' (v. 20). 'For many years you were patient with them. By your Spirit you admonished them through your prophets' (v. 30). In this passage, the Spirit of God is seen as responsible for giving the instruction contained in the Torah, and for speaking through the prophets who constantly challenged the people's unfaithfulness to the Torah.

From a Christian perspective, therefore, there is a close connection between the Holy Spirit and the Mosaic Law attested in both the Old and New Testaments.

The Holy Spirit and Wisdom

There is also a close connection between the Holy Spirit and Wisdom. Isaiah prophesied about the Messiah, the Branch from the stump of Jesse, that 'The Spirit of the Lord will rest on him – *the Spirit of wisdom*

---

[11] Fee, *God's Empowering Presence*, 29, 510.
[12] Romans 7:14; C.E.B. Cranfield, *A Critical and Exegetical Commentary on the Epistle to the Romans* Vol. 1, 355.

and of understanding, the Spirit of counsel and of power, the Spirit of knowledge and of the fear of the Lord,'[13] and he went on to state the effects of the Messiah being Spirit-filled: 'he will delight in the fear of the LORD. He will not judge by what he sees with his eyes, or decide by what he hears with his ears; but with righteousness he will judge the needy, with justice he will give decisions for the poor of the earth.'[14] In Isaiah's vision of the future, the Messiah was filled with the Spirit of wisdom in order to be able to do justice.

The Apostle Paul appropriated ideas that Jewish writers had given to divine Wisdom (*sophia*)[15] and attributed them to Christ. In Proverbs 9:22–31, she is described as the 'craftsman at [God's] side', intimately involved in the creation of the world.[16] Paul made this a focal point in his Christological hymn in Colossians 1:15–20.[17] '[Paul] saw Christ as Wisdom come in the flesh, and therefore whatever had been said of Wisdom in early Jewish thought, including its existence in heaven before creation was now predicated of Christ.'[18]

'The crucified Christ is the embodiment of God's plan of salvation, the true measure and the climactic expression of God's wisdom and power.'[19] The effect, therefore, of regarding Christ as God's Wisdom is to unveil the paradoxical nature of that wisdom, which confounds the supposed wisdom of the world system.[20] A true understanding of the nature, the purposes and the glory of God is therefore mediated by a grasp of the person and work of Christ. And all of this can only be grasped by a revelation from the Holy Spirit.[21]

The Antiochene School of theology preferred to attribute wisdom to the Holy Spirit, and could refer to the Holy Spirit in the feminine as 'Lady Wisdom'. But an either/or choice between linking Christ and wisdom or the Holy Spirit and wisdom is a false dichotomy because the Holy Spirit

---

[13] Isaiah 11:2.

[14] Isaiah 11:3–4a.

[15] E.J. Schnabel, 'Wisdom', in G.F. Hawthorne et al (eds.), *Dictionary of Paul and his Letters*, 967–73; Ziesler, *Pauline Christianity*, 32–5; 128–31.

[16] See also Job 28; Sirach 24; Wisdom of Solomon 8–9.

[17] N.T. Wright provides a convincing account of how this is done in *Climax of the Covenant*, 99–119. See also *What St Paul Really Said*, 68–9.

[18] See also 1 Corinthians 1:24, 30; 8:6. B. Witherington, 'Christology', in G.F. Hawthorne et al (eds.), *Dictionary of Paul and his Letters*, 103, 107; D. Guthrie and R.P. Martin, 'God', in G.F. Hawthorne et al (eds.), *Dictionary of Paul and his Letters*, 355–6; Schnabel, 'Wisdom', 971; Wright, *Climax of the Covenant*, 90–8, 131; S. Westerholm, *Preface to the Study of Paul*, 66; E.P. Sanders, *Paul: A Very Short Introduction*, 96; and Cranfield, *On Romans*, 51–68.

[19] Schnabel, 'Wisdom', 970, apparently quoting Dunn although no reference is given.

[20] 1 Corinthians 1:10–2:10.

[21] 1 Corinthians 2:10.

is the Spirit of Christ (Rom. 8:9)[22] and the Holy Spirit is the Spirit of wisdom (Eph. 1:17).

Law is not enough

But if the Mosaic Law is spiritual, if it was given by the Holy Spirit, and it has been affirmed by Christ; why has it received such a bad press, and why was it necessary for Christ to die? The answer is, because the practical result of the Law, before and without Christ, was death.[23] In Romans 7, Paul is at pains to explain how this came about. It was not the fault of the commandments, he stresses. Commandments such as 'Do not covet' are holy, righteous and good.

It is the absence of the Holy Spirit's power and the all-pervading presence of sin that turned Law's wise guidance into a bondage and a slavery, bringing condemnation and death in its wake.

The problem of the old covenant is not to do with the nature of the Law and its commandments; it is to do with human nature. '[T]he very commandment that was intended to bring life actually brought death'[24] because 'sin, seizing the opportunity afforded by the commandment, deceived me, and through the commandment put me to death'.[25] '[T]he law was powerless ... in that it was weakened by the sinful nature.'[26]

The problem is not the Law's nature or moral content; it is its powerlessness in the face of human sin-fullness.[27] As N.T. Wright clearly spells out 'the "problem of Romans 7" ... is emphatically *not* that of "man under the law" ... but of "the law under man", or, more specifically, under flesh.'[28]

Paul was not the first biblical writer to identify this difficulty with the Torah:

> There is an awareness in the Old Testament itself that the law is limited in its capacity for sustaining righteousness and justice in society, if there is determination to avoid its demands ... In the Old Testament there are three aspects of this awareness. First of all, just laws may be unjustly used, or simply ignored

[22] The juxtaposition of 'the Spirit of God' and 'the Spirit of Christ' in this verse and the two following, without conscious transition between the phrases, is ample evidence of their identity in Paul's thought: see G. Fee, *Paul, the Spirit and the People of God*, 31; Witherington, 'Christology', 107–8 and T. Paige, 'Holy Spirit', in G.F. Hawthorne et al (eds.), *Dictionary of Paul and his Letters*, 408–11.

[23] Romans 7:7–11.

[24] Romans 7:10.

[25] Romans 7:11.

[26] Romans 8:3.

[27] Romans 8:3. See Fee, *God's Empowering Presence*, 513.

[28] Wright, *Climax of the Covenant*, 209.

... Secondly, where the law could be twisted or evaded, those with sufficient power and influence could promulgate unjust laws to their own advantage ... Thirdly, mere changing of the law or invoking of old laws is an inadequate remedy, once injustice has taken deep root and become structurally ingrained ... in a society.[29]

The reason for the failure of the Torah to secure righteousness and shalom was the obdurate sinfulness of the human spirit:

> The failure of the former covenant, the covenant of law, was that even though the Torah was 'Spiritual' in the sense that it came by way of Spirit-inspiration (Rom. 7:14), and even though it came with glory (2 Cor. 3:7), it was not accompanied by the empowering Spirit. Indeed, it was written on stone tablets, which for Paul represented its deadness, its basic inability to set people free. It had become a covenant of letter (a merely written code of laws requiring obedience) leading to death (Rom. 2:29; 7:6; 2 Cor. 3:5–6).[30]

The history of the Israelite kingdoms is that time and again, the Old Testament prophets called the people of God back to live lives of covenant faithfulness and obedience to Torah. Time and again, they proved unwilling and incapable of doing so. Eventually, the predictions of judgement came true and the people of first Israel and then Judah were taken into exile.

The failure of the Mosaic Law to establish righteousness/justice is the demonstration that the best of laws, even those mediated by angels and expressing God's will for his people, are inadequate if treated as an external written code of rules.

The need for a change of heart

In the Old Testament, the Deuteronomist presents in chapters 4 to 26 the laws by which the people are to live in the Promised Land. Then in Deuteronomy 28, after the pronouncement of ritual curses in the previous chapter, he promises blessings for obedience and warns of curses for disobedience. The prediction is of the disobedient people of Israel being uprooted from the land and scattered among the nations (Deut. 28:63, 64). This will happen because of the people's unfaithfulness. The dire pronouncements are repeated at the end of Deuteronomy 29 (vv. 19–28), and given with prophetic certainty that this will come to pass (Deut. 30:1). Moses looks forward to the day when, after judgement and exile, the people will return to the Lord God and obey him with all their heart and soul (Deut. 30:2). In order for this to happen, it will be necessary for the Lord God himself to circumcise the hearts of his people (Deut. 30:6).

---

[29] Wright, *People of God*, 171–2.
[30] G. Fee, *Paul*, 100.

The realisation of the deficiencies of law alone, first seen in Deuteronomy, reaches its fullest expression in Jeremiah. Jeremiah prophesied in Judah at the time of its exile into captivity. The book that bears his name communicates a clear sense of the Lord's patience having been exhausted. Despite the warnings given through the prophets (Jer. 7:13), the people have persisted in their sinfulness; indeed, 'They ... did more evil than their forefathers' (Jer. 7:26).

There is a tension in Jeremiah between the call for the people to repent (Jer. 7:3, 5–7; 26:2–4) and the recognition that they are past turning (Jer. 7:27–29), and that judgement can no longer be averted, expressed in the prohibition against praying for them (Jer. 7:16), and in the pronouncement that 'the LORD has rejected and abandoned this generation that is under his wrath' (Jer. 7:29).

McConville skilfully explains this apparent dichotomy on the basis of a developing understanding of the prophet Jeremiah that the people's hardness of heart makes repentance out of the question (Jer. 7:24–26), unless God initiates it. What is then revealed to him is the disclosure that things have gone so far that deliverance is only possible beyond and through judgement and exile,[31] but that beyond the exile the Lord promises a new covenant and a return to the land.

What the Lord required of his people was heartfelt repentance. In Jeremiah 4:14, he pleads with Jerusalem to 'wash the evil from your heart and be saved'. God's complaint against Judah in Jeremiah 3:10 is that despite seeing him give her faithless sister Israel a certificate of divorce, '[she] did not return to me *with all her heart*, but only in pretence'. Significantly, this prophecy is one of the few in Jeremiah dated to Josiah's reign,[32] a time superficially of great religious zeal and revival.

But God's judgements are not based on externals alone. The Lord judges righteously, and tests 'the heart and mind'.[33] He proclaims, "I the LORD search the heart and examine the mind, to reward a man according to his conduct, according to what his deeds deserve' (Jer. 17:10). This examination, this heart-searching, extends not only to the unjust but also to his servants.[34]

The people's reaction to Jeremiah's Temple sermon, recorded in Jeremiah 26, showed that, 'Judah could not or would not repent'.[35] The experience of Josiah's reforms 'revealed to [Jeremiah] the inability of even the best of laws to reach the heart of a people for God'.[36]

---

[31] McConville, *Judgment and Promise*, 43–5, 50–1, 86–8, 96–7.
[32] Jeremiah 3:6.
[33] Jeremiah 11:20.
[34] See Jeremiah 12:3; 20:12.
[35] McConville, *Judgment and Promise*, 87. For my part, the order ought to be 'Judah would not' or as Jeremiah slowly discerned 'could not repent'.
[36] Kidner, *Jeremiah*, 17, 59.

The depressing conclusion of the first half of Jeremiah is therefore that, 'The heart is deceitful above all things and beyond cure.'[37] The position which has been reached is reminiscent of the one just before the Flood: 'The Lord saw how great man's wickedness on the earth had become, and that every inclination of the thoughts of his heart was only evil all the time' (Gen. 6:5).[38]

The mature Jeremiah realised that we are ourselves incapable of changing our hearts.[39] It is as difficult for us to do as it is for an Ethiopian to change his skin colour or for a leopard to change his spots.[40] In short, the condition of the human heart is incurable.[41] Yet without a change of heart people's behaviour and attitudes will not change.

Then, to both Jeremiah[42] and his contemporary, Ezekiel, writing in Babylonia, were given visions of a new covenant, in which God himself would cleanse his people, and give them a new heart and a new spirit.[43] Under this new covenant, God promised to '*put my Spirit in you and move you to follow my decrees and to be careful to keep my laws*'.[44] For Ezekiel, the purpose of the gift of the life-giving Spirit was explicitly to move God's people to follow his decrees. Heart surgery was what was required and God was going to perform it.

God promised Jeremiah that he himself would initiate the move to inward repentance and obedience. 'I will give them a heart to know me, that I am the LORD ... [then] they will return to me with all their heart.'[45] The new covenant will be written on human hearts,[46] the very place where rebellion had previously been engraved.[47] 'The law of God would then be obeyed, not merely because it was known, but because it was revered, the motivating force thus coming from within rather than from outside.'[48]

To Jeremiah, the Lord revealed the genius of the new covenant. Just as the problem is the human heart, so the solution will be divine action on that heart. No longer will the moral law just be written on tablets of stone; henceforth it will be written in the hearts of God's

---

[37] Jeremiah 17:9.
[38] Genesis 6:5.
[39] Kidner, *Jeremiah*, 166.
[40] Jeremiah 13:23.
[41] Jeremiah 30:12. See Harrison, *Jeremiah*, 106.
[42] Jeremiah 31:33–34.
[43] Ezekiel 36:26.
[44] Ezekiel 36:27; see also Ezekiel 11:19–20. Goldsworthy, *Gospel and Kingdom*, 81; Taylor, *Ezekiel*, 215.
[45] Jeremiah 24:7.
[46] Jeremiah 31:33. See Mason, *Jeremiah*, 155.
[47] Jeremiah 17:1.
[48] Harrison, *Jeremiah*, 42.

people. Yahweh himself will bring about the change of heart that was otherwise impossible.

Yahweh offers to his people a new covenant, described in Jeremiah 32:40 as an 'everlasting covenant'. The promise is the old one: 'They will be my people, and I will be their God' (Gen. 17:7; Exod. 6:7; Lev. 26:12; Hos. 2:19, 23b). What is new is the revelation of how this relationship will be achieved. Yahweh himself says '*I will give them singleness of heart and action ...*' (Jer. 32:39). The need is for a cure which only Yahweh himself can offer.[49]

The revelation which Jeremiah received was that the moral law could only be obeyed in the power of the Spirit and under the guidance of the Spirit. The true meaning of the Torah can only be grasped, not by treating it as an external written code but by meditating upon it under the internal guidance of the Spirit.

When Jesus came, through his life, his teaching and his legacy Jesus fulfilled the new covenant promises to Jeremiah and Ezekiel. Quite simply, *Jesus turned the Law inside out.* Whereas Torah observance focussed on external purity, Jesus made it clear that it was not what was on the outside that made a man pure, but rather what was in his heart.[50] Jesus taught that at the heart of the commands 'Do not murder' and 'Do not commit adultery' was an obligation not to cherish anger and lust in our hearts.[51] The early church's discovery that what God wanted was circumcision of heart not circumcision of foreskin[52] was in line with Jesus' teaching that what mattered to God was not (or was no longer) external ritual purity, but rather inward purity of heart.

Given his theological training in Old Testament studies and his declaration to Felix that 'I believe everything that agrees with the Law and that is written in the Prophets' (Acts 24:14b), it is a mistake to read Paul's theology of the Holy Spirit otherwise than as the outworking of those new covenant prophecies of Jeremiah and Ezekiel. For Paul, part of the reason why the Holy Spirit was given is in order that 'the righteousness of the law might be fulfilled in us' (Rom. 8:4), so that Ezekiel's prophecy that under the new covenant, God's people will 'walk in my statutes and keep my ordinances and obey them' (Ezek 11:19–20) might be fulfilled.[53]

The Holy Spirit and the limits of Law

In the New Testament, despite the fact that many aspects of Paul's thought about (the) law are the subject of vigorous debate, there is no

---

[49] Jeremiah 3:22a; Jeremiah 30:12–17 sees YAHWEH promise to heal the incurable wound!

[50] Matthew 15:11, 16–20.

[51] Cf. Matthew 5:21–22 and 27–28 respectively.

[52] Acts 15. Cf. Deuteronomy 30:6; Jeremiah 4:4.

[53] Cf. Ezekiel 36:26–27. See K. Prior, *The Way of Holiness*, 121.

doubt that Paul 'expresses extreme skepticism about the ability of an external law-code to control human wrongdoing'.[54] There is no possibility for true righteousness apart from the Holy Spirit.

Therefore laws, even laws framed in accordance with God's divine intention for human societies, even laws given by God through his angels to Moses (Gal. 3:19), can only restrain external wrongdoing to a limited extent. They are incapable of achieving the change of heart which God deserves. Wholehearted obedience to God's moral law cannot be expected of those who are not 'in Christ'.

The most fundamental of the limits of law is its inability to make us moral. Law alone cannot produce self-sacrifice; it cannot require virtue. As Catholic moral theology recognises, any fully developed ethical system requires both *virtues and rules*, i.e. enforceable minimum standards of behaviour (*mandata*) and desirable higher standards of behaviour (*concilia*). Minimum standards of behaviour can be enforced but the law can, at most, encourage virtues.[55]

In this connection, David Harte considers 'the use of law to enforce particular standards and its use as a means of enabling or facilitating human liberty and fulfilment'.[56] Therefore, although Law cannot make us moral, it can enable and encourage us to behave in more moral ways. There is a real, but limited, extent to which this is possible.

Truly 'Christian morality' must be heartfelt obedience to God's good moral laws and to the Holy Spirit's moral guidance. It is not only immoral and/or impractical for the church to enforce its vision of morality; it is impossible.[57] The most that can be achieved is a form of legalism that Jesus denounced as not pleasing to God (Mt. 23:27).[58]

However, while force is not apt to produce heartfelt obedience to God,[59] it can stop people starving or being permanently excluded from a

---

[54] Marshall, *Beyond Retribution*, 11.

[55] O'Donovan, *Resurrection*, 170–2.

[56] D. Harte, 'The Legal Framework for Religion in Schools in England and Wales: Enforcement or Enablement?', in P. Beaumont (ed.), *Christian Perspectives on the Limits of Law*, 35–70. Harte adopts this principle as a rationale for maintaining the 'broadly Christian character' and presence of worship in schools. Beaumont himself, in his introduction to the volume, at 1–4, adopts a contrasting position on the educational question, arguing for the presentation of the 'full extent of the beliefs of people adhering to the major world religions, and that these beliefs conflict', without the State adopting a partisan preference for any particular one of them.

[57] Colwell, *Living the Christian Story*, 248. See also M. de Blois, 'Freedom of Religion as the Fruit of the Radical Reformation' in R. O'Dair and A. Lewis (eds.), *Law and Religion*, 174–7.

[58] Martin Luther, quoted in Witte, *Law and Protestantism*, 91–2. See also M. Luther, *Works*, 31:345–54.

[59] O'Donovan, *Desire*, 217.

real stake in society. If Christian morality cannot be enforced, the poor, the weak and the needy should nonetheless be protected from the worst excesses of unrestrained unChristian immorality.

Structural Sin

But the Holy Spirit is not the only spiritual being or spiritual power that the Bible recognises. It acknowledges the spiritual realm as having a number of different classes of occupants, and this recognition of the importance of unseen realities grows through the history of biblical revelation.

In the Old Testament, the prophets frequently addressed the nations as corporate entities:

> there are hints in the Old Testament of an awareness that there is a "personal" world of spiritual, invisible powers that lies behind the institutions and "person-ifications" of states, the overwhelming force of political power, the distinctive "character" of different social systems ... Whatever they are, they are subject, like men, including men who have exercised unbridled power under their influence, to the final judgement of God: "In that day the LORD will punish the powers in the heavens above and the kings on the earth below (Is. 24:21)."[60]

In the New Testament, the Apostle Paul clearly writes about super-earthly entities in his letters, referring to them variously as 'principalities and powers', 'authorities', 'dominions', 'thrones', 'rulers' and so on.[61] The idea that evil resides not only in the hearts of individual human beings but also in the social structures which human beings inhabit is to be found in the Bible's apocalyptic literature in both the Old and New Testaments.[62]

Protestant theology lost sight of this when miracles were being de-bunked, but there has been a radical rediscovery of the realities behind Paul's terms. Experience confirms the truth of the Bible when it speaks of 'very real cosmic spiritual powers that manifest themselves in the very real structures of our very real world'.[63]

The all too evident evils of fascism, communism and capitalism have again forced upon the twentieth century church the realisation that 'Structures do have a life of their own.'[64] Above and beyond the actions of individuals, there are the activities of the institutions that govern and control our lives:

[60] Wright, *People of God*, 108.
[61] Romans 8:38; 1 Corinthians 2:8; Ephesians 1:21; 3:10; 6:12; Colossians 1:16, 2:10, 15. See also 1 Peter 3:22.
[62] de Coninck, *La justice et la puissance*, 93.
[63] R. Foster, *Money, Sex and Power*, 180.
[64] I. Linden, 'People before Profit: The Early Social Doctrine of John Paul II', in P. Vallely (ed.), *The New Politics*, 95.

It is just as meaningful to emphasize that in South Africa apartheid structures made people sinful, as to say that people made sinful apartheid structures. South Africans were, of course, free to resist apartheid and qualify for prison ... everyone wishing to stay out of prison ... compromised to some extent with the sinful structures.[65]

Social structures exert powerful pressures on people, excluding certain options and making others seem natural, almost inevitable. The prophet Samuel accurately discerned the tendency of centralised authority to create a society marked by social stratification, privilege and oppression and that the baleful effects of monarchy would dangerously threaten the distinctive social shape of Israel.[66] Far from being unique to Israel, his predictions have proved to be a recurrent theme in human societies ever since.

Traditional theological models that focus exclusively on the salvation of individuals are incomplete. The traditional prescription that sociopolitical issues will sort themselves out once men and women are converted to Christ is an insufficient remedy for the problem.[67] Something more needs to be addressed.

The experience of the twentieth century has made apparent the extent to which we become passive participants in the social systems which govern our lives. 'Every evil system is sustained by evil people but, far more, by the vast multitude of people who do not resist because they are structurally embedded in it.'[68] This takes us back to Edmund Burke's observation that all that is required for evil to triumph is for good men to do nothing. And it is easiest of all for good men to reconcile themselves to the fact that they are doing nothing if they believe that there is nothing that can be done.

Psychology recognises that institutions have their own personalities that exert considerable influence on the lives of the people in them.[69] Psychologists acknowledge the truth that social structures affect us. Some Protestant theologians argue that this is because of the spiritual realities which underlie them.

Hendrik Berkhof[70] and Walter Wink[71] identify the spiritual powers referred to by the Apostle Paul in his letters as the energising forces behind human beings and social structures. Their thesis is that the very

---

[65]   Linden, 'People before Profit', 94.
[66]   Wright, *People of God*, 61.
[67]   Michael Cassidy, *Partnership* No.5. (Sept. 1976), quoted in Burnett, *Healing of the Nations*, 130.
[68]   Linden, 'People before Profit', 95.
[69]   B. Sells, *The Soul of the Law*, 14–15. Arguably this idea can be traced all the way back to Plato's Forms.
[70]   H. Berkhof, *Christ and the Powers*.
[71]   W. Wink, *Naming the Powers: The Language of Power in the New Testament* Vol. 1.

power structures of our world were created by God but have been affected by the Fall and are in revolt and rebellion against God their Creator. Demons can possess not only individuals but also the structures of society.[72] Richard Foster identifies some of the gods of our age that hold power over our societies: money, sex, religious legalism, technology, efficiency, narcissism, militarism, and absolute scepticism.[73]

Theological insight into the reality of the power structures in our world runs on a twin track. First, there is the insight that the structures of our society influence our lives and need to be changed. The church therefore needs to be concerned not only about the conversion of individuals but also the transformation of structures. This is the conviction of the liberation theologians.[74]

Secondly, there is an increasing acknowledgement that behind the human structures may lie malevolent spiritual influences:

> the Christian involved in any branch of … human life needs to remember that the issues are not merely material or physical … "our struggle is not against flesh and blood" (Eph. 6:12) … It is against spiritual powers and forces which, by their invasion of and influence over human … relationships and structures, can wield an oppressive tyranny over mankind.[75]

Thus the charismatic movement places emphasis on 'spiritual warfare', on the church taking on the challenge of Ephesians 6:12 to use the spiritual weapons at its disposal to 'struggle … against the rulers, against the authorities, against the powers of this dark world and against the spiritual forces of evil in the heavenly realms'.[76]

The church's approach to structural sin must be holistic, taking account of the full dimensions of the situation. The individuals caught up in the sin must be challenged about their individual behaviour, as the Catholic concept of the 'indirect employer' does effectively with regard to Western consumers' responsibility for inhumane working conditions in the Third World.[77] The structures must be challenged, where this is practical and not quixotic. Christenson asserts: 'the structures of society will not succumb to a frontal attack by the church. There is a more effective way – the way of example.'[78] But there comes a time when the church needs to move from abolishing slavery and racism in its own midst

---

[72] Foster summarises their ideas in *Money, Sex and Power*, 180–3.

[73] Foster, *Money, Sex and Power*, 186–9.

[74] A. McGrath, *Christian Theology: An Introduction*, 116–18.

[75] Wright, *People of God*, 74.

[76] Foster, *Money, Sex and Power*, 183–5, 189–93; Burnett, *Healing of the Nations*, 202–3; S. Hawthorne and G. Kendrick *Awaking our Cities for God: A Guide to Prayer-Walking*.

[77] Vallely (ed.), *New Politics*, 17, 95.

[78] L. Christenson, *A Charismatic Approach to Social Action*, 81. See also de Coninck, *La justice et la puissance*, 55–74.

to dismantling slavery and racism in its society.[79] Lawyers have a particular role to play because of the fact that 'Structural evil is usually supported by an unjust legal system.'[80] The prophets should be our example in exposing social evil.[81] But, finally, the church has a unique role to play in combating the evil spiritual realities which lie behind the unjust structures of our fallen world. It alone can wield the spiritual weapons with which God has equipped it.[82] It is not for nothing that the Apostle Paul urges us to pray for our rulers.[83]

However, the recognition of the reality of structural evil must not be at the expense of the primacy of personal responsibility. Neither the 'oppressors' nor the 'oppressed', who may in certain lights both be regarded as the 'victims' of structural evil, are free from personal responsibility for their actions. Structures may render certain options easier or more costly, but our choices remain our responsibility.

Conclusion

Ultimately, the evils in this world will not be wholly eradicated until the moment when the kingdoms of this world have become the kingdoms of our God and of his Christ. When that happens, 'a king will reign in righteousness and rulers will rule with justice' (Isa. 32:1). Security will no longer be required; fortresses, citadels and watchtowers will be abandoned (Isa. 32:14). This moment awaits the outpouring of the Spirit among us (Isa. 32:15), when 'Justice will dwell in the desert and righteousness live in the fertile field. The fruit of righteousness will be peace; the effect of righteousness will be quietness and confidence forever' (Isa. 32:16–17).

With regard to human law making and law enforcement in the meantime, the lesson for us is clear. Because of the paradoxical nature of Christ's kingdom, the absence of the indwelling presence of the Holy Spirit, the inability of law to make human beings truly moral, and the temptations and evil lurking in the power structures of our world there are important limits on the extent to which human laws can be used to achieve a just, righteous, peaceful and holy society.

---

[79] See Christenson, *Social Action*, 52–5; Burnett, *Healing of the Nations*, 128–30.
[80] Burnett, *Healing of the Nations*, 87.
[81] Burnett, *Healing of the Nations*, 213.
[82] Ephesians 6:10–18.
[83] 1 Timothy 2:1–2.

8

Submission to the Authorities

Reprise

A consideration of the character of God as revealed in the Bible has shown him to be a God of order and a God of justice, a God of grace and a God of mercy. God's actions in creation saw him endow human beings with his good gifts of life, dignity, liberty and the ability to engage in rewarding work and to enjoy meaningful relationships. The perfect world that he had created, in which human beings were to enjoy perfect communion with God and with one another was, however, marred and defaced by the human choice to reject God's authority. This original sin has entailed the Fall of all of creation and has led to the distortion both of the reflection of God presented by creation and the disruption of the ability of human beings to perceive that reflection. From the moment of the Fall, God has pronounced the penalty of death against sin.

However, God did not abandon his world to the ravages of sin. On the contrary, he has ordained human government as a means of restraining it, and he is personally active within it curbing the effects of sin until the time of judgement.

Through the Torah, God gave to his holy people guidance in the form of a 'law' which would help them to reflect his character. This law placed a strong emphasis on social justice, on ensuring that no one was excluded from the community. It also placed a strong emphasis on holiness. Within Israel, justice/righteousness was conceived of as a matter of public importance as well as personal morality. It was understood as a lifestyle to be internalised, rather than a mere framework of rules imposed from the outside. Through the practice of righteousness (*tsedeq*) by the people and the administration of justice (*mishpat*) by the judges, a state of shalom could be preserved.

God's people failed, however, to live up to these ideals. A lack of both effective authority and communal standards of morality led to the chaos, anarchy and bloodshed of the time of the judges. The people's response was to demand a king. This amounted again to a rejection of God's kingship. However, God graciously wove the human institution of kingship into his covenant purposes. Israelite kingship was characterised by its separation from the priesthood, by its circumscribed nature, and by the king's obligation to do justice on behalf of his people. This was not merely a passive preservation of the status quo ante, but an active obligation to deliver from oppression.[1]

---

[1] O'Donovan, *Resurrection*, 128.

Israelite kingship failed too to live up to the standards of justice God had revealed. The prophets called the kings back, again and again, to do justice. The prophets also revealed that God's purposes for justice were not limited to his people but extended to the whole world. Despite the warnings of the prophets, the kings, the leaders and the people failed to do justice and to live righteously, and for these sins they were taken into exile.

In this time of exile, Daniel had a vision of the true nature of power. He saw human empires as bestial in nature and looked forward to the day when a truly humane king, a Son of Man, would arise and take the throne. So, we saw in chapter 6, the coming of Jesus – the Christ – the King.

Jesus' kingship is paradoxical in nature: he embodied and demonstrated God's saving justice, he displayed servant leadership and executed deliverance but he eschewed political power. And in the context of the present study, we understood the kingship of Jesus as the dethroning of all human pretensions to absolute power or absolute authority.

Then, in chapter 7, we reflected on the giving of the Holy Spirit and saw in him the fulfilment of the promises of a new covenant. We saw how the Holy Spirit's power is necessary for the fulfilment of God's law, and Paul's conclusion that law alone, even God-given law, is insufficient to make human beings moral. We also reflected on the nature of power, and observed how the power structures in our fallen world can be forces for evil.

Such is the biblical context into which studies of Romans 13:1–7, where Christian reflections on power have all too often begun and finished, must be placed.

Government has a Role within God's Purposes

Christianity flourished, in its early years, in a hostile empire whose representatives had executed its founder, Jesus the Christ. The question which therefore arose as a matter of urgency was what attitude should Christians have to the governing authorities of the Roman Empire?

Paul gave the fullest answer to that question in Romans 13. The chapter begins: 'Everyone must submit himself to the governing authorities, for there is no authority except that which God has established. The authorities that exist have been established by God.'[2]

From verse 1 Paul concludes in verse 2 that rebellion against the established authorities amounts to rebellion against God. What makes Paul's assertion about the need to submit to governing authorities all the more remarkable is that he was someone who knew from painful first hand experience that his theoretical rights as a Roman citizen were often rendered illusory in practice because of what seemed expedient to local

2 See also Titus 3:1 and 1 Peter 2:13–14. For an exploration of the idea of 'authorities' (*exousiai*), see O'Donovan, *Resurrection*, 122–4.

officials. In Philippi, he was beaten and thrown into prison without trial (Acts 16:22–39). In Caesarea, Paul languished in Felix's prison while the governor hoped that Paul would offer him a bribe (Acts 24:26).[3]

Jesus in Matthew 22:15–22, when asked whether he would pay the Roman taxes, said, 'Give to Caesar what is Caesar's and to God what is God's.'

Both Jesus and Paul affirmed the legitimacy of government within its proper role. For Christians, almost any form of social organisation is better than anarchy.[4] 'The Apostles advocated submission [to the authorities] in spite of [their] injustice.'[5]

The current theological vogue is to relativise the importance of Romans 13. This is a mistake. However, it is important to read Romans 13 in its rightful context both within the letter in which it is to be found, and in the overall context of the Bible's teaching. Romans 13 is *not* addressed to the Roman political authorities, giving them a Christian charter for their actions or a Christian list of their role and responsibilities.

Instead, Romans 13 is written to an embattled Christian church, to instruct them on how to view those in secular authority.[6] It is written in a letter whose central concern is arguably the righteousness/justice of God. It is written in a letter where Paul has wrestled at length with the relationship between Christians and the Mosaic Law, and as Christopher Marshall rightly points out: 'given the social, moral and civic functions of the Mosaic law in first-century Judaism, Paul's perspective on the law cannot be limited to purely theological concerns'.[7]

Viewed as part of the textual whole of the Epistle to the Romans, as Cranfield says:

> it ought to be recognized as highly significant that [Romans] 13.1–7 has been placed between [Romans] 12.9–21 and 13.8–10, two passages concerned with love. Was not Calvin right in saying that the fulfilment of what is

---

[3] Peter too in 1 Peter 2 links his discussion of submission to governing authorities with the duties of a slave to his master, and in particular the virtue of bearing up under the pain of unjust suffering (1 Pet. 2:19).

[4] J.W. Montgomery, 'Law and Morality: Friends or Foes?', *Law & Justice* 122 (1994), 87 at 91.

[5] de Coninck, *La justice et la puissance*, 67; see also M. de Blois, 'Freedom of Religion as the Fruit of the Radical Reformation', in R. O'Dair and A. Lewis (eds.), *Law and Religion*, 165.

[6] Marshall, *Beyond Retribution*, 235–6. I do not find the thesis that the specific reason for the teaching was to urge Christians not to join in a popular campaign of tax resistance convincing; nor am I persuaded that such an explanation, even if correct, substantially alters the meaning of the passage within its canonical context.

[7] Marshall, *Beyond Retribution*, 11.

enjoined in [Romans] 13.1–7 "constitutes not the least part of love"?[8] Must we not recognise that trying seriously to fulfil our political responsibility as Christians, which in a democracy is a very onerous matter, is an important part of the love of our neighbour for which the Holy Spirit sets us free, an important part of our sanctification?[9]

Yoder,[10] too, points out that it is not incidental that the remainder of Romans 13 (especially vv. 8–10) is a reprise of the second great commandment as the summation of our obligations under the law to our fellows. Christian political responsibility is an expression of the love which is 'the fulfilment of the law' (Rom. 13:10).

Paul urges Christians to submit to the governing authorities because they are God's servants (*diakonos*). Paul in Romans 13:3–5 endows government with the quality of being 'God's servant' in two distinct ways. On the one hand, he declares: 'do what is right and [the one in authority] will commend you for he is God's servant to do you good'. On the other hand, he warns that '[the one in authority] does not bear the sword for nothing [for] he is God's servant, an agent of wrath to bring punishment on the wrongdoer.' Another apostle, Peter wrote in 1 Peter 2:13, 'Submit yourself for the Lord's sake to every authority instituted among men … sent by him *to punish those who do wrong and to commend those who do right.*'

Governments exist to do and to encourage good/right and to punish and discourage wrong. If they are doing that, they are acting as God's servants and fulfilling the purpose for which they have been instituted. If they are not doing that, they are acting in disobedience and rebellion to God.

Paul goes on in Romans 13 verses 6–7 to affirm another aspect to the role of government. He says 'This is also why you pay taxes, for the authorities are God's servants, who give their full time to governing.' Paul confirms that the collection of taxes is within the proper powers of government. He also recognises the value of *governing*, the fact that human societies need administering and organising, and confirms that governments are entitled to collect taxes to pay for the costs of running a government. This was a bold statement within the context of the Roman Empire where the similarity between taxation and expropriation was marked.

---

[8] J. Calvin, *The Epistles of Paul the Apostle to the Romans and to the Thessalonians*, 285.

[9] Cranfield, *On Romans*, 44. See also I. Leigh, 'Towards a Christian Approach to Religious Liberty', in P. Beaumont (ed.), *Christian Perspectives on Human Rights and Legal Philosophy*, 49.

[10] Yoder, *Politics of Jesus*, 197.

The Proper Aims of Government

God is in favour of order. God loves good and hates evil. God loves justice. Speaking at the Lawyers' Christian Fellowship Annual Dinner in 2001, Dr Brian Mawhinney identified these three functions of government as emerging from Romans 13: (1) the preservation of order; (2) the promotion of good and the punishment of evil; (3) the raising and spending of taxes in the interest of the common good.

The obligation on governments to preserve order is uncontroversial, although Christians disagree about the extent to which it is right for governments to impose moral conformity, and about the degree to which government's coercive powers should be exercised or constrained. It is the second and third functions of government that have given rise to far greater debate among Christians.

Christians differ about what Paul is referring to when he says that government should commend right and punish wrong. Some on the political right insist that the Bible limits the appropriate role of the state to such areas as national defence, the adjudication of disputes, the defence of private property and the monitoring of certain public goods.[11] Others, whether liberation theologians or dominion theologians,[12] go to the other extreme and declare that the state is to usher in the kingdom of God as Christians take control of the institutions of the state and use them to apply biblical principles to every aspect of life. On the one hand, we would have little more than Nozick's ultra-minimalist state,[13] on the other, no distinction at all between state, church and civil society.

Most Christian thinkers, however, reject both of those alternatives. As we have seen in chapter 6, Jesus himself destroys the argument of the liberation and dominion theologians. When asked by Pilate whether he was king of the Jews, he declared, 'My kingdom is not of this world' (Jn. 18:36). The kingdom of God will only be fully realised in heaven, among the society of believers there.

Conversely, the ultra-minimalist state fails to take account of government's God-given responsibility for governing, and underplays the biblical teaching on government's obligation to provide for its citizens'

---

[11] Views summarised by Gay, *Liberty and Justice*, 92, 106–7.

[12] Also called 'theonomists' or 'Christian reconstructionists'.

[13] Nozick, *Anarchy, State and Utopia*, ix: 'Our main conclusions about the state are that a minimal state, limited to the narrow functions of protection against force, theft, fraud, enforcement of contracts, and so on, is justified; that any more extensive state will violate persons' rights not to be forced to do certain things, and is unjustified; and that the minimal state is inspiring as well as right.' See also 26–8 for a more detailed description of the ultra-minimalist state. This is, in effect, the position argued for by theonomists such as G. DeMar, *Ruler of the Nations: Biblical Principles of Government*, 77ff.

welfare to be found in the story of Joseph in Egypt,[14] the legislation of the Pentateuch regarding widows, orphans, aliens and the poor, or the tirades of the prophets against the unconcerned rich and rulers. The ultra-minimalist state falls short of God's purposes because it fails to provide justice for its people.

It is a fundamental, but recurrent, theological error to relegate to charity *alone* ethical demands that are in fact matters of justice.[15] There is no doubt that the church should be at the forefront of movements to alleviate poverty, to overturn injustice and to provide proper medical care. There is no doubt that the teaching and the example of Christ give Christians a distinctive motivation for doing so, for we serve Christ as we serve each of the divine image-bearers (Mt. 25:31–46).

But the obligation to 'Love your neighbour as yourself' is *not* the ethical originality of Christ's teaching. The obligation to 'Love your neighbour as yourself' is an obligation given to God's people in Leviticus, but to a people who were without the indwelling presence of the Holy Spirit and whose *polity* was to be an example to all the nations of how their social affairs should be structured. The obligation to ensure that everyone participates in the blessings of living in society and that none is deprived of their life, their dignity, their liberty, and their ability to enjoy meaningful work and relationships, is inherent in the created order of the world as God made it, not merely in the redeeming actions of God within that world.

The ethical innovation of Christ is in the command given to his disciples in the upper room on the night he was betrayed when he commanded them to 'Love one another *as I have loved you*' (Jn. 15:12).[16] Jesus' love for his disciples was not limited to a neighbour love that took the form of a sharing of resources. Jesus' love for his disciples expressed itself in humility, in service, in being prepared to go all the way to death for them. The new ethic Jesus taught went beyond a love which shares to a love which sacrifices itself for the good of others. Such a love deserves the name 'charity' (*agape*); law cannot enforce such a love; such a love, in this fallen world, is what is required in order that all may be led to share with one another.[17]

What can be, and is, demanded of human laws and legal systems by God is that they do such justice as is possible in this fallen world.[18]

Defining the Good and the Right

Paul talks in Romans 13 blithely about right and wrong, about good and evil. But how are right and wrong to be discerned? And within those

---

[14]   Genesis 41–45.
[15]   It is the trap into which Christenson slips in *Social Action*, 85–9.
[16]   Cf. Ricoeur, 'Golden Rule', 392–7.
[17]   Wright, *People of God*, 87.
[18]   O'Donovan, *Desire*, 148.

categories, what does government have a mandate to enforce and what is not to be enforced by human law?

For Christians, right and wrong can be discovered in two ways. On the one hand, there is what can be observed from nature (general revelation);[19] on the other hand, there is what God has revealed in Scripture (special revelation). Both general and special revelation are objective. General revelation refers to the objective realities of the created order; special revelation to the objective reality of the incarnate Christ and the objective truth revealed in the Bible. Right and wrong are therefore not, in the Christian conception, sociological constructs nor is right derived from or dependent on state authority, although it may need the backing of state force.[20]

Basing themselves on natural law theory, some Christian thinkers[21] and politicians argue that the task of the state is simply to enact laws which are consistent with natural law and natural justice. In other words, the role of the state is no more and no less than to create a level playing field within which individuals and groups are free to pursue their own conceptions of what is good without undue interference. Others argue that natural law thinking cannot define the content of the rights it seeks to uphold, and that it is only by looking at Scripture that we can discern the way a society should be going.[22] The role of government is therefore to promote those things that God has said in Scripture are good and to discourage those things which God has said in Scripture are bad.

In practice, theories which propose legislation on a natural law basis and those which would seek to make laws based on Scripture are on a continuum. This is what one would expect to find if the same Holy Spirit is at work in both nature and Scripture, revealing the same God. In order to create a viable, coherent set of propositions from natural law, it is necessary to interpret nature in the light of Scripture.[23] On the other

---

[19] Natural law theory is based on this idea, to be found in Hebrews 8:10, Romans 1:20; 2:14–15 and developed in the *Summa Theologica* of Thomas Aquinas, *Natural Theology comprising "Nature and Grace"* by Emil Brunner, and most recently by Finnis, *Natural Law*. It is closely associated with the idea of 'common grace'. Further, see chapter 2.

[20] Wortley, 'Christian Tradition', 10.

[21] Montgomery, 'Law and Justice', 12 at 17–18 reviews some contributions to this field.

[22] Montgomery, 'Law and Justice', 19; P. Devlin, *The Enforcement of Morals*.

[23] Cf. Finnis, *Natural Law*, 101, where he stresses that although Aquinas believed in the self-evidence of primary principles, he emphasised that moral principles such as those in the Ten Commandments were *conclusions from* those primary self-evident principles. I differ from Aquinas in that I give priority to revelation rather than to reason: cf. O'Donovan, *Resurrection*, 133–4. Luther's view was that the Ten Commandments were the clearest expression of natural law: Witte, *Law and Protestantism*, 113.

hand, if Christianity is not to be brought into disrepute, Christians must be able to demonstrate the social utility of the laws they are proposing;[24] in other words, it would be wrong to impose on society a law whose benefit could not be argued from nature.

This congruence between God's requirements as revealed in nature and as revealed in Scripture is to be expected if, as we have seen in the Old Testament, insights derived from the created order and from the Torah are intertwined. It is also to be expected if, as theologians are increasingly recognising, the consummation of all things is not the doing away with of the created order but its transformation and renewal.[25]

The right

No law is value free.[26] All laws are inevitably morally loaded in that they imply that there is right and wrong, and institutionalise rational or irrational prejudices. Christians believe that Christian values lead to a good life and that some Christian values will bring benefit to the lives of whoever abides by them, whether a Christian or not. How do we discern which Christian values government should promote or enforce and which it should not?

Calvin's answer was that 'the duty of magistrates ... extends to both tables of the law',[27] i.e. that civil government should enforce the Ten Commandments, both those relating to the worship of God and to the respect for others.

But it is not clear why, even on Calvin's account (nor on Luther's), given the duality between church and state and between the first and second tables of the Decalogue, the church should not be conceived of as having primary responsibility for the first and the state for the second. Given the duality, why should the sanctions for violation of the first table of the Decalogue extend beyond discipline by, and in the last resort, excommunication from, the church?

As well as the practical difficulties of enforcing the first table of the Decalogue, which proved insuperable in European history, Calvin's approach is vulnerable to two fundamental objections. The first is that the Ten Commandments are not, in their entirety, susceptible to enforcement by government, whose concern is only with 'the external regulation of manners'.[28] The tenth commandment, 'Do not covet', cannot be

---

[24] J.W. Montgomery, 'Law and Morality', 105, and *The Shaping of America*, 154–6, J.N.D. Anderson, *Morality, Law and Grace*, 82; B. Mitchell, 'Should Law Be Christian?', *Law & Justice* 96 (1988), 12 at 18, 21.

[25] This is at the heart of, for example, O'Donovan's thought.

[26] D.H. McIlroy, 'A Christian State?', *Law & Justice* 120 (1994), 32 at 33; I.H. Jones, 'A Truly Christian Lawyer?', *Christian Lawyer* 36 (1993), 16–17.

[27] Calvin, *Institutes* Book IV, ch. 20, para. 9.

[28] Calvin, *Institutes* Book IV, ch. 20, para. 1.

policed, and it is arguable that the same difficulty also applies to the first. It is highly significant for the shape of Christian thought about the relationship between human laws and divine laws that, 'The Tenth Commandment indicates that, while having done nothing illegal by human standards, a person can nevertheless be morally guilty before God.'[29]

Within the Ten Commandments themselves there is, therefore, a disjunction between the requirements of divine law and the realities of human law enforcement. The disjunction is made even more marked in the New Testament through Jesus' emphasis on internal attitudes.

The second objection is that the Ten Commandments were revealed to Israel, who were, uniquely, God's chosen people and God's chosen polity. Israel stood in a unique position before God. For the legal institutions of any other polity or nation to assert jurisdiction over religious questions is, implicitly, to lay claim to the same right to a 'special relationship' with God as was enjoyed by Israel. Such an identification of nation and religion is a betrayal of the transnational nature of Jesus' kingdom.

Quite apart from our changed social conditions, the Torah cannot be applied literally today because no nation stands in the same relationship to the Lord God as Old Testament Israel did. Today, for the Christian and despite some pretensions to the status in the past (e.g. in Puritan England and Anabaptist Munster) it is the church and not any nation or state which can validly claim to be Israel.[30]

I have argued in chapter 2 that rather than beginning directly with the Ten Commandments,[31] human government should find its justification and its jurisdiction instead in the implications of the creation narratives. Such an approach lays the stress on justice rather than on moral conformism.

At its finest, Christianity has a long history of tolerance, based on a 'confidence in the ability of the Truth to vindicate itself without instruments of State coercion'.[32] Non-Christians are not to be forced to behave as Christians.[33] The state should, within reason, respect the moral autonomy of its subjects, and their right to choose how they wish to live.[34] As

---

[29] Wright, *God's People in God's Land*, 138.

[30] M. and A. Schluter, 'Gender co-operation: some implications of God's design for society', *Cambridge Papers*, 12.2 (June 2003), 5.

[31] I am not, for a moment, denying the universal moral validity of the Ten Commandments, but I am, instead, challenging the wisdom, desirability and capability of human enforcement of them *all*.

[32] Quoted in *The Cambridge Papers*, March 1992 Vol.1, No.1.

[33] A. Castrey, 'Christian Lawyer', *Fulcrum* (December 1991), 18. Temple, *Christianity and Social Order*, 114, wrote: 'If we have to choose between making men Christian and making the social order more Christian, we must choose the former.'

[34] Jones, 'A Truly Christian Lawyer', talks of Christianity embodying a 'tolerance principle'. See also McIlroy, 'A Christian State?', 36–7; Mitchell,

de Coninck puts it, 'The obligation to love one's enemy, which criss-crosses the New Testament, finds a form of fulfilment in the creation of a public space where none will be assaulted for his beliefs.'[35]

However, we do not live as isolated individuals. To achieve a just social order, it is not sufficient to create an 'exclusion zone' of non-interference in questions of conscience. Our decisions and choices affect one another. Human life is infinitely valuable to God, which is why he sent Jesus Christ to die for us. The second great commandment is 'to Love your Neighbour as you Love yourself'. Government is under an obligation before God to intervene whenever the 'Life' of one or more of its citizens, seen in its broadest terms, is threatened by the wrong choices of others.[36]

As the creation theology of the Bible demonstrates, there is a role for government in protecting human life and respecting human dignity, taking into account human liberty and the human needs for rewarding work and meaningful relationships. To the extent that the Ten Commandments and other aspects of the Torah are to be reflected upon and applied in contemporary situations, it is precisely because they embody creation principles of what is good for human beings, even those who do not acknowledge the kingship of God.[37]

For Western society, social justice would require a greater concern to ensure that all have adequate housing, proper nourishment, meaningful work, shared leisure time and leisure facilities, and appropriate education.[38] '[Christians] should have, in the front of our minds, the lives of the excluded, the poor, the handicapped and the vulnerable as we test the adequacy of what is proposed and done [by government].'[39]

However, the message of the Old Testament prophets may present an ever-greater challenge to the West. If, as the oracles against the nations demonstrate, God is deeply concerned about the way in which nations treat one another, the deprivation of life and of quality of life caused by

---

[34] *(continued)* 'Should Law Be Christian?', 17; de Blois, 'Foundation of Human Rights', 14; and P. Beaumont, 'Christian Perspectives on the Law: What Makes them Distinctive?', in R. O'Dair and A. Lewis (eds.), *Law and Religion*, 529.

[35] de Coninck, *La justice et l'abondance*, 50.

[36] Our 'Life' in this context includes our home, our possessions, and provision for our basic needs, such as food, water, shelter, education, health care, etc.

[37] In this connection, the distinction between the first and second tables of the Decalogue is not watertight. It may be legitimate to enforce the Sabbath-rest command to some extent, because, as Isaiah noted, the need for a common day of rest is a matter of obvious social utility. Cf. O'Donovan, *Desire*, 186.

[38] It is perhaps a reflection both of the consistency of Christian insight and the intractability of the human condition that the above needs are largely the same as those identified by William Temple sixty years ago in *Christianity and Social Order*, 32–5, 86–7, 97.

[39] Gladwin, *Good of the People*, 19.

unjust economics falls under his condemnation just as much as the deprivation of life and of quality of life caused by unjust wars.

Social justice is, of course, only one side of the coin. The other side of the coin is criminal justice. The two are inseparable because it is one of the lessons of history that the force of criminal justice is used disproportionately against those who have the most complaints to make about the lack of social justice. Paul expresses his views on the function of government in penal justice with the warning that, '[the one in authority] does not bear the sword for nothing [for] he is God's servant, an agent of wrath to bring punishment on the wrongdoer' (Rom. 13:4).

Although the better reading is one that the 'sword' is a general description of the state's power of enforcement,[40] or 'the symbol of penal authority, of the power legitimately possessed by a civil authority to coerce recalcitrant citizens to maintain order and strive for the common good by obeying the law of society',[41] the image evoked by Paul probably included, in the first century context, a reference to use of capital punishment.[42]

Lest there be any doubt about the legitimacy of government's role in punishing wrongdoing:

> the terms used in [Romans 13:4 and 1 Peter 2:14] for the state's punishment of crime – "wrath" (*orge*) and "vengeance" or, better, "requital" (*ekdikos, ekdikesis*) – are elsewhere reserved for God alone. ... This means that the state is said to do what God alone has the right to do, and which Christians are expressly forbidden to do – namely, avenge wrongdoing. In some sense, then, the state acts as God's instrument or "servant" (*diakonos*, Rom. 13:4) for visiting wrath on wrongdoers in present history.[43]

Reading Romans 13:1–7 in its context it is impossible to avoid the conclusion that it is intimately linked to the preceding passage, Romans 12:9–21 in which Paul is discussing the Christian's responsibility to love others, both one's Christian brothers (vv. 9–13, 15–16) and one's enemies (vv. 14, 17–21).[44] In verse 19, Paul writes, 'Do not take revenge, my friends, but leave room for God's wrath, for it is written: "It is mine to avenge; I will repay," says the Lord.'

> It is not so much that God instructs or empowers human courts to administer vengeance *autonomously* on God's behalf. Rather the state's punishment of

---

[40] J.A. Ziesler, *Paul's Letter to the Romans*, 312. See also Yoder, *Politics of Jesus*, 203–5. O'Donovan, *Desire*, 152, points out that the distinction Yoder draws between the police function of government on the one hand and war and capital punishment on the other is an anachronism.

[41] J. Fitzmyer, *Romans*, 668.

[42] Marshall, *Beyond Retribution*, 234ff. Marshall, himself an opponent of capital punishment, rightly makes this concession.

[43] Marshall, *Beyond Retribution*, 147; O'Donovan, *Desire*, 148–9.

[44] de Coninck, *La justice et le pardon*, 73.

evil deeds may, in certain circumstances, be seen as a vehicle for God's wrath against sin. ... In other words, ... it acts as a servant of God, albeit unawares.[45]

Jesus' teaching on the non-recourse to violence by Christians is dependent on this context: that there is a government authority to whom appeal can be made regarding questions of law-enforcement. 'While Christians are to eschew violence in their personal relations, the maintenance of justice by force [by legitimate government authority] is the assumed social context of that self-denying ordinance.'[46] The abandonment of one's right to retaliate or to demand retribution, presupposes the pre-existence and hence, by implication, the legitimacy of that right. Christopher Marshall's examination of the New Testament vision for justice, crime and punishment is rightly entitled *Beyond Retribution* because retribution, the concept that our deeds lead to morally justified deserts, is the beginning, but not the end of biblical conceptions of delivering justice.[47]

Therefore, '[to accept] Christ's injunction to personal non-violence is to accept that the existence of government is morally required. Love both justifies and sets limits to the use of force.'[48] However, if government is seen as an instrument of God's justice, the ends it pursues in its administration of justice ought to be those which God pursues in his justice-making actions on earth. Except *in extremis*, those aims are the restoration of the peace of the community, and the reformation and re-integration of the wrongdoer into that community.

Colson's assessment is:

Only a biblical worldview can produce a system of true justice, one that holds individuals responsible for their actions under an objective rule of law but always in the context of community and always with the chance of transformation of the individual and healing of fractured relationships and of the moral order.[49]

'Paul's point is that when "the authority" [*ten exousian*] is a terror to bad conduct, it serves as God's agent of wrath and vengeance ... It is the punitive or protective *function* of the state that is affirmed, not the *methods* it uses.'[50] But what Paul leaves implicit within Romans 13:1–7 is a description of the good which governing authorities are to promote, and the wrongdoing which they are to prohibit.

---

[45] Marshall, *Beyond Retribution*, 148, emphasis mine.
[46] A.J. Rivers, 'The new world order?', *Cambridge Papers* 8.4 (1999), 2. See also Marshall, *Beyond Retribution*, 87, where he discusses Jesus' teaching about handing over to the lender one's cloak, and O'Donovan, *Resurrection*, 129 where he 'defines' justice as public right action.
[47] See especially Marshall, *Beyond Retribution*, 121, 189, 195.
[48] Rivers, 'The new world order?', 2.
[49] C. Colson, *Justice that Restores*, 101. See also 8, 21, 45, 61.
[50] Marshall, *Beyond Retribution*, 236, 239.

The good

Inherent, but undeveloped, therefore, in Paul's account of the role of government in Romans 13:3–5 is the concept of the good, a concept which is missing from modern Liberalism.

The backdrop to modern Liberalism is utilitarianism, and a form of utilitarianism sometimes described as 'preference-utilitarianism' which traces its roots all the way back to Jeremy Bentham. The preference-utilitarian view of society is this: each person is free to decide for himself what is his good, what he thinks will make him happy. For one it might be ice cream, for another model aeroplanes, for a third lifelong mono-gamy, for still another pornography.[51] The job of government is then to arrange society in such a way that happiness is maximised, so that more people are able to achieve their vision of the good than are frustrated in their attempts to achieve it. People are treated equally in that the interests of all are put into the equation to determine what social order will achieve the greatest overall happiness. This is the just society. For the utilitarians, if the majority are happy, then this more than compensates for the unhappiness of the minority.[52] The utilitarian notion of justice is inadequate because it fails to value individuals sufficiently. Those who lose out in the utilitarian calculus can have no complaint that society's treatment of them is unjust. Christianity draws very different conclusions from its belief in the fundamental equality of people. It 'takes individuals seriously' in a way that utilitarianism does not.

Rawls' revision of the utilitarian account is to the effect that justice requires the interests *of all* to be considered. The starting point must therefore be equality for all, and this can only be deviated from to the extent that giving some extra resources will mean that everyone in the commu-nity, and especially the worst off, will be better off (the 'maximin' princi-ple).[53] Only then will we have a just society. Rawls' account is better than the utilitarians because he at least does take individuals seriously. But, as Rawls' critics point out, Rawls' account of justice merely seeks to include all in the benefits of being able to choose and work towards their own individual conception of the good. Like Bentham, and unlike J.S. Mill,[54] Rawls himself has no account of the good to offer.[55] He remains an

---

[51] See, e.g., R. Dworkin, 'Do we have a right to pornography?', in *A Matter of Principle*, at 353, 359–72.

[52] Assuming that their relative degrees of happiness and unhappiness are balanced.

[53] Rawls, *Theory of Justice*, 130–5, 266–7.

[54] For a comparison of the thought of Bentham and J.S. Mill, see W.T. Bluhm, *Theories of the Political System*, 448–54 and K. Britton, 'Utilitarianism', in J.O. Urmson (ed.), *The Concise Encyclopedia of Western Philosophy and Philosophers*, 287–9.

[55] In the first edition of his book *A Theory of Justice*, Rawls wrote, at 303: 'All social primary *goods* – liberty and opportunity, income and wealth, and all

inheritor of the Benthamite idea that if desired equally 'push-pin is as good as poetry'. In Rawls' account, justice as the primary social virtue is instead substituted for any substantive description of what is good.

A Christian critique of Rawls' theory of justice focuses around two points: his lack of an account of the good, and on his anthropology.

1. A description of what is good

With regard to the first aspect of that critique, Rawls' omission of a description of the good is far from accidental. The theorists who originally proposed liberalism as a framework for the legal order sought a system of law which was neutral between various conceptions of the good, i.e. they aimed to create a body of rules which maximised people's opportunities to do what they wanted.

However, within liberalism itself, there is a growing realisation that the view of liberalism as a philosophy which is completely neutral between all possible conceptions of the good is unrealistic and incomplete. The suggestion is that the best law can hope to achieve is neutrality between a limited number of recognised 'goods' which people are free to choose between. The alternative is a chaos in which people's views of what society should be like and of what counts as a fulfilled human existence are so radically different that any coherent form of community quickly disintegrates.

In fact, what liberalism is missing is a description of what it is good for individuals to pursue. It has a developed account of what are 'goods' at the level of society (or at least contractarian pre-society), in the form of the twin values of liberty and equality.[56] Although different liberal thinkers use them in different ways and combine them in different combinations, they are constant features of any political theory that is truly 'liberal' in nature.

The liberal account of the polity adopts liberty and equality as public goods leaving each individual free to pursue his or her own private ends. Liberal political theory therefore represents an inversion of what has happened to Christian morality. Liberalism has developed a public morality without a private morality. Conversely, Christian moral thought has, at least in certain circles and with some notable exceptions,

---

[55] (*continued*) the bases of self-respect – are to be distributed equally unless an unequal distribution of any or all of these goods is to the advantage of the least favoured.' (Emphasis mine). In the second edition, a revised version of this passage is given greater prominence. At 54, Rawls says that his two principles of justice, set out at 52–3, 'are a special case of a more general conception of justice that can be expressed as follows: "All social *values* – liberty and opportunity and income and wealth, and all the social bases of self-respect – are to be distributed equally unless an unequal distribution of any, or all, of these *values* is to everyone's advantage."' (Emphasis mine.) The highlighted amendment is surely a significant one.

[56] O'Donovan, *Desire*, 279–80.

moved since the time of the Enlightenment in the direction of developing a private morality but without a corresponding public morality.

The problem with the total absence in Rawls' theory of justice of any attempt to identify what it is good for human beings to pursue in life is that this agnosticism deprives his principles of justice of a meaningful claim to moral primacy. In the words of Michael Sandel:

> Only in a universe empty of *telos* ... is it possible to conceive a subject apart from and prior to its purposes and ends. Only a world ungoverned by a purposive order leaves principles of justice open to human construction and conceptions of the good to individual choice.[57]

The impact of his critique is that, 'once it is conceded that our conceptions of the good are morally arbitrary, it becomes difficult to see why the highest of all (social) virtues should be the one that enables us to pursue these arbitrary conceptions "as fully as circumstances permit." '[58]

The holistic Christian worldview I have argued for as revealed in the Bible is one in which the 'public' liberal values of liberty and equality hold a significant place. However, it has, in contrast to the theories of Rawls and other 'liberal' thinkers, a defined vision of the ultimate good and a view of what makes for a 'good life' even leaving God out of the equation. There is, therefore, a stronger framework upon which to build a social construct than the one proposed by Rawls whilst at the same time preserving an important space of individual moral decision-making.

2. A view of human beings in relationship with one another

After much bloodshed and at considerable cost to the visible unity of the church, the Reformation secured for its inheritors freedom of conscience. From that time on, there has been an ever-increasing emphasis on the human being *as an individual*. In Rawls' theory, the human being as an individual is reduced to a Kantian abstraction, a hypothetical being unencumbered by emotional attachments, able to enter into and dissolve relationships at will, without cost to his or her personal integrity.[59]

In a timely corrective, Protestant theologians are rediscovering the importance of community, and the need for a doctrine of the church which expresses that just as God created human beings to be in relationship with one another so he inaugurates a new community which not only enjoys restored communion with him but also renewed fellowship with one another.[60]

Therefore, unlike standard liberalism, Christianity conceives of human beings not as unrelated individuals, whose attachments are only ever contingent, but as social beings-in-relationship.

[57] M.J. Sandel, *Liberalism and the Limits of Justice*, 175.
[58] Sandel, *Liberalism*, 167.
[59] Cf. O'Donovan, *Desire*, 276.
[60] For an important example of this trend, see Fee, *Paul*.

Placing an emphasis on community has an important effect on how one views Rawls' theory of justice. One of Rawls' communitarian critics, Sandel argues that in a true community, with shared values and final ends, and a background of implicit practices and understandings, justice need not be the primary virtue.[61] This may be true of the church. But the whole reason why Rawls makes his principle of justice primary is that Western liberal society is increasingly lacking the shared final ends and the background of implicit practices and understandings which make real community possible.

There is a further danger, however, in the emphasis on justice as primary, in the limited Liberal sense of rights protected.[62] Rawls' emphasis on rights, coupled with his conception of the individual, has the potential of denuding the public square of all other social actors.[63] And law *alone* cannot provide a satisfactory basis for the interactions of the individuals within a society.

In the words of Alwyn Thompson and Caroline McAdam:

> No functioning society can rely on the law alone as a means of defining relationships within that society. Relationships are mediated and defined through a host of social institutions operating in a multiplicity of ways. Some function on the basis of agreement, consensus and compromise; others on the basis of mutual trust and respect. Between the individual and the state are families, schools, trade unions, churches, community, and voluntary groups, businesses and many more.[64]

In every community there are social 'conventions', sometimes expressed in legislation, but 'more often a matter of non-enforceable mutual expectations and felt obligations'.[65] Such conventions:

> are *possible* because men are capable of moral insight, of agreeing in the recognition of moral insight, and of committing themselves to maintain it; they rest on a presupposition of fidelity to a common interest and purpose. Conventions are

---

[61] Sandel, *Liberalism*, 172.

[62] For an analysis of the Liberal position, see Rivers, 'Bill of Rights?', 30–1, also I. Leigh, 'Religious Liberty', 31, and 'Clashing Rights, Exemptions and Opt-Outs: Religious Liberty and "Homophobia" ', in R. O'Dair and A. Lewis (eds.), *Law and Religion*, 247.

[63] An associated danger is that Rawls' account of permissible discourse in the public square disenfranchises non-Liberals or seeks to foreclose the debate against them: see Leigh, 'Clashing Rights', 251–3, 271–3; also Rex Ahdar, 'Religious Group Autonomy, Gay Ordination and Human Rights Law', 275–7; and Gary Watt, 'Giving unto Caesar: Rationality, Reciprocity and Legal Recognition of Religion', in R. O'Dair, and A. Lewis (eds.), *Law and Religion*, 45 at 46–52, 59–63 in the same volume.

[64] Thompson and McAdam, *A Shared Vision?*, 23. See also Griffiths, *Morality and the Marketplace*, 10–11.

[65] Wright, *People of God*, 113; G.R. Dunstan, *The Artifice of Ethics*, especially chapter 1, 'Community and Convention', 1–17.

necessary because men fail conspicuously to follow their moral insights and are capable of ruthlessly exploiting one another in the pursuit of self-interest; they rest on a presupposition of infidelity to the community purpose.[66]

These conventions develop most naturally and are sustained most easily within the smaller communities of interest which make up civil society. By processes which sociologists are far more qualified to describe and explain than a humble lawyer, extended family groups, neighbourhoods, trade unions, churches, community groups, sports and social clubs arrive at a shared understanding of 'acceptable behaviour' which may or may not be buttressed by any explicit or visible sanction.

There is, to use American parlance, a 'clear and present danger' that the distinctive and cohesive nature of such social organisations will collapse under the combined pressures of the *imperium* of economics in all aspects of society, the atomistic individualism of standard liberalism and the enforcement *ad absurdem* of human rights ideology. Thompson and McAdam note:

> The danger with human rights ideology is that ... it threatens to subvert the myriad structures and relationships that constitute civic and political society. All relationships become absolute, based not on negotiation, compromise or respect, but on legal resolution of competing claims to rights. This is destructive socially and politically.[67]

William Temple emphasised the extent of the danger. He argued that liberty itself depends on a free civil society:

> Liberty is actual in the various cultural and commercial and local associations that men form. In each of these a man can feel that he counts for something and that others depend on him as he on them. The State which would serve and guard Liberty will foster all such groupings, giving them freedom to guide their own activities provided these fall within the general order of the communal life and do not injure the freedom of other similar associations.[68]

The Christian vision of liberty is of liberty as expressed in solidarity.

Conclusion on the right and the good

Unlike preference-utilitarianism, Christianity values people as individuals and insists that none may be sacrificed simply because their misery is outweighed by the greater happiness of others. Unlike Rawlsian Liberalism, Christianity recognises that relationships are fundamental to human being. Unlike both preference-utilitarianism and Rawlsian Liberalism, Christianity does have an account of the good to offer, a doctrine of creation in

---

[66] Wright, *People of God*, 114.
[67] Thompson and McAdam, *A Shared Vision?*, 23. See also M. Ignatieff, *The Needs of Strangers*, 13.
[68] Temple, *Christianity and Social Order*, 70.

which God gave good gifts to all people, 'common grace' for all to enjoy in this lifetime whether or not they acknowledge his claim to their life.

As we saw in chapter two, against the Rawlsian vision of unrelational human beings, existing in a world without purpose and able to construct a system of justice in their own image, the Christian vision is of human beings, made in the image of God, for relationship with God and relationship with one another, beings of inherent dignity and value, who should be free to labour and love. These are the good gifts of God to us both as individuals and as part of the human race. Justice is the exercise of power and authority in order to preserve and protect the good gifts of God, given as his common grace. If justice is exercised as the expression of love in social organisation, then its claim to pre-eminence can be acknowledged.[69] But the biblical vision of justice is more defined than that of Rawls. It rests on stronger ethical and anthropological foundations.

The Dangers of a Christian Vision of the Good and the Right

Any political theory that places a value on individual liberty must demonstrate its ability to navigate a path between the Scylla of totalitarianism and the Charybdis of anarchy. The facile accusation against any Christian political theory would be that as soon as you give a religion any form of political power, it tends to institutionalise itself to preserve its position within society, and then the more sinister aspect is that it begins to consider the possibility of coercing people into following its dictates.[70]

However, the state and the church have different roles and responsibilities within God's purposes. Each is valid, but neither should attempt a takeover of the other's domain.[71] 'The church's most important contribution to the polity is simply to *be* the church.'[72]

> We cannot expect the state to do the church's business. Where it attempts to do so or is made to do so, the result is utter confusion of Law and Gospel, and the mixing of the Two Kingdoms. In C.S. Lewis' terms, Aslan (the

---

[69] Temple, *Christianity and Social Order*, 78.

[70] Tan, *Lost Heritage*, 74: 'When religion and politics go hand in hand, what results is a monolithic totalitarian system that will murder to enforce its will. That was why, in the Old Testament, the function of king and priest were separated in Israel. The other religions had their king and priest together in one person.' See also Haugen, *Good News*, 89–90.

[71] This idea is reflected in the Catholic concept of 'subsidiarity' and the neo-Calvinist idea of 'sphere sovereignty'. The interrelationship between these two concepts is explored in D.H. McIlroy, 'Subsidiarity and Sphere Sovereignty: Christian Reflections on the Size, Shape and Scope of Government', *Journal of Church and State* 45 (2003), 739–64.

[72] Gay, *Liberty and Justice*, 225.

Christ symbol) and Tash (the Antichrist) are syncretically blended into the monster "Tashlan".[73]

Christianity, rightly understood, is inherently anti-totalitarian. For thinkers like John Owen in Britain and Roger Williams in America, 'Tolerance was a virtue born of confidence in the ability of the Truth to vindicate itself without instruments of State coercion.'[74] Christianity involves a voluntary response to God's love; and the only Christian faith worthy of the name is that which is freely chosen.[75]

Coercion is emphatically *not* God's preferred method of dealing with his human creatures. If Jesus' attitude to the Pharisees on the one hand and the prostitutes, tax collectors and other social outcasts is anything to go by, heartfelt obedience and love matter to God far more than outward moral conformity. For all his strengths, Augustine of Hippo's most devastating error was to legitimise the use of force to maintain the unity of the institutional church.[76] This runs directly contrary to Paul's teaching in 2 Corinthians 10:3b–6 that the church does not wage war as the world does and does not fight with the weapons of the world.

Christianity stands on two major principles that avoid totalitarianism on the one hand and anarchism on the other: the value of human life and the value of human liberty. These twin principles are neatly drawn together in Kant's assertion that, 'Human beings are ends not means'. In Christian thought about the structures of government, a firm emphasis on the importance of individual liberty is balanced against the needs of justice in preserving human life, human dignity and maintaining opportunities for rewarding work and meaningful relationships for all the members of society.

The Calling of Secular Authorities: The Common Good

This emphasis on the responsibility of government to do justice and to look after the interests of *all* its citizens can be summarised in the notion of the 'common good'.[77] A just government is one that pursues the com-

[73] J.W. Montgomery, *The Shaping of America*, 154.
[74] Quoted in (1992) 1(1) *Cambridge Papers*.
[75] O'Donovan, *Resurrection*, 168. For an exploration of how this works in the context of children, see F. Bridger, *Children Finding Faith: Exploring a Child's Response to God*.
[76] Forster, *Kingdom of Jesus*, 5.
[77] Finnis writes: 'Justice, as a quality of character, is in its general sense always a practical willingness to favour and foster the common good of one's communities, and the theory of justice is, in all its parts, the theory of what in outline is required for that common good.' *Natural Law*, 165.

mon good, seeking the interests of all and therefore paying special attention to the needs of the weakest in society.

As well as reflecting the biblical emphasis on justice, this concept of the 'common good' comes very close to the ideas of the political philosopher John Rawls,[78] in which the aim of government must be to maximise the resources available to the poorest. Because each individual is made in the image of God none can be sacrificed merely because their misery is outweighed by the increased happiness of others.

The Christian vision of a just society is therefore one in which government works for the common good, that is to say, for the good of all. It is one in which people acknowledge their solidarity with one another, based on their common humanity. It is one in which every person and family has access to the necessary resources to be able to earn a decent living and participate as dignified members of their community. It is one in which people are socially rich, with sufficient time and resources to be able to enjoy good relationships. It is a society in which the poor and the powerless are considered. It is one in which government recognises its duty to do justice and yet acknowledges that its role should be one of facilitating rather than controlling, allowing smaller unions and institutions within civil society to function relationally, enriching the social capital of society.

How different is such a vision from Rawls' maximin principle of justice? There is something intuitively attractive from a Christian point of view about statements such as 'While the distribution of wealth and income need not be equal, it must be to everyone's advantage.'[79] '[T]he basic structure [of society] should allow inequalities [of income, wealth, authority and responsibility] so long as these improve everyone's situation, including that of the least advantaged, provided that they are consistent with equal liberty and fair opportunity',[80] as well as 'Injustice … is simply inequalities that are not to the benefit of all'.[81] But who is borrowing from whom? After all, is it not the case that Rawls' veil of ignorance in his original position is a device to avoid the effects of original sin![82] By denying his actors knowledge of their own personal characteristics, abilities or preferences,[83] Rawls prevents them making the sort of self-regarding choices which bedevil any attempt to establish a just society on earth. Perfect justice has to be divine in origin, and only perfect men, or as Christians believe, *the* perfect man, Jesus, could begin to bring it into effect.

[78] Set out in Rawls, *Theory of Justice*, 130–5, 266–7.
[79] Rawls, *Theory of Justice*, 53.
[80] Rawls, *Theory of Justice*, 133.
[81] Rawls, *Theory of Justice*, 54.
[82] But not to avoid original sin *per se* as his actors continue to have only limited altruism.
[83] Rawls, *Theory of Justice*, 11, 16–19.

Social Justice and the Just Society: The Role of Government

Nonetheless, the proper role of government is limited. Government alone cannot create a just society.[84] A just society requires that individuals and groups within it act justly. Hence the biblical emphasis on justice/ righteousness as an issue for everyone in society not just those concerned with making, administering and enforcing the law.[85]

Law plays a part in setting and in reinforcing social moral conventions. But it cannot bear the weight of upholding the moral order alone. If society as a whole or a particular section of it rejects the validity, necessity or appropriateness of the law then it will not be obeyed. Whether it is businessmen breaching accounting standards, young people taking drugs or the general population speeding, the law *alone* cannot create a social morality.

But if law alone is not sufficient to maintain society's cohesion, it is nonetheless necessary. As the law on abortion demonstrates, once something has been legalised, the way is open for it to become acceptable, even routine and banal.[86]

The tension for legislators is to recognise and support the institutions of civil society in the positive and necessary contribution that they can make to public morality, without at the same time requiring them all to function as 'liberal associations'.[87] Liberty and dignity may find powerful expression in groupings that are smaller than the modern state. The danger, at the beginning of the twenty-first century, is of over-regulation, of the disregard of 'sphere sovereignty'.[88] In Western democracies, which suffer from legislative diarrhoea, we need again to heed Paul's words to Timothy to pray for 'kings and all who are in high positions, so that we may lead a quiet and peaceable life in all godliness and dignity' (1 Tim. 2:2).

Nonetheless, in the biblical conception of delivering justice, government would intervene and provide a safety net where other social

---

[84] See Rivers, 'Bill of Rights?', 39–40.

[85] Cf. O'Donovan, *Desire*, 185. John Locke, the father of political liberalism, insisted that religious belief in particular was needed to foster moral values such as law-abidingness and self-restraint: see S. Kessler, 'John Locke's Legacy of Religious Freedom', *Polity* 17 (1984–5), at 495.

[86] In the context of homosexuality, Ian Leigh sets out the graduations of responses that might be adopted to such moral questions, but which liberal society is today in danger of neglecting. See his Leigh, 'Clashing Rights', 246.

[87] P. Marshall, 'Liberalism, Pluralism and Christianity: A Reconceptualization', *Fides et Historia* 21 (1989), 4 at 9. See also Temple, *Christianity and Social Order*, 70; Leigh, 'Clashing Rights', 263–7, also Ahdar, 'Religious Group Autonomy', at 275 in the same volume.

[88] J.E. McGoldrick, *Abraham Kuyper: God's Renaissance Man*, 52, 61–72, 74–6, 80–1, 151, 153–4, 158–66, 177–9, 191, 196, 228–9; Gay, *Liberty and Justice*, 133–5; McIlroy, 'Subsidiarity and Sphere Sovereignty', 739; O'Donovan, *Desire*, 242.

institutions have failed in their responsibilities, rather than supplanting them and aggregating their rightful functions to itself.

Therefore, although there is a presumption in favour of the free market, government is justified in intervening both to ensure that the market remains genuinely free, and to palliate the consequences of market failure. As de Coninck notes, the 'free market' has a tendency to ignore the demands of the poor and to overvalue the views of the richest.[89] Government, informed by the Christian ideas of justice, solidarity and the common good, must ensure that the needs of all are taken into account.

Order and the Practical Importance of Justice

But justice is not the sole criterion by which human laws are to be judged. The maintenance of public order also matters. Human law is often an attempt at a compromise between justice and order. Lord Denning, half a century ago, expressed the conundrum in this way:

> The law, as I see it, has two great objects: to preserve order, and to do justice; and the two do not always coincide. Those whose training lies towards order, put certainty before justice; whereas those whose training lies towards the redress of grievances, put justice before certainty. The right solution lies in keeping the proper balance between the two.[90]

Human law has a significant place in God's ordering of his universe in a creation which has fallen. On occasion, Christian accounts of the role of law within human social organisation have over-emphasised its role in the preservation of order to the exclusion of sufficient reflection upon the ample biblical witness to the importance of justice. Human laws and legal systems ought to be, in some measure, a reflection of divine justice. Although there is a tension between law and gospel, we can say, unequivocally, that God is in favour of law.

As Lord Denning noted, ideally a legal system ought to promote and pursue the twin objectives of order and justice. However, in times of (perceived) crisis, people tend to choose security/order over justice. Thus Hitler was an attractive option in the chaos of inter-war Germany, as it struggled through the Great Depression. Thus many in Eastern Europe today, exposed to the vagaries of the supposedly 'free markets', hanker after the old certainties of state-planned communism. Thus Americans did not hesitate for a moment after 9/11 to exchange their civil liberties for a broth of anti-terrorist legislation.[91]

Recognising this fact, Charles Colson says:

[89] de Coninck, *La justice et l'abondance*, 55.
[90] Quoted in Anderson, *Freedom under Law*, 39.
[91] The criticism focuses mainly on the US Patriot Act.

it might be said that before a society can reflect God's righteousness, it must reflect God's order. This is not a matter of exalting order over righteousness; it is merely pointing out that you have to build the first floor before you can build the second floor.[92]

In a similar vein, although he himself was well aware of the importance of justice, William Temple wrote:

> Now the most fundamental requirement of any political and economic system is not that it shall express love, thought that is desirable, nor that it shall express justice, though that is the first ethical demand to be made upon it, but that it shall supply some reasonable measure of security against murder, robbery and starvation.[93]

In one sense they are right. You cannot build a just social order unless you have a social order to begin with. However, the relationship between order and justice is not so straightforward. Injustice creates insecurity. And ultimately it creates insecurity not only for the oppressed but also for their oppressors. Those who are oppressed and alienated by the system, who feel that they have no stake in it, who are left with nothing to lose; they are the ones amongst whom the terrorists, the rebels and the suicide bombers will arise.

In the shanty towns of the world, terrorism and the causes of terrorism cannot be eradicated by 'security measures'. The only way to a lasting peace is through a just settlement: one which recognises the sins committed by the terrorists *and* the sins committed by the oppressors.

The tragic example of Rehoboam in 1 Kings 12 is a vivid illustration of the biblical proverbs on kingship and justice. Whereas Proverbs 28:2 proclaims that, 'a man of understanding and knowledge maintains order' (cf. Prov. 8:12–21), Rehoboam lost his throne by rash vows of repression and forced labour.

Peace–Order–Justice are far more closely linked than our analytical minds, trained in the Greek tradition of dissection of ideas, realise. In fact, in Hebrew thought they could be encompassed by a single word, shalom. Colson sees the importance of this concept, and recognises its dimensions of order, righteousness and wholeness.[94] This recognition is not a novelty in Christian thought. In *The City of God*, Augustine talks about the *tranquillitas ordinis*, the peace of the community, which is a reflection of biblical order and justice. And Paul in 1 Corinthians 14:33 makes the link explicitly, describing the Lord as the God 'not … of disorder but of peace'.

Therefore, quite apart from the moral arguments, social justice can be commended to rulers on purely prudential grounds. The proverbial

---

92 Colson, *Justice that Restores*, 48.
93 Temple, *Christianity and Social Order*, 61.
94 Colson, *Justice that Restores*, 100–1.

truths about justice and faithfulness establishing a ruler's throne[95] are a sound analysis of vulnerability of governments at all places and in all times. Poverty, especially in the midst of gross inequalities of wealth, is a breeding ground for riots, revolts, terrorism and revolution.[96] The partisans of a right wing 'law and order' agenda will never be able to deliver shalom, because a social order can only be stabilised over the longer term when it exhibits a modicum of social justice.[97]

In our fallen world, the state of shalom is unattainable, at least by means of the coercive authority of government. Therefore, Christians have a special calling to live at peace.[98] The role of government is to contribute to the peace of society, which involves a positive obligation to maintain order and social justice, and a negative obligation of non-interference when the common good is not at stake. Just as Romans 13 stresses the positive obligations incumbent upon government, so 1 Timothy 2:1f. emphasises the negative obligation. By creating a social space in which people can live 'peaceful and quiet lives' in accordance with their private conscience, government can help to establish the conditions in which people can 'come to a knowledge of the truth' (1 Tim. 2:3).[99] This non-interference is, as is its use of the sword, 'good and pleases God'. It involves the recognition by government that there is 'a sphere of individual responsibility before God in which the public good is not immediately at stake'.[100]

The Accountability of Government

In the pursuit of order and justice, Christianity places governments not in the place of God but in a place of accountability to God. Paul's teaching is that the authority of government is not an absolute authority but an

---

[95] Proverbs 20:28; 29:14. See chapter 4.

[96] de Coninck, *La justice et l'abondance*, 18.

[97] Cf. H. Zehr, *Changing Lenses: A New Focus for Crime and Justice*, 109–10; J. Ive, 'Peace-building from a biblical perspective', *Engage* 2 (Summer 2003), 3: 'The achievement of justice is a necessary prerequisite for the establishment of peace, but the justice to be worked for cannot simply be identified with the demands of any one class or party grouping'. Finnis, *Natural Law*, 260: 'The authority of the law depends … on its justice or at least its ability to secure justice.'

[98] Luke 10:5; Romans 12:18; 14:17, 19; 1 Corinthians 7:15; 14:33; Galatians 6:16; Ephesians 4:3; Colossians 3:15; 1 Thessalonians 5:13; Hebrews 12:14; James 3:18; 1 Peter 3:11; 5:14; Jude 1:2.

[99] O'Donovan, *Desire*, 146–7. At this point, as at others in this outline of a biblical value of human law, are linked the four 'Kingdom values' of political theology identified by E. McDonagh, *The Gracing of Society*: 'justice, freedom, peace and truth'.

[100] O'Donovan, *Desire*, 255.

authority given, according to Romans 13:4b, to the rulers as God's servants. Government can be challenged and resisted whenever it steps outside of its God-given authority. Government has no authority to demand the worship of idols, to proscribe the spreading of the gospel, to impose laws that are directly contrary to God's standards of justice. Nor does government have the authority to *require* the worship of the triune God, still less to enforce a particular style of worship of him. The reason is simply that for the God who looks upon the heart, any worship that does not come from the heart is not pleasing to him.

As N.T. Wright notes:

> Romans 13 is very far from being a charter for big or bullying governments. On the contrary, it places the authorities of this world where they belong: accountable to the one who is Lord of all. In a world where there is still such a thing as great wickedness, we need a judiciary just as we need locks on our front doors. But it must be seen to be accountable to something higher than itself. If it is accountable to the God revealed in Jesus there will be certain quite specific things that follow about the way in which, and the ends for which, it exercises its power.[101]

Government has potential to be used by God, sometimes because of its calling to promote good and to punish wrong, and sometimes in spite of the failure of its leaders to live up to that calling. But government also has the potential for great evil, as the horrors of Nazi Germany, Soviet Russia and Apartheid South Africa all too aptly demonstrate. The Bible which gives us the vision of government's true calling in Romans 13 also gives us the picture of the Beast warring against the saints in Revelation 13. At its worst, government can be a demonic institution, capable of far more evil than disorganised groups of individuals could have ever dreamt up.

The Bible which recognises the necessary fact of governmental authority also acknowledges the potentially brutish nature of that authority.[102] In Daniel 7, four earthly empires are all described in bestial terms.[103] The only truly humane kingship is that of the Son of Man. Even as exemplary a king as David was guilty of abusing his power to seduce the wife of another man, and then to have her husband killed in order to 'hush up' the consequences of his sexual impropriety (2 Sam. 11). Revelation 13 is an important counter-balance to Romans 13.

Beginning with Ambrose and notwithstanding the phenomenon of Christendom, mediaeval Christian thought placed emphasis on the phrase in Romans 13 that he who wields political power is the 'minister of God unto you for good'; this was interpreted so that only political power founded on justice could be regarded as having a sacred sanction.

---

[101] Wright, *What Saint Paul Really Said*, 157; cf. O'Donovan, *Desire*, 231.

[102] Haugen, *Good News*, 130–1.

[103] de Coninck, *La justice et la puissance*, 13.

The Epistle thus contains *a doctrine of the sacred character of authority, not of the divinity of power.*[104]

The message throughout the Bible is that political authority does not come solely through the will of the people, or the strength of the army behind the ruler, but is given by God. With divinely given authority comes accountability.

Political and legal authorities are not exempt from sinfulness that affects humanity as a whole. Christians ought also to be mindful of the truth expressed in the adage 'Power tends to corrupt, and absolute power corrupts absolutely.' Therefore, Christians should support the rule of law, the limited state and the separation of powers, as all being instruments apt to mitigate the effects of the Fall and to reduce the scope of influence for the adage.[105]

The nature of the conundrum is expressed well by de Coninck:

> We need to find a balance between two demands: on the one hand, the need to protect the weak and the poor requires a minimum of constraints; on the other hand, the existence of too many constraints gives too much control to the one in power, who can then merrily indulge in exploiting it.[106]

The Christian Witness to the True Role of Human Law

1. Upholding the law

Christians believe in law. It is a form of address through which God has spoken. Even in this country where the name of God seems to be little honoured, the sixth (murder), eighth (theft) and ninth (no false testimony) commandments still form an integral part of our system of justice. Many of our legal procedures and our substantive laws are reasonable reflections of divine justice. They deserve to be commended, promoted and honoured. A society is in grave danger where there is no respect for the law.[107] The fear of detection and punishment is insufficient glue to keep a society from chaos. There has to be a common assent that the laws are good if they are to be effective.

---

[104] A. Passerin d'Entrèves, *The Notion of the State*, 183; cf. O'Donovan, *Resurrection*, 72.

[105] Haugen, *Good News*, 47; Calvin, *Institutes* Book IV, ch. 20, para. 8 '… Owing, therefore, to the vices or defects of men, it is safer and more tolerable when several bear rule, that they may thus mutually assist, instruct, and admonish each other, and should any one be disposed to go too far, the others are censors and masters to curb his excess.' See also J.A. Kirk, *The Meaning of Freedom: A Study of Secular, Muslim and Christian Views*, 245.

[106] de Coninck, *La justice et l'abondance*, 59.

[107] Montgomery, 'Law and Justice' 16 affirms that the legal positivists were right to place emphasis on preserving the rule of law for this reason.

The law has enough critics and cynics. Christians are called to be neither dismissive nor disrespectful of human laws, on the one hand, nor fearful of the power of human governments on the other. Instead, Christians should be respectful and prayerful about the role of law as having an important, although subsidiary, place in God's purposes in this world.[108] Christians should be positive and enthusiastic in their endorsement of what is good about the laws and the legal system under which they live.

2. *Enforcing the law*

Theoretical rights are little use. A country may have the most impeccable set of laws, but if its citizens do not have the ability to rely on those rights in their everyday lives those rights almost need not exist at all. As we saw from looking at the Old Testament prophets, it matters to God whether or not the courts do justice and whether everyone has someone who is prepared to plead their cause.

> We need to grapple with this important issue of peace. Clearly, there is a place for individual Christians to be involved in society – including maintaining law and order. There has to be a use of force to restrain the criminal and subversive elements within society.[109]

Gary Haugen identifies coercion and deception as the two great weapons wielded by oppressors.[110] Often, the law does provide means of redress but the poor and the ill-educated are unable to vindicate their rights. To take a contemporary example, one landlord in this country recently told his tenant that the tenant had no choice but to pay the vastly increased rent or to leave the flat he was living in. In fact, even under the Housing Acts brought in under the last Conservative government, a tenant can apply to have his rent assessed by a Rent Assessment Committee. The landlord was lying but how will the tenant, who could not afford to pay for legal representation, know that?

As de Coninck says:

> It is true that the rule of law, where the same rules apply to everyone is an improvement in comparison with the mediaeval state, where privilege ruled … But the laws, the rules, the procedures, the factors to be taken into account have become so complex that the weak and the destitute can no longer understand them. There is therefore a factual inequality between those who can navigate in the marshland of the rules which structure our lives, and those who are drowning in it.[111]

---

[108] O'Donovan, *Desire*, 148.
[109] Tan, *Lost Heritage*, 226.
[110] Haugen, *Good News*, 119.
[111] de Coninck, *La justice et la puissance*, 95, translation mine.

Enforcement of the law matters to God.[112] Christians should be committed to ensuring that *all* people, whether rich or poor, British or foreign, have effective access to their entitlements and to the protection which the law offers them.

3. Reforming the law

How do we devise practical rules which do not collapse into totalitarianism and excessive paternalism on the one hand, and anarchism on the other?

There is a clear Christian mandate for constructive criticism of human laws. We have a higher standard of justice by which to criticise positive (i.e. human) laws.[113] We should be ready to do so whenever necessary. However, what should be our aim in reforming the law?

J.W. Montgomery helpfully points to the limits of what is appropriate for us to seek to legislate:

> Believers should not endeavour to legislate even genuine scriptural moral teachings where the value of the given teaching will only be recognized by those who have already accepted Christ as Lord and the Bible as the Word of God ... To legislate such biblical teachings is to confuse law and gospel by forcing non-Christians to practice Christianity apart from personal acceptance of it.
>
> Believers should strive to legislate all those socially valuable moral teachings of Scripture whose value can be meaningfully argued in a pluralistic society ... offer[ing] arguments on scientific, social, and ethical grounds potentially meaningful to the non-Christian.[114]

The message of the prophets is that social justice is not the least part of morality. The church and Christians within it who have anything to do with the legal system should be reminding government of its obligations to do justice, and to make sure that the voice of the poor is heard and recognised as a legitimate claim on government.[115]

> As 'salt' and 'light' Christians should persistently present to authority moral arguments with persuasive force and practical relevance. This should characteristically be on behalf of the weak, powerless and those wronged by injustice or callous neglect ... And it is most likely to be effective at the level of specific issues and achievable, limited objectives.[116]

---

[112] Rivers, 'Bill of Rights?', 48.
[113] de Blois, 'Foundation of Human Rights', 11.
[114] 'The Limits of Christian Influence', *Christianity Today*, 23 January 1981. Montgomery's position is directly in line with that of Philip Melanchthon – see Witte, *Law and Protestantism*, 76.
[115] de Coninck, *La justice et l'abondance*, 55.
[116] Wright, *People of God*, 120.

Jesus predicted that his followers would be persecuted just as the prophets had been. This illustrates the central nature of the church's role in bringing about social justice. The church's ministry, *qua Church*, to the state is to be prophetic. But individual Christians may be called to take up governmental positions, as Daniel and Joseph were called to serve in the world's administrations.

Above all, it must be our concern that the laws we promote will favour the spread of the gospel. Subject to difficult questions regarding abortion and euthanasia where the sanctity of life itself is at stake, if we have to choose between legislating Christian values and ensuring that people are prepared to listen to the gospel, then it is the gospel which must be given primacy over the law.[117] William Temple wrote, 'If we have to choose between making men Christian and making the social order more Christian, we must choose the former.'[118]

Law reforms inspired by Christian reflection ought also to be realistic. Above all others, Christians should be mindful of the depth of human sinfulness and the limits of human foresight. All Christian legislative initiatives must recognise that the presence of sin and the absence of the (indwelling presence of the) Holy Spirit limit what it is possible to achieve through legislation. Law making can only constrain and encourage; it cannot change hearts.

4. Challenging the law

Christians are called to live as citizens of two kingdoms: the earthly kingdom and the heavenly kingdom.[119] Each kingdom has claims it can properly make of us. But when the claims of the two kingdoms conflict, it is the obligations placed upon us as citizens of heaven which must prevail.[120]

During the Second Gulf War of 2003, the wisdom of the American President being represented at press conferences by Ari Fleischer, a Jewish spokesman, was questioned. The response of the US Administration was to dismiss the criticism on the basis that Mr Fleischer was an American first and a Jew second. It should not be so for Christians. Christians should always be citizens of heaven and, if push comes to shove, strangers on earth (Phil. 3:20).

---

[117] The exact calculation in any given case may be a difficult one but J.W. Montgomery suggests some guidelines in *The Shaping of America*, 152–8. See also Leigh, 'Religious Liberty', 51, and Andrew Bramwell Bartlett in Cundy (ed.), *Law – Some Christian Perspectives*, 32: 'The highest good is not law but love.'

[118] Temple, *Christianity and Social Order*, 114.

[119] Augustine, *The City of God*; Calvin, *Institutes* Book IV, ch. 9, para. 1; Gay, *Liberty and Justice*, 119, D.M. Lloyd-Jones, 'Render Unto Caesar', in *Unity in Truth*, at 190–1.

[120] Forster, *Kingdom of Jesus*, 2.

In Acts 4, after the healing of the cripple at the Beautiful Gate of the Temple, the Apostles Peter and John were summoned before the Sanhedrin. The Sanhedrin's jurisdiction at that time, accepted by the occupying Roman powers, included regulation of all matters relating to the Jewish faith, of which the apostles still felt themselves a part at this early stage in the Christian mission. A clash of wills was inevitable following Peter's declaration in Acts 4:12 that Jesus Christ was the only way to salvation. The Sanhedrin's response was to charge the Apostles not to speak or teach at all in the name of Jesus (Acts 4:18). Peter and John's reply was the earth-shattering: 'Judge for yourselves whether it is right in God's sight to obey you rather than God' (Acts 4:19).

Obedience to God permits or requires disobedience to government when government is acting outside of its God-given authority, when it is enacting laws which are contrary to divine law, when its laws prohibit the spreading of the gospel and when it is seeking to enforce religious obligations. In all these things, Christian disobedience is not a rejection of governmental authority but rather a witness to its true nature and limitations.[121]

5. A vision for justice making

Upholding, enforcing, reforming, and challenging the law are all part and parcel of a Christian vision for justice making. N.T. Wright emphasises the importance of:

> think[ing] through the question of justice – God's justice for the world, in eventual future, and anticipated in the present – as part of the theme of … the righteousness of God. The word *dikaiosune*, after all, can just as easily be translated "justice" as "righteousness". If it is true that God intends to renew the whole cosmos through Christ and by the Spirit – and if that isn't true then Paul is indeed talking nonsense in Romans 8 and 1 Corinthians 15 – then, just as the holiness of Christian living in the present is a proper, albeit partial, fitful and puzzling, anticipation of the future life of the resurrection, so acts of justice, mercy and peace in the present are proper, albeit inevitably partial, fitful and puzzling anticipations of God's eventual design. They are not lost or wasted; they are not, in the old caricature, a matter of oiling the wheels of a machine that is about to run over a cliff. They are signs of hope for a world that groans in travail, waiting for its promised liberation.[122]

---

[121] C.E.B. Cranfield, *On Romans*, 169; 'The Christian's Political Responsibility according to the New Testament' in *The Bible and the Christian Life: A Collection of Essays*, 48–68.

[122] Wright, *What Saint Paul Really Said*, 164. The same idea is repeatedly stressed in O'Donovan's conception of redemption as the vindication, restoration, and fulfilment of *this* creation: *Resurrection*, 55, 67, 105.

The importance of social justice as an integral part of the *missio Dei* has now been rediscovered by evangelicalism. Article 5 of the Lausanne Covenant on Evangelism and Christian Social Responsibility declares:

> We affirm that God is both Creator and the Judge of all men. We therefore should share his concern for justice and reconciliation throughout human society and for the liberation of men from every kind of oppression. Because mankind is made in the image of God, every person, regardless of race, religion, colour, culture, class, sex or age, has an intrinsic dignity because of which he should be respected and served, not exploited. Here too we express penitence both for our neglect and for having sometimes regarded evangelism and social concern as mutually exclusive. Although reconciliation with man is not reconciliation with God, nor is social action evangelism, nor is political liberation salvation, nevertheless, we affirm that evangelism and socio-political involvement are both part of our Christian duty. For both are necessary expressions of our doctrines of God and man, our love for our neighbour and our obedience to Jesus Christ. The message of salvation implies also a message of judgement upon every form of alienation, oppression and discrimination, and we should not be afraid to denounce evil and injustice wherever they exist. When people receive Christ they are born again into his kingdom and must seek not only to exhibit but also to spread its righteousness in the midst of an unrighteous world. The salvation we claim should be transforming us in the totality of our personal and social responsibilities. Faith without works is dead.[123]

Conclusions

As has been argued earlier in this chapter, human structures of government have a distinct but limited role to play in God's purposes in our world. This recognition avoids the errors at either end of the spectrum, from the view which treats the state as irredeemably pagan, and therefore outside the perfection of Christ, to the view which treats the state as God's regent.

Human law is a good thing. It should, and often does, reflect divine justice. It is the principal means by which government exercises its God-given authority. Law has an important role to play in God's providential ordering of our fallen world.

Christians should be concerned to uphold, enforce and reform the law. However, although law is a good thing, gospel, the good news about Jesus Christ, is an even better thing. When Jesus Christ ascended into heaven, he did not leave behind him a political party or a nation-state to continue his mission. Instead, he left a different form of society, the

---

[123] See also Wright, *What Saint Paul Really Said*, 153 and Cranfield, *On Romans*, 170.

church, and promised it the power, direction and comfort of the Holy Spirit. It is the church not the state that is the primary vehicle for God's redemptive purposes in this world. The role of the state is limited. It is not the function of government to make men Christians. It is the role of the church to be prophetic, to call all people and all social structures to acknowledge the lordship of Christ and the rule of God.

Human law has a proper, but limited, role in God's purposes for humanity. It is not to seek to create heaven on earth, however, but rather to promote those Christian values, derived from God's revelation of himself, which can be demonstrated to have social utility. Key among those values are the protection of human life, the respect of human dignity and human liberty, and the creation of space in which people are free to labour and love in meaningful and rewarding ways.

In the words of Tom Rose:

> The worldly goal of civil government, from the Christian viewpoint, is not to build an earthly utopia, but only to establish a *workable justice* that will serve to restrain man's evil heart, on the one hand, and to free him from the evil inclinations of others, on the other, so that he can be free and self-responsible to his Creator and Lord.[124]

---

[124] T. Rose, *Economics, Principles and Policy from a Christian Perspective*, 80.

9

The Last Judgement

The Cross and the Injustice of Human Laws

What is life like at the moment? What do you see as you look at the world around you? Is everything right in the world, or is it a world full of trouble and problems? Global warming, famine in Africa, wars, religious persecution, racial hatred, violent crime, drug abuse, overwork, unemployment, family breakdown – these are the evils which blight our world. The rock group U2 wrote a song called, 'When I Look At The World',[1] which repeats the accusation Voltaire made 250 years ago against those who peddle a naïve view that somehow we live in 'the best of all possible worlds'.

In the Old Testament, the writer of Ecclesiastes considered the state of the world around him. He was not comforted by what he saw: 'I looked and saw all the oppression that was taking place under the sun: I saw the tears of the oppressed – and they have no comforter' (Eccl. 4:1).

The people(s) of this world do not deal justly with one another. There is a crying need for justice, for intervention, for deliverance. Those in government, those in power, should be acting to rescue the poor, the weak and the oppressed.

But, in many places, the legal system that should have put things right and given justice to the oppressed has become part of the problem. Laws and legal systems are not framed in ways which protect the rights of the oppressed, and even those that are can be manipulated by those with the means to do so. This is not a new problem. The writer of Ecclesiastes says: 'I saw something else under the sun: In the place of judgement – wickedness was there, in the place of justice – wickedness was there' (Eccl. 3:16).

Something is fundamentally wrong with this world – good people suffer and evil people prosper. The Bible does not pretend that things are as good as they could be; but it does promise that God is ultimately in control and that things are not as bad as they could be, although at some times and in some places they may get pretty close.

Ultimately, the Bible's answer to the injustice of human laws and legal systems is to be found at the cross. At the cross, the one who should have been acknowledged as the ruler of the world and its just judge was executed. Two of the finest legal systems of the ancient world: the Roman and the Jewish, combined and conspired to put to death a man who, in the opinion of the Roman judge, had committed no crime

---

[1] From their album *All That You Can't Leave Behind*.

(Lk. 23:4). An innocent man was put to death, and the rightful king was assassinated. God himself knows all about the depths of human injustice: he has experienced the worst of it for himself.

So, if the present world is unfair and human legal systems are prone to injustice; will the scores ever be settled, will justice ever be done, and wrongs ever be righted?

A strange thing happened when Jesus was dying on the cross. One of the robbers who was being executed alongside him said, 'Jesus, remember me when you come into your kingdom' (Lk. 23:42). It was a remarkably odd thing for one dying man to say to another. And yet the robber's words were proved to be true, because although Jesus died, he did not stay dead. He was raised again to life, ascended into heaven, and is waiting by the side of God to return to earth one day to reclaim his kingdom.

The Bible tells us that one day Jesus will return to earth. And next time he is coming with his whole army. Next time Jesus comes to Jerusalem it will not be on a donkey, it will be with thunder and lightning. Next time he is coming to take charge over his kingdom and to destroy his enemies and defeat the rebels. Next time it truly will be: 'the Mother of all Battles'; a war to end all wars, which the Bible calls Armageddon.

Yet the truth is that the outcome is certain. Jesus has *already* by his death and resurrection won the victory over the powers of darkness. The world *already* by its rejection of Jesus stands condemned (Jn. 3:18).[2]

But until the time of his return, Jesus by his death has offered an amnesty to the rebellious human race. He has given us a chance to return to him, to acknowledge him as our king, and to have an amnesty for our past crimes and rebellions. But time is short: one day, he will return to reclaim the whole earth. The question facing all humanity is: is Jesus the king of your life?

The Last Judgement[3]

The Old Testament prophets looked forward to 'the Day of the Lord'. That 'Day of the Lord' had two components to it: salvation for God's people and judgement on God's enemies. From their perspective the Old Testament prophets thought that the two bits would go together. Isaiah 61:1–2 says:

> The Spirit of the LORD is on me,
> because he has anointed me to preach good news to the poor.
> He has sent me to proclaim freedom for the prisoners
> and recovery of sight for the blind,

---

[2] Burridge, *John*, 61 rightly stresses that, for John, the eschaton is realised in the Jesus event.

[3] Matthew 13:24–30, 36–43; 25:31–46; 2 Corinthians 5:10; Hebrews 9:28.

to release the oppressed,
to proclaim the year of the Lord's favour
and the day of vengeance of our God.

These were the words quoted by Jesus in Luke 4:17–19 as his 'Nazareth manifesto' when he read in the synagogue. Yet he stopped before, 'the day of vengeance of our God', when he declared, 'Today this Scripture is fulfilled in your hearing' (Lk. 4:21).

When he ascended into heaven after his resurrection, his work on earth was not over. He is coming back again. Jesus came the first time as Saviour. He will come again as Judge. We live now in the in-between times, between the comings of Christ, in what the New Testament writers refer to as 'the last days'.

The world awaits the consummation of Jesus' kingdom that was promised by Isaiah. It awaits his second coming. Then the world will see that, 'Of the increase of his government and peace there will be no end. He will reign on David's throne and over his kingdom, establishing and upholding it with justice and righteousness from that time on and forever' (Isa. 9:7).

When will the end come?

Both the Apostles Peter and Paul had to write to groups of Christians who, two thousand years ago, were already wondering when and whether Jesus would return. Peter wrote in 2 Peter 3:3–4: 'First of all, you must understand that in the last days scoffers will come, scoffing and following their own evil desires. They will say, "Where is this 'coming' he promised? Ever since our fathers died, everything goes on as it has since the beginning of creation."' But, says Peter, people were saying that sort of thing at the time of the Flood, which overwhelmed them as a sudden disaster (2 Pet. 3:6).

There is a reason for the delay: 'The Lord is not slow in keeping his promise, as some understand slowness. He is patient with you, not wanting anyone to perish, but everyone to come to repentance' (2 Pet. 3:9).[4]

Why is the second coming important?

Although it is delayed, the second coming is a vital part of Christian doctrine. The second coming is the guarantee that God is in control of history. The second coming is the affirmation that life is not fundamentally unjust; that it does have meaning and that there will be a day of reckoning. Lawyers see justice being done but they also see, and sometimes participate in, injustice being done. The second coming will lead to the holding of the divine court where justice will be done perfectly.

---

[4] See also 1 Timothy 2:4.

Future justice

For the Christian church, with its record of producing martyrs for their beliefs, the promise that God sees and will one day act is crucial. A key part of Paul's message to the Thessalonians was that 'pay-back time' is coming. Their present sufferings would be rectified. He says in 2 Thessalonians 1:6: 'God is just: He will pay back trouble to those who trouble you and give relief to you who are troubled and to us as well.' God is not blind. He sees the evil that is being committed on this earth. 'The Lord will punish men for their sins' (1 Thess. 4:6b).

When will this happen? Paul wrote in 2 Thessalonians 1:7: 'This will happen when the Lord Jesus is revealed from heaven in blazing fire with his powerful angels.' In fact, some sins are dealt with (partially) on this earth. Human justice does reflect divine justice, but the final, perfect reckoning awaits the day of judgement.

Jesus' promise to the murderer on the cross – the moment at which his glory was displayed (Col. 2:15) is a powerful demonstration of the fact that all human verdicts are only *provisional*. 'Definitive judgment on human evil is reserved for the returning Christ, for he alone has adequate knowledge and wisdom to do justice to sin.'[5]

One day the judge who alone knows the full facts and can see into the hearts of men will impose true and perfect justice. He was watching on every street corner the rapes, murders, robberies that have ever occurred. He could see into the houses where the domestic violence and child abuse was happening. He saw the embezzlement and abuse of power in all the workplaces and government offices that have ever existed. God was there and he will judge.[6] 'There is nothing hidden that will not be made known' (Mt. 10:26; Mk. 4:22; Lk. 8:17). Paul in Romans 2:5b–6 writes: 'you are storing up wrath against yourself for the day of God's wrath, when his righteous judgement will be revealed. God "will give to each person according to what he has done".'

> Genuine justice requires that all relevant factors be taken into account, but human beings can never know all these factors and are simply not equipped to make final judgements on people. In practice we can achieve only a rough justice, which may be preferable to no justice at all but is still less than ideal. By contrast, God deals with people not merely on the basis of their external deeds but on the basis of their intentions, motivations, and enduring moral character, which God alone can know perfectly.[7]

Human laws are finite; only God's justice is infinite.

---

[5] Marshall, *Beyond Retribution*, 261.
[6] Lamentations 3:36.
[7] Marshall, *Beyond Retribution*, 128. See 2 Chronicles 6:30.

The Last Judgement will be a Revelation[8]

1. A revelation of the kingship of Jesus

Christians believe that Jesus is the pinnacle of God's revelation of himself, to the point where Jesus could say: 'He who has seen me has seen the Father' (Jn. 14:6–13). Seeing Jesus is as good as seeing God himself.

But the Jesus-event is not complete. The self-disclosure of God through his chosen Christ has not yet finished. Jesus has come, he has lived, he has died, he has been raised again to life, he has ascended into heaven, but he has not yet come again in glory.

This return in glory is described as the *parousia*, a word used in the Greek of New Testament times to designate the visit of a ruler.[9] It is also referred to as an *apokalypsis*, an 'unveiling' or 'disclosure' when the power and the glory which are rightfully Christ's will be revealed to the world.[10]

Until the second coming, there is an element of hiddenness, of veiling, about the rule of God.[11] On the Last Day, then 'they will know that I am the LORD' (Ezek. 30:19). On that day, 'the LORD Almighty will be exalted by his justice, and the holy God will show himself holy by his righteousness' (Isa. 5:16).

In Revelation 19:11, John writes: 'I saw heaven standing open and there before me was a white horse, whose rider is called faithful and true. With justice he judges and makes war.' God's kingdom is established through the display of the two key functions of kingship: the waging of a war of deliverance and the delivering of justice, which vindicates the righteous and condemns their enemies.[12] We saw, in chapter 4, how *hesed* and *emeth*, covenant faithfulness and truth, should exemplify the rule of the king. Here, in the last act of history, God sends his king, Jesus, into the fallen, sinful world in order to consummate God's victory over evil, to complete the deliverance of God's creation from evil.

The second coming will be the revelation of divine justice – the proclamation of the sovereignty of the Lord, the confirmation of forgiveness to those rebels who had laid down their arms and accepted his amnesty, and the execution of judgement against those who have refused to have him as their king. The *parousia* is therefore 'an act of God in Christ for the salvation of the world and its judgment'.[13] Just as sitting in judgement and carrying out justice was an essential hallmark of Old Testament kingship, so it will be the hallmark of Jesus' return as king (Mt. 25:31–33).

---

[8] Gunton, *Revelation*, 112, 120.
[9] G.E. Ladd, 'Eschatology', in *The New Bible Dictionary*, 387.
[10] Ladd, 'Eschatology', 387.
[11] O'Donovan, *Desire*, 146.
[12] O'Donovan, *Desire*, 287.
[13] G.R. Beasley-Murray, *Jesus and the Kingdom of God*, 341.

The reign of God and of his Christ that the second coming will make manifest will be a reign characterised by righteousness and justice (Pss. 9:7–8; 45:6). The prophecy of Isaiah 16:5 will be fulfilled: 'In love a throne will be established; in faithfulness a man will sit on it – one from the house of David – one who in judging seeks justice and speeds the cause of righteousness.' As was predicted in Proverbs, and as we saw in chapter 4, the throne established in perfect love, justice and righteousness will endure forever.

2. A revelation of the truth of human lives

God made us – he is entitled to set the standards by which we should live, and to punish us when we do not live up to those standards. He made us for relationship with himself, and he is entitled to be angry when we ignore him. God created a good world, and we, who have chosen to do evil, have poisoned it, defaced it and destroyed it. In the final analysis, as James says: 'There is only one Lawgiver and Judge, the one who is able to save and destroy' (Jas. 4:12).

The revelation of Jesus as God's chosen King will be accompanied on that last day by the realization of the rejection of him and of his rule by human beings. '[In] the biblical perspective sin is ultimately rebellion against God.'[14] The true nature of human selfishness and self-centredness will be revealed at the *apokalypsis*.

Some of the evil that lives in human hearts rises to the surface. In other people it remains hidden. The fact that what emerges about people's lives after their death is radically different from the public image they presented illustrates the truth that Paul wrote in 1 Timothy 5:24: 'The sins of some men are obvious, reaching the place of judgement ahead of them; the sins of others trail behind them.'

The last judgement will be a revelation; it will be an exposure, a bringing into the light of all the dark deeds, words, and thoughts of human beings.[15] Throughout the Bible it is made clear that God's judgement is not just based on what we do, but also on what we think, and in the final analysis, upon who we are.[16] In Jeremiah, God declares: 'My eyes are on all their ways; they are not hidden from me, nor is their sin concealed from my eyes' (Jer. 16:17). All of our wickedness, whether carried out in secret or in public, will be exposed for what it is on the day of judgement (Mt. 10:26). As Jesus declared, 'What you have said in the dark will be heard in the daylight, and what you have whispered in the ear in the inner rooms will be proclaimed from the roofs' (Lk. 12:3).

---

[14] Beasley-Murray, *Kingdom of God*, 342.

[15] 1 Corinthians 4:5. Cf. O'Donovan, *Desire*, 38.

[16] 1 Samuel 16:7; Matthew 15:10, 11, 17–20. Cf. Marshall, *Beyond Retribution*, 191; and chapter 10 of O'Donovan's *Resurrection and Moral Order*.

3. A revelation of God's judgement

Just as the sending of Jesus to die on a cross was an act of God's love and of his justice, so too will be the last judgement. 'He will not let evil disfigure his creation and bring suffering to his creatures forever. There must be a day of reckoning for evil and for evildoers.'[17]

The writer of 2 Peter declared the 'Day of the Lord' to be a day of judgement (2 Pet. 3:7), a day of disclosure (2 Pet. 3:10), a day of fire (2 Pet. 3:7), a day for the destruction of ungodly men (2 Pet. 3:7, 10, 11). Paul wrote in 2 Thessalonians 1:7–9:

> when the Lord Jesus is revealed from heaven … He will punish those who do not know God and do not obey the gospel of our Lord Jesus. They will be punished with everlasting destruction and shut out from the presence of the lord and from the majesty of his power.

Paul warned about 'the day of God's wrath, when his righteous judgement will be revealed' (Rom. 2:5). On that day, those with stubborn and unrepentant hearts would discover the wrath that they had stored up against themselves. Paul said that on that day:

> God "will give to each person according to what he has done." To those who by persistence in doing good seek glory, honour and immortality, he will give eternal life. But for those who are self-seeking and who reject the truth and follow evil, there will be wrath and anger.
> (Rom. 2:6–7)

At the last judgement we will get what we asked for.[18] Those who have sought after God will get the presence of God (see 1 Thess. 4:17). Those who have lived this life wanting nothing to do with God will find God wanting nothing to do with them. God has given the atheist so much: sun and rain, food, talents, skills and abilities, even life itself – everything of value that we have is ultimately a gift from God. The atheist or the agnostic wants nothing from God. In hell, the atheist will get nothing from God. What is promised for those 'who do not know God and do not obey the gospel of our Lord Jesus' is, in the original Greek 'eternal destruction away from the presence of the Lord'. Hell will be awful and eternal, whether conscious or annihilation. There will be no second chances (Lk. 17:26).

Those who reject God's offer of forgiveness will get what their deeds deserve, or to put it another way, will receive the consequences of their

---

[17] Lucas, *Ezekiel*, 53.

[18] Cf. Marshall, *Beyond Retribution*, 198: 'Those who refuse to appropriate the benefits of God's saving justice in the work of Christ … face the prospect of final destruction. This is not because in the final analysis retribution wins out over mercy but because their destiny remains determined by Adam's transgression rather than by the Second Adam's obedience (Rom. 5:12–21).' See also 189, 193, 195.

choices. Those who have chosen to live life without allegiance to God's chosen king, Jesus Christ; without a grateful acknowledgement of the good gifts of God; and without a recognition of their obligations towards him and their fellow creatures, will experience an eternity in which they are excluded from the presence of the king and in which his good gifts are withdrawn as unwanted presents returned to the giver.[19]

Destruction and damnation are not God's preferences: they are not what he wants to do to his sinful human creatures. He would much rather embrace them as errant children who are at last returning home, as rebels who have laid down their arms and surrendered to their rightful king. As the prophet Ezekiel realised, the sovereign Lord takes no pleasure in the death of the wicked, he would far rather that they turn from their evil ways and live (Ezek. 33:11). Yet if evil is what we persist in choosing, despite all the good gifts God has given us, and all the chances he has offered us to return to him, then we will be judged according to the choices we have made and the path we have chosen (Ezek. 33:20).

But what is in store for God's holy people? Jesus is coming back 'to be glorified in his holy people' (2 Thess. 1:10). Paul, writing to the Christians in Rome, said this: 'our present sufferings are not worth comparing with the glory that will be revealed in us' (Rom. 8:18).

God's people look forward to glorification – to glorious new bodies (1 Cor. 15), and to a glorious new heaven and new earth, in which sin, suffering, sickness, decay and death are no more (Rev. 21). We look forward to being in the presence of God forever (1 Thess. 4:17b; 2 Thess. 1:9; Rev. 21:3, 22–23). We look forward to God's reign of justice.

So is the Christian faith all 'pie in the sky when you die'? In one sense, it is. If there is no future resurrection, then Paul admits: 'If only for this life we have hope in Christ, we are to be pitied more than all men' (1 Cor. 15:19). As C.S. Lewis retorted to the allegation that Christianity is just pie in the sky when you die: 'either there is "pie in the sky" or there is not' – and that is the real question.[20]

In another sense, it isn't. 'This is eternal life – to know God' (1 Jn. 5:11). Christians can enjoy something of the reality of God's presence in this life. Eternal life starts the moment you become a Christian.

But the truth of future judgement and eternal life is dependent upon the resurrection of Jesus. It is the resurrection of Jesus that is the assurance of the Christian hope. As Paul told the Athenians at the Areopagus, God 'has set a day when he will judge the world with justice by the man he has appointed. He has given proof of this to all men by raising him from the dead' (Acts 17:31).

On the day of judgement, the whole world will be held accountable to God.

---

[19] Whether this experience in eternity will be one of conscious damnation, 'living death', or extinction/annihilation is beyond the scope of this book to explore. The options are considered in the ACUTE report, *The Nature of Hell*.

[20] C.S. Lewis, *The Problem of Pain*, 132–3

Rulers will be judged at the last judgement

The prophet Isaiah wrote:

> Woe to those who make unjust laws,
> to those who issue oppressive decrees,
> to deprive the poor of their rights
> and withhold justice from the oppressed of my people,
> making widows their prey and robbing the fatherless.
>
> What will you do on the day of reckoning,
> when disaster comes from afar?
> To whom will you run for help?
> Where will you leave your riches?
> Nothing will remain but to cringe among the captives
> or fall among the slain.
> (Isa. 10:1–4a)[21]

God will hold those who have wielded power in this world accountable for the way in which they have used it.[22] God will judge the oppressors and dictators of this world for the misery they have caused, and condemned for it. Like Babylon, they will be treated in the way in which they have treated others unless, like Nineveh in the book of Jonah, they repent and plead for God to be merciful.

The oppressed will be vindicated at the last judgement

In the contrast to the behaviour of the unjust rulers of this present age, the actions of Jesus as judge will be just. 'With righteousness he will judge the needy, with justice he will give decisions for the poor of the earth. He will strike the earth with the rod of his mouth; with the breath of his lips he will slay the wicked' (Isa. 11:4). In Malachi, the Lord declares: 'I will come near to you for judgment ... I will be quick to testify against sorcerers, adulterers and perjurers, against those who defraud labourers of their wages, who oppress the widows and the fatherless, and deprive foreigners of justice, but do not fear me' (Mal. 3:5).

'God is a God of justice. He must establish right rule on the earth. The cries of his people and, indeed, of all the slain of the earth come to him and must be avenged.'[23]

Jesus illustrated this righting of wrongs through the parable of the rich man and the beggar in Luke 16:19–31. He told how there was a rich man who ignored the sufferings of a diseased beggar. After their deaths, the

---

[21] See also Proverbs 22:22–23.

[22] In relation to the institution of slavery, Paul warned human masters that they would be accountable to their Master, God, for the way in which they had treated their slaves (Eph. 6:9). See also Job 31:13–14; O'Donovan, *Desire*, 234.

[23] Mason, *Jeremiah*, 240, commenting on Jeremiah 51:49. See also Job 16:18 and Revelation 6:9–11.

rich man went to hell and the beggar went to heaven. Jesus uses the figure of Abraham to explain to the rich man: 'Son, remember that in your lifetime you received your good things, while [the beggar] received bad things, but now he is comforted here and you are in agony.'

God must be capable of and willing to provide more than adequate compensation for the miseries and injustices of this present life, otherwise the biblical exhortations to endure patiently in the face of them become nothing other than a cruel mockery of human suffering and exploitation.[24] It must be true that, in the words of Thomas Moore, 'Earth hath no sorrow that heaven cannot heal.'[25]

Justice as deliverance and justice as destruction

What we want others to experience is justice; what we hope we will experience is mercy. Such is the dichotomy of our desires; such are the double standards of our morality. Yet this duality in the structure of morality is inescapable. Judgement is the essential context in which mercy can take effect. Without just judgement, without a recognition of the penalty that could rightfully be imposed by just Judge, mercy is indistinguishable from casual indulgence or moral indifference to evil. There has to be a recognition of 'what might have been' had mercy and forgiveness not been extended and accepted in order to make sense of the transaction of grace by which relationship is restored.

God wants to offer us restorative justice: a judgement that combines justice and mercy. He wants to bring us back to himself and he has done everything to make that possible, while respecting the freedom he gave us to choose to reject his overtures of love:

> God's concern is not with an abstract administration of justice, but that people should live in a right relationship with him and with one another. To make this possible, strict justice has to be tempered with mercy. Because no one who turns to God is perfect, that relationship has to begin on the basis of forgiveness ... God's declared willingness to accept those who turn to him, to forgive, is the only ground of hope for the future.[26]

But as we have seen, the freedom God has given us is a responsible freedom. Our actions and choices have *real* consequences.

'If God willed the dire consequences that ensue on sin ... [it] may be that he has willed them as the only way of doing justice to the freedom and responsibility of the human personality, as he has created it.'[27] The

---

[24]   1 Corinthians 4:12; 2 Thessalonians 1:5; 2 Timothy 2:3, 12; James 5:10; 1 Peter 2:19–20.

[25]   Irish poet, 1779–1852.

[26]   Lucas, *Ezekiel*, 169.

[27]   C.F.D. Moule, 'Punishment and Retribution: An Attempt to Delimit Their Scope in New Testament Thought', *New Perspectives on Crime and Justice* 10 (1990), 6.

possibility of hell, of an eternal separation from God, is a theological necessity in order to make sense of an atonement in which the Son of God had to die.

But Jesus, who died a criminal's death, has been vindicated. He has exhausted the curse of the law (Gal. 3:13–14). The Christian hope is that, because of God's vindication of Jesus, one day before the judgement seat of God; all unjust verdicts will be reversed, all corrupt decisions will be nullified and all wrongful sentences will be cancelled. In this moral universe, evil will one day be expunged. Its presence will be extinguished. At the last judgement, all the decisions of secular law makers will be shown up for what they are – merely contingent pronouncements awaiting confirmation or reversal from the one who looks not only on the outside but also on the heart.

But in that moment, when all wrongs are put right, something even more remarkable will happen. Grace and mercy will flood into the situation, so that those who are accounted 'in Christ' will receive a pardon for the wrongs they have committed against him, an amnesty for their rebellion against their Maker. The price of justice will be found to have been paid by the only one who had infinite resources that he expended in paying it.

Historic Christianity teaches that the judgement comes first. All have been weighed in the balance and all have been found to 'fall short of the glory of God'. All are deserving of the sentence of death pronounced on Adam and Eve and their heirs. But judgement is not necessarily the last word.[28] Paradoxically it is only those who acknowledge their guilt, their unworthiness, in this life who are assured that they will receive mercy in the life to come. Those who persist in defying the Lord, the Holy One of Israel, will be repaid for their deeds.[29]

Human Justice in the Meantime

The relationship between human justice and divine justice can be seen as another instance of the truth of that famous quote from Paul: 'Now we see but a poor reflection as in a mirror; then we shall see face to face. Now I know in part; then I shall know fully, even as I am fully known' (1 Cor. 13:12). Human justice is a shadow of divine justice, an incomplete and sometimes indistinct image, but one that brightens as the light of the good news about what God has done in Christ is shone upon it.

The question is: will the legal systems we have been participating in be recognised as a reflection or a shadow, however faint, of divine justice or merely as a parody of it?

---

[28] Cf. Ezra 9:13.
[29] Jeremiah 50:29b; Obadiah 15.

I have argued in this book that earthly authorities are incompetent to resolve questions relating to the ultimate good of knowing God. Their concerns can only relate to penultimate goods, given as good gifts of God in creation, marred by the Fall but open to possibilities of redemption because of the work of Christ. So human laws and legal systems should promote and protect the value of human life, human dignity, human liberty and provide opportunities for their subjects to enjoy rewarding work and meaningful relationships. In order to do so, human legal systems have to take action against those who disturb the social order, who attack these public goods, and in doing so are to be regarded as acting as agents of God's wrath. However, as should by now be clear, earthly authorities should act in accordance with God's gracious wrath, intervening, providing compensation and punishing to the minimum extent necessary for the protection of the community and with the hope of reintegrating the wrongdoer into the community if at all possible.

Human justice is imperfect. Human fact-finding mechanisms are imperfect. We lack omniscience. Human judgements are imperfect. We lack perfect wisdom. Human laws are inadequate. We lack perfect foresight of the future.

But even more fundamental than any of the other indications of the finitude of human justice is the fact that all human pronouncements of guilt and innocence, of right and wrong, are provisional.[30] Ultimately, we are fully accountable for 'every careless word' (Mt. 12:36) to the perfect, omniscient judge of the universe – The Lord God. He reserves to himself the power to overturn every human judgement. He will, on the last day, declare a man executed as a Judaean blasphemer and rebel to be his chosen instrument for saving the Universe! On that day those imprisoned, tortured, martyred for their faith in him will be vindicated.

Human justice is, and can only ever be expected to be, a provisional or qualified good.[31] But in the present state of affairs, in the present world-order, *pending the second coming of Christ*, it remains a good nonetheless. When justice is done, God's will is carried out, and God is pleased. The perfect justice of God stands both as a paradigm to emulate and as a standard against which all human systems of justice will be judged.

Now, such a doctrine is uncomplicated and relatively easy to expound in a Byzantine system, where the Emperor is the representative of God on earth (the regent of Christ). It can also be easily accommodated within a political theology which accepts that the Christian prince has been given authority by God to wield temporal power in his name.

It is much more difficult to make the easy comparison between human justice and divine justice in the post-Enlightenment world, where the French/American project of separating the church and the state has

---

[30] And that must include the judgements of church authorities, cf. Gunton, *Revelation*, 96–7.

[31] O'Donovan, *Resurrection*, 72, 130.

detached government from a recognition that its power is from God, although it is one of the curiosities of history that the American motto is still 'In God We Trust'. For the most part, however, Western government is no longer even pretending that it is exercising power on God's behalf.

The difficulty is that government which is self-consciously claiming its authority from God tends to absolutise itself to the point where 'The King can do no wrong'; whereas government which does not make such claims tends to become wholly indifferent to the demands of God upon the exercise of its functions. Neither is a justifiable position on the biblical evidence. The teaching of the Bible is, as we have seen, that human government has been given responsibility by God, and is accountable to God for the discharge of that responsibility.

> In biblical thought human righteousness is an expression of divine righteousness. Human justice should be a reflection of God's justice. That is to say, the responsibilities laid down in the law are a response to God's initiative in saving Israel from Egypt and giving the law to Israel. Human righteousness, strictly speaking, arises out of gratitude for God's initiative. This is also to recognize that the system of human justice is not a self-sustaining system. Because of human greed and failure it cannot be self-sustaining. Left to itself it will always break down in disorder and chaos. From the Jewish and Christian perspective the system of human justice can only work if it is seen as a reflection of God's justice. It can be sustained only by the energy of gratitude to God and as a response to his generous purpose in his dealings with humankind.[32]

The reality of final judgement is meant to operate as a spur to human justice. 'This is what the LORD says: "Maintain justice and do what is right, for my salvation is close at hand and my righteousness will soon be revealed"' (Isa. 56:1). The human law maker, lawyer or judge is to act justly because he or she knows that one day they will have to give an account of themselves to God.

The prospect of final judgement ought also to affect the substantive content of human justice. The Christian message is that the world does not divide neatly into 'them' and 'us', into the criminals and the victims. Judged against God's perfect standards, 'all have sinned'.[33] We are all in the same boat; all of us are dependent on God's mercy. Therefore, the human judge should be mindful of his or her common humanity with the criminal who falls to be sentenced or with the litigants whose case requires judicial resolution.[34]

> The relative justice which is all that is possible in this sinful broken world, the justice which comes from the balancing of claims and interests and acts to

---

[32] Dunn and Suggate, *Justice of God*, 36.

[33] See Romans 3:20, 23.

[34] Cf. M. Volf, *Exclusion and Embrace: A Theological Exploration of Identity, Otherness, and Reconciliation*, 124; O'Donovan, *Desire*, 261, 278.

restrain sin, must constantly be measured against the divine justice and love we know in Jesus Christ, and in our experience of justification.[35]

Christians therefore have an important witness to human legal systems about the importance of mercy in judgement, and about the pursuit of reconciliation in justice.[36] Nonetheless, human justice cannot be redemptive *as such*; the most it can do is to point beyond itself to the redemption available through the justice of God.[37]

In the meantime, pending final judgement, human law is meant to be a reflection of God's law. At all times and in all places it is, to a greater or lesser extent. Whenever a court system is set up to reduce the risk of people settling matters themselves by violence, God's design is reflected. Laws against murder and theft reflect God's rules in the Ten Commandments. God's justice is transcendent perfection. Human law is the imperfect, man-made copy. Just how careful a copy depends on those framing the laws and enforcing the laws and administering the legal system. It depends on the lawyers and on the state.

Conclusions

From the preceding study it should be clear that, 'The biblical mandate to seek justice and rescue the oppressed is an integral and magnificent theme of the Christian heritage.'[38] In the words of de Coninck: 'To be a Christian is to live today according to the values which will reign tomorrow ... it is to fix one's eyes on what will last: "justice, mercy and faith" (Mt. 23:23).'[39]

In biblical thought, the knowledge of God and the practise of delivering justice and mercy are inextricably linked:

> Let not the wise man boast of his wisdom or the strong man boast of his strength or the rich man boast of his riches, but let him who boasts boast about this: that he understands and knows me, that I am the LORD who exercises kindness, justice and righteousness on earth, for in these I delight. (Jer. 9:23)

Just as God himself exercises kindness, justice and righteousness on earth, so his servants too should exercise justice, righteousness and kindness.

The pursuit of God's justice in human relationships is in biblical terms one of the most important expressions of a life lived in accordance with

[35] D.B. Forrester, 'Political Justice and Christian Theology', *Studies in Christian Ethics* 3.1 (1990), 13.

[36] de Coninck, *La justice et le pardon*, 72; O'Donovan, *Desire*, 200, 202–3, 256.

[37] O'Donovan, *Desire*, 269.

[38] Haugen, *Good News*, 62.

[39] de Coninck, *La justice et l'abondance*, 79.

God's standards of righteousness and holiness. There is therefore a clear mandate for Christian involvement in human legal and administrative institutions seeking to influence them towards a greater demonstration of the gracious servant-rule of the Son of Man.

Postscript

Having emphasised, throughout this study, the imperfections, failures and finite nature of human laws and legal systems, it behoves me to confess and acknowledge the patent limitations of the present book. It is inadequate as a Christian justification for the modern nation-state; it is incomplete as a criticism of it; it is inchoate as a Christian political theology. It underplays the traditional emphasis on the responsibility of government for maintaining 'law and order' and skirts over the complexities of government's responsibility for criminal justice. Perhaps most significantly of all, in its discussion of human laws it has not fully explored the place of law in relation to the gospel of grace.

All these omissions are deliberate. Most of them can be explained on the basis that space does not permit a sufficient exploration of them in the present volume.

In relation to law and order, criminal justice, and law and gospel, the omissions have been calculated to provoke. All these subjects have been discussed by others elsewhere and used as the lens through which to view human laws. The present account offers a change of lens in order to illuminate that which otherwise is in danger of receding into the background – the fundamental duty of human governments to do justice.

In relation to political theory more generally, however, the omission is made for different reasons. It is a fondly cherished belief of most lawyers (other than the Legal Realist and the Critical Legal Studies Schools) that there is more to law than just 'frozen politics'. Lawyers even have their own name for that branch of enquiry that is concerned with the philosophy of law; we call it 'Jurisprudence'. Doubtless, such a discipline is a sub-set of moral philosophy and/or political philosophy, but lawyers maintain the semi-autonomous nature of legal reasoning within the general flow of practical reasoning.[1]

Therefore it is possible to give a theoretical account of the nature and functions of law without going on to complete the work of giving a comprehensive account of the actual or the desirable political order. Questions of who has power, why they in particular have it and whether, and on what terms they should have it, can be deferred (although the boundaries of enquiry are not impermeable). It is possible to state in isolation an account of the means for which that power should be used, exploring it in relation to the use of law as a tool.

Within the limited sphere of this study, what I have sought to demonstrate is that the witness of the Bible is that there is an authority given to

---

[1] Cf. Finnis, *Natural Law*, 316–17. See also 269, 282.

human institutions to maintain social order, but that the social order is only truly secure when it is administered in accordance with God's standards of justice, and that these standards of justice involve the recognition of the protection of the value of human life, human dignity and human liberty, and opportunities for all in society to enjoy rewarding work and meaningful relationships.

Bibliography

ACUTE Commission, *The Nature of Hell* (Carlisle: Paternoster, 2000)

Ahdar, R.J., 'Religious Group Autonomy, Gay Ordination and Human Rights Law', in R. O'Dair, and A. Lewis (eds.), *Law and Religion* (Oxford: Oxford University Press, 2001), 275–98

Alexander, P. (ed.), *The Lion Encyclopedia of the Bible* (Tring: Lion, 1978)

Anderson, J.N.D., *Freedom under Law* (Eastbourne: Kingsway, 1988)

——, *Morality, Law and Grace* (London: Tyndale Press, 1972)

Aquinas, T., *Selected Writings* (Harmondsworth: Penguin, 1998)

——, *Summa Theologica* (Westminster: Christian Classics, 2000)

Aristotle, *Nichomachean Ethics* (Ware: Wordsworth: 1996)

——, *Politics* (tr. T.A. Sinclair; Harmondsworth: Penguin, 1962)

Augustine, *The City of God* (tr. H. Bettenson; Harmondsworth: Penguin, 1955)

Bainton, R., *Here I Stand* (Oxford: Lion, 1987)

Baldwin, J.G., *1 and 2 Samuel: An Introduction and Commentary* (Tyndale Old Testament Commentary; Leicester: Inter-Varsity Press, 1988)

Barth, K., *Church Dogmatics* (tr. G.W. Bromiley and T.F. Torrance; Edinburgh: T. & T. Clark, 1956–62)

Barth K. and E. Brunner, *Natural Theology comprising 'Nature and Grace' by Professor Dr Emil Brunner and the Reply 'No!' by Dr Karl Barth* (tr. P. Fraenkel; London: Geoffrey Bles, 1946)

Beasley-Murray, G.R., *Jesus and the Kingdom of God* (Carlisle: Paternoster, 1986)

Beaumont, P. (ed.), *Christian Perspectives on Human Rights and Legal Philosophy* (Carlisle: Paternoster, 1998)

——, *Christian Perspectives on Law Reform* (Carlisle: Paternoster, 1998)

——, 'Christian Perspectives on the Law: What Makes them Distinctive?', in R. O'Dair, and A. Lewis (eds.), *Law and Religion* (Oxford: Oxford University Press, 2001), 529–46

——, *Christian Perspectives on the Limits of Law* (Carlisle: Paternoster, 2002)

Beaumont, P. and K. Wotherspoon (eds.), *Christian Perspectives on Law and Relationism* (Carlisle: Paternoster, 2000)

Berkhof, H., *Christ and the Powers* (tr. J.H. Yoder; Scottdale, Penn.: Herald Press, 1962)

Birch, B.C., W. Brueggemann, T.E. Fretheim and D.L. Petersen, *A Theological Introduction to the Old Testament* (Nashville: Abingdon, 1999)

Blenkinsopp, J., *Wisdom and Law in the Old Testament: The Ordering of Life in Israel and Early Judaism* (revd edn.; Oxford: Oxford University Press, 2001)

de Blois, M., 'The Foundation of Human Rights: A Christian Perspective', in P. Beaumont (ed.), *Christian Perspectives on Human Rights and Legal Philosophy* (Carlisle: Paternoster, 1998), 7–30
——, 'Freedom of Religion as the Fruit of the Radical Reformation', in R. O'Dair and A. Lewis (eds.), *Law and Religion* (Oxford: Oxford University Press, 2001), 163–84
Bluhm, W.T., *Theories of the Political System* (Englewood Cliffs: Prentice-Hall, 1965)
Bridger, F., *Children Finding Faith: Exploring a Child's Response to God* (2nd edn.; Bletchley: Scripture Union, 2000)
Britton, K., 'Utilitarianism', in J.O. Urmson (ed.), *The Concise Encyclopedia of Western Philosophy and Philosophers* (2nd edn.; London: Hutchinson, 1967), 287–9
Brown, P., 'L'élitisme païen' in P. Ariès and G. Duby (eds.) *Histoire de la vie privée* (Paris: Editions du Seuil, 1985), Tome I, 239–41
Bruce, F.F., 'Messiah', in *The New Bible Dictionary* (London: Inter-Varsity Press, 1962), 811–18
——, *The Epistle of Paul to the Romans: An Introduction and Commentary* (Tyndale New Testament Commentary; 2nd edn.; Leicester: Inter-Varsity Press, 1985)
Brueggeman, W., *Theology of the Old Testament: Testimony, Dispute, Advocacy* (Minneapolis: Augsburg Fortress, 1997)
Bryant, C., *Possible Dreams: A Personal History of the British Christian Socialists* (London: Hodder, 1996)
Burnett, D., *The Healing of the Nations* (Carlisle: Send the Light Ltd, 1986)
Burnside, J., 'Inspired Justice', *Justice Reflections* 1 (2002), JR-1
Burridge, R.A., *John: The People's Bible Commentary* (Oxford: BRF, 1998)
Calvin, J., *The Epistles of Paul the Apostle to the Romans and to the Thessalonians* (tr. R. Mackenzie; Edinburgh: Banner of Truth, 1961)
——, *The Institutes of Christian Religion* (tr. F.L. Battles; London: SCM Press, 1961)
Castrey, A., 'Christian Lawyer', *Fulcrum* (December 1991)
Catherwood, F., *A Better Way: The Case for a Christian Social Order* (London: Inter-Varsity Press, 1975)
——, *Pro-Europe?* (Leicester: Inter-Varsity Press, 1975, 1991)
Chantry, W.J., *God's Righteous Kingdom: Focusing on the Law's Connection with the Gospel* (Edinburgh: Banner of Truth, 1980)
Charles, J.D., 'Crime, The Christian and Capital Justice', *Journal of the Evangelical Theological Society* 38.3 (1995), 429–41
Chesterton, G.K., *Orthodoxy* (London: Hodder, 1996)
Christenson, L., *A Charismatic Approach to Social Action* (London: Lakeland, 1975)
Colson, C., *Justice that Restores* (Leicester: Inter-Varsity Press, 2000)
Colson, C. and R. Neuhaus (eds.), *Evangelicals and Catholics Together* (London: Hodder, 1996)

Colwell, J.E., *Living the Christian Story: The Distinctiveness of Christian Ethics* (Edinburgh: T. & T. Clark, 2001)

de Coninck, F., *La justice et l'abondance* (Québec: Editions la Clairière, 1997)

——, *La justice et la puissance* (Québec: Editions la Clairière, 1998)

——, *La justice et le pardon* (Québec: Editions la Clairière, 2003)

Copp, S., 'A Christian Vision for Corporate Governance', in P. Beaumont (ed.), *Christian Perspectives on Law Reform* (Carlisle: Paternoster, 1998), 105–54

Cranfield, C.E.B., *The Bible and the Christian Life: A Collection of Essays* (Edinburgh: T. & T. Clark, 1985)

——, *A Critical and Exegetical Commentary on the Epistle to the Romans* (2 vols.; Edinburgh: T. & T. Clark, 1975, 1977)

——, *On Romans and Other New Testament Essays* (Edinburgh: T. & T. Clark, 1998)

Creighton, L. *Life and Letters of Mandell Creighton* (London & C.: 1904)

Cundall, A.E., *Judges: An Introduction and Commentary* and Morris, L., *Ruth: An Introduction and Commentary* (Tyndale Old Testament Commentaries; Leicester: Inter-Varsity Press, 1968)

Cundy, J. (ed.), *Law – Some Christian Perspectives* (Glasgow: Lawyers' Christian Fellowship, 1990)

Davies, W.D., *The Gospel and the Land: Early Christianity and Jewish Territorial Doctrine* (Berkeley: University of California Press, 1974)

DeMar, G., *Ruler of the Nations: Biblical Principles of Government* (Forth Worth: Dominion, 1987)

Denning, A.T. *The Influence of Religion on Law* (LCF; King's College: Newcastle upon Tyne, 1953)

Devlin, P., *The Enforcement of Morals* (London: Oxford University Press, 1959)

Douglas, J.D. (ed.), *The New Bible Dictionary* (London: Inter-Varsity Press, 1962)

Drane, J., *Jesus and the Four Gospels* (revd edn.; Tring: Lion, 1984)

Dumbrell, W.J., *Covenant and Creation: A Theology of the Old Testament Covenants* (Carlisle: Paternoster, 1984, 2000)

Dunn, J.D.G. and A.M. Suggate, *The Justice of God: A Fresh Look at the Old Doctrine of Justification by Faith* (Carlisle: Paternoster, 1993)

Dunstan, G.R., *The Artifice of Ethics: The Morehouse Lectures, 1973* (London: SCM Press, 1974)

Dworkin, R., *A Matter of Principle* (Cambridge, MA: Harvard University Press, 1985)

Ellison, H.L., *The Message of the Old Testament* (Carlisle: Paternoster, 1969)

——, *The Prophets of Israel: From Ahijah to Hosea* (Exeter: Paternoster, 1969)

Ellul, J., *Le Fondement Théologique du Droit* (Neuchâtel: Delachaux & Niestlé, 1946)

——, 'Concerning the Christian Attitude Toward Law', *Christian Scholar* 42.2 (1959), 139ff.

Fee, G., *God's Empowering Presence: The Holy Spirit in the Letters of Paul* (Peabody, MA: Hendrickson, 1994)

——, *Paul, the Spirit and the People of God* (London: Hodder & Stoughton, 1997)

Finnis, J., *Natural Law and Natural Rights* (Oxford: Clarendon, 1980)

Fitzmyer, J., *Romans: A New Translation with Introduction and Commentary* (New York: Doubleday, 1993)

Fletcher, J. and Montgomery, J.W., *Situation Ethics* (Minneapolis: Bethany, 1972)

Forrester, D.B., 'Political Justice and Christian Theology', *Studies in Christian Ethics* 1 (1990), 1–13

Forster, R., *The Kingdom of Jesus* (Carlisle: Authentic Lifestyle, 2002)

Foster, R., *Money, Sex and Power: The Challenge of the Disciplined Life* (London: Hodder & Stoughton, 1985)

France, R.T., *The Gospel According to Matthew: An Introduction and Commentary* (Tyndale New Testament Commentary; Leicester: Inter-Varsity Press, 1985)

Freeman, H.E., *An Introduction to the Old Testament Prophets* (Chicago: Moody, 1968)

Gay, C.M., *With Liberty and Justice for Whom? The Recent Evangelical Debate over Capitalism* (Grand Rapids: Eerdmans, 1991)

Gladwin, J., *The Good of the People: A Christian Reflection on Living with the Modern State* (Basingstoke: Marshall Pickering, 1988)

Goldingay, J.E., *Daniel* (WBC 30; Dallas, TX: Word Books, 1998)

Goldsworthy, G., *Gospel and Kingdom: A Christian Interpretation of the Old Testament* (Carlisle: Paternoster, 1981, 1994)

Green, J.B., 'Death of Christ', in G.F. Hawthorne, R.P. Martin and D.G. Reid (eds.), *Dictionary of Paul and his Letters* (Downers Grove/ Leicester: Inter-Varsity Press, 1993), 201–9

Griffiths, B., *Morality and the Marketplace* (London: Hodder, 1982)

Gundry-Volf, J.M., 'Expiation, Propitiation, Mercy Seat', in G.F. Hawthorne, R.P. Martin and D.G. Reid, (eds.), *Dictionary of Paul and his Letters* (Leicester: Inter-Varsity Press, 1993), 279–84

Gunton, C.E., *A Brief Theology of Revelation: The 1993 Warfield Lectures* (Edinburgh: T. & T. Clark, 1995)

Guthrie, D. and Martin, R.P., 'God', in G.F. Hawthorne, R.P. Martin and D.G. Reid (eds.), *Dictionary of Paul and his Letters* (Leicester: Inter-Varsity Press, 1993), 354–69

Harrison, R.K., *Jeremiah and Lamentations: An Introduction and Commentary* (Tyndale Old Testament Commentary; Leicester: Inter-Varsity Press, 1973)

Hart, H.L.A., *The Concept of Law* (2nd edn.; Oxford: Clarendon Press, 1994)

Harte, D., 'The Legal Framework for Religion in Schools in England and Wales: Enforcement or Enablement?', in P. Beaumont (ed.), *Christian Perspectives on the Limits of Law* (Carlisle: Paternoster, 1998), 35–70

Haugen, G.A., *Good News About Injustice: A Witness of Courage in a Hurting World* (Leicester: Inter-Varsity Press, 1999)

Hawthorne, G.F., R.P. Martin and D.G. Reid (eds.), *Dictionary of Paul and his Letters* (Leicester: Inter-Varsity Press, 1993)

Hawthorne, S. and G. Kendrick, *Awaking our Cities for God: A Guide to Prayer-Walking* (Milton Keynes: Word, 1994)

Hill, C., *Puritanism and Revolution: Studies in Interpretation of the English Revolution of the 17th Century* (London: Panther, 1968)

Hobbes, T., *Leviathan* (ed. R. Tuck; Cambridge, Cambridge University Press, 1991)

Hubbard, D.A., *Joel and Amos: An Introduction and Commentary* (Tyndale Old Testament Commentary; Leicester: Inter-Varsity Press, 1989)

Ignatieff, M., *The Needs of Strangers* (London: Chatto & Windus, 1984)

Isasi-Diaz, A.M., 'Justice and Social Change', in L.M. Russell and J.S. Clarkson (eds.), *Dictionary of Feminist Theologies* (Louisville: Westminster John Knox, 1996), 150–62

Ive, J., 'Peace-building from a biblical perspective', *Engage* 2 (Summer 2003)

Jackson, B.S., 'Historical Observations on the Relationship between Letter and Spirit', in R. O'Dair and A. Lewis (eds.), *Law and Religion* (Oxford: Oxford University Press, 2001), 101–10

Jones, I.H., 'A Truly Christian Lawyer', *Christian Lawyer* 36 (1993), 16–17

Kant, I., *Foundations of the Metaphysics of Morals* (1785; tr. L.W. Beck, Indianapolis: Bobbs-Merrill, 1959)

Kärkkäinen, V-M., *Pneumatology: The Holy Spirit in Ecumenical, International and Contextual Perspective* (Grand Rapids: Baker Book House, 2002)

Kessler, S., 'John Locke's Legacy of Religious Freedom', *Polity* 17 (1984–5), 484–503

Kidner, D., *The Message of Jeremiah* (Leicester: Inter-Varsity Press, 1987)

Kirk, J.A., *The Meaning of Freedom: A Study of Secular, Muslim and Christian Views* (Carlisle: Paternoster, 1998)

Kline, M., *The Treaty of the Great King* (Grand Rapids: Eerdmans, 1963)

Knibb, M.A., *The Qumran Community* (Cambridge: Cambridge University Press, 1987)

Knight, G.A.F., *A Christian Theology of the Old Testament* (London: SCM Press, 1959)

Ladd, G.E., 'Eschatology', in *The New Bible Dictionary* (London: Inter-Varsity Press, 1962), 386–91

LaSor, W.S., D.A Hubbard and F. Wm Bush, *Old Testament Survey: The Message, Form and Background of the Old Testament* (2nd edn.; Grand Rapids: Eerdmans, 1996)

Lebacqz, K., 'Justice', in L.M. Russell and J.S. Clarkson (eds.), *Dictionary of Feminist Theologies* (Louisville: Westminster John Knox, 1996), 158–9

Leigh, I., 'Clashing Rights, Exemptions and Opt-Outs: Religious Liberty and "Homophobia"', in R. O'Dair and A. Lewis (eds.), *Law and Religion* (Oxford: Oxford University Press, 2001), 247–74

——, 'Towards a Christian Approach to Religious Liberty', in P. Beaumont (ed.), *Christian Perspectives on Human Rights and Legal Philosophy* (Carlisle: Paternoster, 1998), 31–72

Lewis, C.S., *The Problem of Pain* (London: Geoffrey Bles, 1940)

Linden, I., 'People before Profit: The Early Social Doctrine of John Paul II', in P. Vallely (ed.), *The New Politics: Catholic Social Teaching for the Twenty-first Century* (London: SCM Press, 1998), 84–96

Lloyd-Jones, D.M., *Romans: Atonement and Justification* (Edinburgh: Banner of Truth, 1970)

——, *Unity in Truth* (Darlington: Evangelical Press, 1991)

Lucas, E., *Ezekiel: The People's Bible Commentary* (Oxford: BRF, 2002)

Marcel, P., 'La Vraie Révolution: L'Intelligence du Coeur', in *Esprit Révolutionnaire et Foi Chrétienne* (Aix-en-Provence: Kerygma, 1988), 71–86

Marshall, C.D., *Beyond Retribution: A New Testament Vision for Justice, Crime and Punishment* (Cambridge: Eerdmans, 2001)

Marshall, I.H., 'Using the Bible in Ethics', in D.F. Wright (ed.), *Essays in Evangelical Social Ethics* (Exeter: Paternoster, 1978), 39–58

Marshall, P., 'Liberalism, Pluralism and Christianity: A Reconceptualization', *Fides et Historia* 21 (1989), 4–17

Martens, E.A., 'Capital Punishment and the Christian', in J.H. Redekop and E.A. Martens (eds.), *On Capital Punishment* (Hillsbor, KA: Kindred Press, 1987), 19–29

Mason, R., *Jeremiah: The People's Bible Commentary* (Oxford: BRF, 2002)

McConville, J.G., *Judgment and Promise* (Leicester: Apollos, 1993)

McDonagh, E., *The Gracing of Society* (Dublin: Gill and Macmillan, 1989)

McGoldrick, J.E., *Abraham Kuyper: God's Renaissance Man* (Darlington: Evangelical Press, 2000)

McGrath, A., *Christian Theology: An Introduction* (2nd edn.; Oxford: Blackwell, 1997)

——, *'I Believe': Exploring the Apostle's Creed* (Leicester: Inter-Varsity Press, 1991, 1997)

McIlroy, D.H., 'A Christian Concept of Law' *Law & Justice* 144 (2000), 49–61

——, 'A Christian State?', *Law & Justice* 120 (1994), 32–40

——, 'A Christian View of the Role of the State', *Law & Justice* 142/3 (1999), 117–21

——, 'Christian Perspectives on Society', *Law & Justice* 145 (2000), 38–51

——, 'God and Justice', *Graya* 115 (2002), 24–35

——, 'Subsidiarity and Sphere Sovereignty: Christian Reflections on the Size, Shape and Scope of Government', *Journal of Church and State* 45 (2003), 739–64

——, 'The Holy Spirit and the Law', *Justice Reflections* 3 (2003), JR-14

——, 'The Relevance of Old Testament Law for Today: Part One', *Law & Justice* 148 (2002), 21–37

——, 'The Relevance of Old Testament Law for Today: Part Two', *Law & Justice* 150 (2003), 21–36

Mead, M., 'Some Anthropological Considerations Concerning Natural Law', *Natural Law Forum* 6 (1961), 51–64

Mendenhall, G.E., *Law and Covenant in Israel and the Ancient Near East* (Pittsburgh: The Presbyterian Board of Colportage of Western Pennsylvania, 1955)

Mitchell, B., 'Should Law Be Christian?', *Law & Justice* 96 (1988), 12–22

Montgomery, J.W., *Human Rights and Human Dignity* (Edmonton, Alberta: Canadian Institute for Law, 1986, 1995)

——, 'Law and Justice', *Law & Justice* 120 (1994), 12–25

——, 'Law and Morality: Friends or Foes?', *Law & Justice* 122 (1994), 87–106

——, 'The Limits of Christian Influence', *Christianity Today*, 23 January 1981, reprinted in *Christians in the Public Square: Law, Gospel and Public Policy* (Edmonton: Canadian Institute for Law, Theology and Public Policy, 1996), 65–7

——, *The Shaping of America* (Minneapolis: Bethany, 1976)

——, 'Whose Life Anyway? A Re-examination of Suicide and Assisted Suicide', in P. Beaumont (ed.), *Christian Perspectives on Law Reform* (Carlisle: Paternoster, 1998), 83–104

——, 'Why a Christian Philosophy of Law?', in P. Beaumont (ed.), *Christian Perspectives on Human Rights and Legal Philosophy* (Carlisle: Paternoster, 1998), 73–94

Morris, L., *The Book of Revelation: An Introduction and Commentary* (Tyndale New Testament Commentary; revd edn.; Leicester: Inter-Varsity Press, 1987)

Motyer, J.A., *Isaiah: An Introduction and Commentary* (Tyndale Old Testament Commentary; Leicester: Inter-Varsity Press, 1999)

Moule, C.F.D., 'Punishment and Retribution: An Attempt to Delimit their Scope in New Testament Thought', *New Perspectives on Crime and Justice* 10 (1990), 1–21

Muilenburg, J., *The Way of Israel: Biblical Faith and Ethics* (Harper Torchbooks, 1961)

Neuhaus, R.J., 'The Catholic Difference', in C. Colson and R.J. Neuhaus (eds.), *Evangelicals and Catholics Together: Toward a Common Mission* (London: Hodder, 1996), 175–228

Newton, J., *Letters of John Newton* (London: Banner of Truth, 1960)

Nobbs, D., *Theocracy and Toleration: A Study of the Disputes in Dutch Calvinism from 1600–50* (Cambridge: Cambridge University Press, 1938)

North, D.C., _Structure and Change in Economic History_ (New York: W.W. Norton & Co., 1981)

Nozick, R., _Anarchy, State and Utopia_ (Oxford: Oxford University Press, 1974)

O'Dair, R. and A. Lewis, _Law and Religion_ (Oxford: Oxford University Press, 2001)

O'Donovan, O., _Resurrection and Moral Order: An Outline for Evangelical Ethics_ (2nd edn.; Leicester: Apollos, 1994)

——, _The Desire of the Nations: Rediscovering the Roots of Political Theology_ (Cambridge: Cambridge University Press, 1996)

Oestreicher, P. _Thirty Years of Human Rights_ (The British Churches' Advisory Forum on Human Rights, 1980)

Packer, J.I., _Knowing God_ (2nd edn.; London: Hodder, 1993)

Paige, T., 'Holy Spirit', in G.F. Hawthorne, R.P. Martin and D.G. Reid (eds.), _Dictionary of Paul and his Letters_ (Leicester: Inter-Varsity Press, 1993), 404–13

Passerin d'Entrèves, A., _The Notion of the State: An Introduction to Political Theory_ (Oxford: Clarendon Press, 1967)

Pelikan, J. and H.T. Lehmann (eds.), _Luther's Works_ (55 vols.; Philadelphia, 1955–68)

Pinnock, C.H., _Most Moved Mover: A Theology of God's Openness_ (Carlisle: Paternoster, 2001)

Plato, _The Republic_ (tr. G.M.A. Grube; London: Pan, 1974)

Prior, K., _The Way of Holiness_ (Carlisle: OM Publishing, 1969, revd. 1982, 1994)

von Rad, G., _Old Testament Theology_; (2 vols. London: SCM Press, 1962)

Rawls, J., _A Theory of Justice_ (revd. edn.; Oxford: Oxford University Press, 1999)

Redekop, J.H. and E.A. Martens (eds.), _On Capital Punishment_ (Hillsbor, KA: Kindred Press, 1987)

Reisinger, E., _The Law and the Gospel_ (Phillipsburg, NJ: P&R Publishing, 1997)

Richardson, A., _The Political Christ_ (London: SCM Press, 1973)

Ricoeur, P., 'The Golden Rule: Exegetical and Theological Perplexities', _New Testament Studies_ 36 (1990), 392–7

Rivers, A.J., 'A Bill of Rights for the United Kingdom?', in P. Beaumont (ed.), _Christian Perspectives on Law Reform_ (Carlisle: Paternoster, 1998), 25–50

——, 'The new world order?', _Cambridge Papers_ 8.4 (1999)

Robinson, J.H., _Readings in European History_ (Boston: Ginn, 1905)

Rose, T., _Economics, Principles and Policy from a Christian Perspective_ (Mercer, PA: American Enterprise Publications, 1986)

Russell, L.M. and J.S. Clarkson, _Dictionary of Feminist Theologies_ (Louisville: Westminster John Knox, 1996)

Sandel, M.J., _Liberalism and the Limits of Justice_ (2nd edn.; Cambridge: Cambridge University Press, 1998)

Sanders, E.P., *Paul: A Very Short Introduction* (Oxford: Oxford University Press, 1991, 2001)

Schluter, M. and A., 'Gender co-operation: some implications of God's design for society', *Cambridge Papers*, 12.2 (June 2003)

Schluter, M. and D. Lee, *R Factor* (London: Hodder, 1993)

Schnabel, E.J., 'Wisdom', in G.F. Hawthorne, R.P. Martin and D.G. Reid (eds.), *Dictionary of Paul and his Letters* (Leicester: Inter-Varsity Press, 1993), 967–73

Scott, A., 'Scripture, Relationism and Contemporary Regulation of Utilities', in P. Beaumont and K. Wotherspoon (eds.), *Christian Perspectives on Law and Relationism* (Carlisle: Paternoster, 2000), 165–88

Seevaratnam, M., 'That there might be equality: an examination of the biblical perspective on economic equality, and its missiological relevance' (unpublished dissertation, All Nations Christian College, 1998)

Sells, B., *The Soul of the Law* (Shaftesbury: Element, 1994)

Shakespeare, W., *The Complete Works of William Shakespeare* (London: Abbey Library, 1978)

Sider, R., *Rich Christians in an Age of Hunger* (; London: Hodder, 1977 [1st edn.], 1997 [4th edn.])

Sippo, A.C., 'Totalitarianism: the Effects of Martin Luther', *St Catherine Review* (Nov/Dec 1996), available on the internet at: www.aquinas-multimedia.com/catherine/total.html

Snaith, N.H., *The Distinctive Ideas of the Old Testament* (London: Epworth, 1944)

Stott, J.R.W., *Issues facing Christians Today* (2nd edn.; London: Marshall Pickering, 1990)

——, *The Message of Romans* (Leicester: Inter-Varsity Press, 1994)

Tambasco, A.J., *A Theology of Atonement and Paul's Vision of Christianity* (ZS: NT; Collegeville, MN: Liturgical, 1991)

Tan, K., *Lost Heritage: The Heroic Story of Radical Christianity* (Godalming: Highland, 1996)

Tate, M.E., *Psalms 51–100* (WBC 20; Dallas, TX: Word Books, 1998)

Tawney, R.H., *The Acquisitive Society* (London: Bell, 1921; London: Collins, 1961)

Taylor, J.B., *Ezekiel: An Introduction and Commentary* (Tyndale Old Testament Commentary; Leicester: Inter-Varsity Press, 1969)

Temple, W., *Christianity and Social Order* (London: Penguin, 1942; London: Shepheard-Walwyn, 1976)

Thompson, A. and C. McAdam, *A Shared Vision? Human Rights and the Church* (Belfast: Centre for Contemporary Christianity in Ireland, 2000)

Thompson, J.A. *Deuteronomy: An Introduction and Commentary* (Tyndale Old Testament Commentary; London: Inter-Varsity Press, 1974)

Urmson, J.O. (ed.), *The Concise Encyclopedia of Western Philosophy and Philosophers* (2nd edn.; London: Hutchinson, 1967)

Vallely, P. (ed.), *The New Politics* (London: SCM Press, 1998)

Van Der Heide, E., 'Justice in International Relations with Less
    Developed Countries', *Transformation* 1 (April–June 1984)
Veyne, P., *Le Pain et le Cirque, Sociologie historique d'un pluralisme politique*
    (Paris: Seuil, 1976)
Volf, M., *Exclusion and Embrace: A Theological Exploration of Identity,
    Otherness, and Reconciliation* (Nashville: Abingdon Press, 1996)
Voute, P., 'In Sickness & Health', *Third Way* (October 2002), 9
Watts, J.D. W., *Isaiah 34–66* (WBC 25; Dallas, TX: Word Books, 1987)
Watt, G., 'Giving unto Caesar: Rationality, Reciprocity and Legal
    Recognition of Religion', in R. O'Dair and A. Lewis (eds.), *Law and
    Religion* (Oxford: Oxford University Press, 2001), 45–64
Westerholm, S., *Preface to the Study of Paul* (Grand Rapids: Eerdmans,
    1997)
Wilberforce, W., *A Practical View of Christianity* (Peabody, MA:
    Hendrickson, 1996)
Wink, W., *Naming the Powers: The Language of Power in the New Testament*
    Vol. 1 (Philadelphia: Fortress Press, 1984)
Wiseman, D.J., *1 and 2 Kings: An Introduction and Commentary* (Tyndale
    Old Testament Commentary; Leicester: Inter-Varsity Press, 1993)
Witherington, B., 'Christology', in G.F. Hawthorne, R.P. Martin and
    D.G. Reid (eds.), *Dictionary of Paul and his Letters* (Leicester: Inter-
    Varsity Press, 1993), 100–15
Witte, J., *Law and Protestantism: The Legal Teachings of the Lutheran Refor-
    mation* (Cambridge: Cambridge University Press, 2002)
Woodhead, L., 'Love and Justice', *Studies in Christian Ethics* 5.1 (1992),
    44–63
Wortley, B., 'The Christian Tradition in English Law', *Law & Justice* 150
    (2003), 10–20
Wright, C.J.H., *Living as the People of God: The Relevance of Old Testament
    Ethics* (Carlisle: Paternoster, 1990)
——, *God's People in God's Land: Family, Land, and Property in the Old
    Testament* (Carlisle: Paternoster, 1997)
——, *Walking in the Ways of the Lord: The Ethical Authority of the Old
    Testament* (Leicester: Apollos, 1995)
Wright, D.F. (ed.), *Essays in Evangelical Social Ethics* (Exeter: Paternoster,
    1978)
Wright, N.T. *The Climax of the Covenant: Christ and the Law in Pauline
    Theology* (Edinburgh: T. & T. Clark, 1991)
——, *The New Testament and the People of God* (London: SPCK, 1992)
——, *What Saint Paul Really Said* (Oxford: Lion, 1997)
Yoder, J.H., *Karl Barth and the Problem of War* (Nashville: Abingdon Press,
    1970)
——, *The Christian Witness to the State* (Newton, KA: Faith and Life
    Press, 1964)
——, *The Politics of Jesus: Vicit Agnus Noster* (2nd edn.; Grand Rapids/
    Carlisle: Eerdmans/Paternoster, 1994)

Young, H., *Major Themes from Minor Prophets* (Grantham: Autumn House, 1996)

Zehr, H., *Changing Lenses: A New Focus for Crime and Justice* (Scottdale, PA: Herald Press, 1990)

Ziesler, J.A. *Paul's Letter to the Romans* (London/Philadelphia: SCM Press/Trinity, 1989)

——, *Pauline Christianity* (revd edn.; Oxford: Oxford University Press, 1990)

Scripture Index

Old Testament

Genesis

1 – 2	17
1:27	22
1:27–28	25
2:2–3	25
2:15	25
2:16–17	18, 24
2:17	22
2:24	25
3:1	18
3:4	18
3:5	18
3:14–19	27
3:17–19	22
4:9	38
4:15	21
4:23	60
6 – 9	7
6:5	150
6:6	7
8:20 – 9:17	6
15:7	46
15:16	109
17:7	151
19:24–25	111
32:28	123
41 – 45	162
47:29	80

Exodus

6:7	151
7:13–14	110
7:22	110
8:15	110
8:19	110
8:32	110
9:7	110
9:12	110
9:35	110
12:12	70
18:13	63
18:15	63
18:21	63, 86
18:22	63
18:26	63
21:15–17	60
21:20–21	62
21:22–25	59
21:26–27	62
21:28–30	60
22:25–27	93
23:3	85
23:6	84
23:7	113
23:11	57
23:19	57
34:6	80

Leviticus

6:8 – 7:21	45
10:11	50
11:44–45	9
11:45	44
16:1–28	45
17 – 26	44–5
18:24–28	66
19	49
19:2	44, 49
19:9–10	55
19:10	57
19:13	55
19:15	85
19:18	38, 48, 129
19:36	54, 78

20:9	60	6:6–9	50
20:22	47	6:7	50
20:22–24	66	6:20–25	50
23:22	57	7:7f.	46
24:17–22	59	8:2	46
25:18	47	8:11	46, 100
25:23	53	8:17–18	37, 46
25:23–31	90	8:19	46, 100
25:35–38	56	9:5	46, 53, 65
25:36f.	56	10:17–18	12
25:39f., 43	52–3	10:17–19	44
25:39–55	56	10:19	52
26:1–13	45	11:19	50
26:3–35	47	12:1	47
26:12	151	13:5	47
26:14–43	45	14:22–29	55
26:45	65	14:28f.	57
27:30–32	55	15:1–3	56
		15:11	57
Numbers		15:15	46, 53, 55
5:6	47, 61	16:11	55
14:18	13	16:12	47
26	53	16:14	55
26:52–56	24	16:18–20	51, 64, 86–7
27:17	77	16:20	47, 87, 91
34	53	17:6	87
35:6–34	60	17:8–13	51, 64
35:30	87	17:12	60
		17:14–20	76
Deuteronomy		17:18–20	74
1:1 – 4:49	46	17:19–20	71
1:15	81	19:14	54
1:16–17	84	19:15	87
4 – 26	148	19:15–21	59
4:1	47	19:16–19	60
4:1–2	43	19:16–21	86
4:5	47	20:10	113
4:5–6	50–1	21:18–21	60, 62, 63
4:6–8	65	23:15	56
4:11–14	42	23:19–20	56
4:14	47, 52, 126	24:1	62
5:1 – 26:19	46	24:6	56, 63
5:9	50	24:12–13	56
5:15	55	24:7	60
5:31	47	24:14f.	55
6:5	48, 129	24:17	84

25:13–16	54	10:6	30
25:15	78	17:1–13	30
26:9	53	17:6	30
26:12ff.	57	18:1	30
27	48	18:27	30
27:1 – 30:20	46	19:1	30
27:17	54	19:22–28	30
27:19	53, 84	20:1–48	30
28	48, 91, 148	21:10–12	30
28:1	43	21:20–23	30
28:1–14	65	21:25	30
28:15	106		
28:58–68	106	*Ruth*	
28:63	148	2:2	55
28:64	148		
29	103	*1 Samuel*	
29:19–28	148	2:8	57
30:1	148	8:3	64
30:2	148	8:8	71
30:6	148, 151	8:11–12	71
30:17–19	106	8:13	72
31:1 – 34:12	46	8:15–17	72
32:4	10	10:25	71
33	45	11	73
33:8	45	12:14	71
33:10	45	12:14–15	74
		13	73
Joshua		13:8–14	72
1:8	50, 54	14	73
2:14	80	15:22	73
5:15	8	16:7	194
13 – 18	24	17	73
13 – 19	53	18	73
20:1–9	60		
		2 Samuel	
Judges		5:2	77
2:12–13	30	6:17	72
2:17	30	7:7	77
2:19	30	8	73
3:7	30	8:15	73, 78, 80
4:5	64, 70	11	181
8:23	71	11:1	73
8:33	30	12:1–14	89
9:5	30	15:1–6	73
9:30–57	30	24:17	77

1 Kings

2:3	75
3	73
3:9	81
3.11	76
3:28	73
4:26	76
5:13	76
6:38 – 7:1	76
8:62	72
9:15	76
9:20–23	76
9:21	76
10:9	78, 80
10:14	76
10:26	76
11	76
11:1–2	76
11:5–8	76
11:38	74
12	179
12:7	81
12:25–33	72
13	89
13:34	72
14:6–16	89
14:7–11	72
15:3	74
5:14	74
18:16–39	9
20:31	113
20:35–43	89
21:1–16	90
21:1–29	89
21:17–28	90
22	73
22:17	77
22:44	74

2 Kings

1:3–17	89
3:9	73
3:11–19	90
6:8–10	90
6:21–23	90
6:22	113

6:33 – 7:2	90
8:7–15	90
8:18	74
8:21	73
8:27	74
8:28–29	73
9:1–10	90
9:7–10	69
10:1–11	69
10:31	74
13:14–19	90
14:3	74
14:9–13	73
14:25, 28	91
15:4	74
15:34–35	74
16:2–3	74
18:3–5	74
18:6	74
19:20–22	74
21:2–6	74
22:2	74
23:25	75
23:25	74
23:32	74
24:4	113
24:9	74
24:18	74

1 Chronicles

11:2	77
16:31	7
17:6	77
17:11–14	74
21:17	77
23:4	64
26:29	64
29:11–12	7

2 Chronicles

6:30	192
9:8	78
18:16	77
19:5	64
19:7	11
19:8	64

19:10	64		33:11	4
19:11	64		35:10	57
			36:5–9	11–12
Ezra			37:27–29	47
7:10	45		40:11–12	80
7:25	78, 82		45:2–6	121
9:13	199		45:6	7, 194
9:13–15	16		47:7–9	7
			57:4	80
Nehemiah			57:11	80
5:3	101		61:8	80
5:4	101		72	75, 80
5:15	101		72:1–9	121
5:17–18	101		72:4	80
9:13	145		73	11
9:20	145		78:70	77
9:30	145		81:11–12	32
			82:1–4	112
Job			85:10	81
5:15	57		85:11	80
8:3	11		89:14	11
16:18	197		89:15	80
24:2f.	54		89:19–20	140
24:2–4	96		89:26–27	140
24:9–10	96		93:1–2	7
28	146		96:5	17
31:13–14	197		96:10	7
34:12	11		97:2	11
34:17	11		99:4	11, 82
36:3	11		101:1	11
37:23	11		103:6	12
			103:19	7
Psalms			104:30	143
1:2	50		106:3	82
9:7	7		106:13–15	32
9:7–8	194		108:5	80
9:9	112–13		111:7	4
9:12	112–13		112:1	50
9:16	11		112:5	63
10:14	57		119	50
11	113		139	21
11:7	83		140:12	12
12:5	113		145:8	5
22:8	7		145:9	5
25:10	80		145:11–13	7
33:5	11		145:13b–17	5

Proverbs
1:1	82
1:3	82
2:6	82
2:9	82
3:3	80
3:29	85
3:30	85
6:16–17	113
6:16–19	85–6
8:12–21	82, 179
9:22–31	146
10:9	82
11:1	54
11:24	54
11:26	55
12:17	85
13:23	84
14:5	85
14:25	85
14:31	84
15:16	82
15:27	86
16:6	80
16:8	82
16:10	78
16:11	54
16:12	78
16:13	86
16:19	54
17:5	84
17:8	86
17:15	83
17:23	86
17:26	83
18:5	83
18:17	87
18:23	85
19:5	85
19:9	85
19:28	85
20:8	83
20:10	54
20:23	54
20:26	83
20:28	80, 180

21:3	98
21:13	84
21:14	86
21:21	82
21:28	86
22:2	84
22:7	84
22:16	84
22:22–23	85, 197
22:28	85
23:10	54
23:10–11	85
24:23–25	83
25:5	78
25:18	85
28:2	69, 179
28:3	85
28:5	81
28:8	63
28:16	82
28:21	83
29:4	78, 87
29:7	83
29:12	86
29:14	86
29:13	84
29:14	85, 180
31:4–5	84–5
31:8–9	84

Ecclesiastes
2:24	25, 35
3:12–13	35
3:16	189
4:1	189
5:18	35,
8:15	35
9:9	35

Isaiah
1 – 36	11
1 – 37	102
1:9f.	111
1:10–17	72
1:11	97
1:15b–17	97

1:21	97	40:15–17	7, 108–10
1:21–31	9	40:22–24	7, 108–10
1:23	97	40:24	108
5:7	97	42	80
5:8–10	24	42:1–9	118
5:16	193	44:28	77
5:22–23	85	45:1–7	107
5:23	97	46	107
6:5	9	46:1–47:15	66
9:6–7	6	47	107, 109
9:7	121	47:1	109
10:1–2	84	47:2	109
10:1–4a	197	47:3	109
10:12–19	111	47:5	109
11:1–10	121	47:7	109
11:2	146	47:8–15	109
11:3–4a	146	48:10	9
11:4	197	49:6	65, 121
11:10–16	121	49:22–26	121
13:1 – 21:17	66	51:4–5	113
13:11	111	56:1	201
13:19	111	58	100, 102, 113
13 – 23	110	58:2	100
14:2	111	58:3	100
14:4–6	111	58:3–14	102
14:13	111	58:4	100
16:5	80	58:6–7	100–1
16:6	111	58:9	100–1
23:1 – 25:12	66	58:9–12	101
23:9	111	59	100, 102, 113
24:21	153	59:2	113
29:20–21	86	59:3–11	101
30:18	10	59:7	113
32:1	156	59:13–18	102
32:14	156	59:16	113
32:15	156	59:18	113
32:16–17	81, 156	59:20	102, 113
33:14	9	60:1–3	65
33:22	70	61:1–2	190
34:1–17	66	61:8	112
37:1–7	90	63:1–6	121
37:16	7		
38 – 55	102	*Jeremiah*	
39, 40	108	3:6	149
39:6	105	3:10	149
40:6–8	108	3:17	106

3:22	99, 151	21:10	75
4:4	151	21:12	57, 97
4:14	149	21:13–14	75
5:16–17	108	22:1–5	77
5:28–29	57, 98	22:3	78, 80
7	99	22:5–7	75
7:3	149	22:9	98
7:5–6	99	22:13–17	24, 98
7:5–7	149	22:15	78, 80
7:5–11	102	22:17	99, 110
7:9	99	22:30	75
7:9–10	99	23:1	77
7:9–11	99	23:1–4	77
7:11	99	23:5	78, 80
7:13	149	23:5–8	117
7:16	149	23:30	117
7:17	99	24:7	150
7:21–23	99	25:8–11	107
7:24–26	149	25:9	105, 107
7:27–29	149	25:9–11	107
9:8	99	25:9–12	108
9:9	106	25:12–14	107, 108
9:23	202	25:15–26	107
9:24	112	25:15–38	66, 110
10:17–18	106	25:26	107
11:20	149	26	149
12:1	11	26:1–6	99
12:3	149	26:2–4	149
12:12	107	26:4	99
12:14–17	106	27:3	106
13:23	150	27:4–5	105
14:11	107	27:4–7	107
15:14	106	27:6	106, 107
16:12	110	27:7	109
16:17	194	27:8–11	106
16:19	106	27:12	107
17:1	150	27:12–15	90
17:3	75	28	106
17:9	150	29:10	105
17:10	149	29:17–18	107
17:19–27	102	29:32	106
18:12	110	30:8–11	121
20:4–6	106	30:12	150
20:12	149	30:12–17	151
21:3–7	107	31:10	77
21:7	106	31:33	150

31:33–34	150
32:5	106
32:24	107
32:25	106
32:27	107
32:28	106
32:36	107
32:39	151
32:40	151
33:6–9	121
33:15	78, 80
34:1–7	90
34:2	106
34:17	107
34:21–22	106
36	75
36:1–24	90
37:1–21	90
38:2	107
38:3	106
38:14–26	90
40:3	106
42:17	107
42:22	107
43:8–13	107
43:10	107
44:22	109
46–51	110
46:1 – 49:39	107
46:1 – 51:64	66
46:24	106
46:25	111
46:26	106
48 – 51	110
48:7	111
48:13	111
48:29–30	111
48:42	111
48:47	106
49:3	111
49:4	111
49:6	106
49:16	111
49:39	106
50:1 – 51:64	107
50:2	111

50:6	77
50:15	109
50:29b	199
50:31	109
50:31–32	111
51	107
51:11	109
51:15–16	107
51:24	109
51:47	111
51:49	109, 197

Lamentations
3:36	192

Ezekiel
1 – 3	8
1:1	8
10:7	9
11:19–20	150, 151
16:49	111
18	25
21:28–32	67
22	99–100
22:1–16	99
22:3–5	99
22:12	100
22:17–22	9
25 – 32	110
25:1 – 32:32	8, 66
27:3	111
28:2	111
28:5–6	111
28:16	111
28:18	111
29:3	111
29:9	111
30:19	193
33:11	196
33:20	196
34	77
34:2–5	77
34:7–8	77
34:15–24	77
34:20–31	117
34:24	139

35	110	1:1 – 2:5	92
36:26	150	1:3	92, 111
36:26–27	151	1:3 – 2:16	91
36:27	150	1:6	111
35:1–15	66	1:9	111, 112
37:24–28	121	1:13	92, 112
37:25	139	2:1	92, 112
38:1 – 39:6	66	2:4	93
44:23	45	2:6–7	57, 93
44:24	64	2:8	93
45:1–8	72	2:9	94
45:1–10	24	2:10	94
45:9	78, 80	2:11	94
45:10–12	54	3:1	94
		3:1 – 6:14	91
Daniel		3:9	92
1:2	107	3:10	95
2:31–45	107	3:11	95
3	69	3:14–15	95
5	109	4:1–2	95
6	69	4:4–5	93
7	107	4:6	94
9	116	4:7–8	94
9:25–26	116	4:9–10	94
		4:10–11	94
Hosea		4:12	95
1:4	69	5:3	95
2:19	151	5:4–6	93
2:23	151	5:4	95
3:4	73	5:6	95
4:1	80	5:7	93
5:10	54	5:10	93
8:7	32	5:11	93, 95
8:11–13	72, 73	5:11–12	24
12	96	5:12	93
12:1	96	5:14–15	93, 95
12:6	96	5:15	93, 95
12:7	96	5:18,20	95
		5:21–24	93
Joel		5:24	79
3:1–16	66	5:26–27	95
3:3	96	6:1–3	91
		6:1–7	92
Amos		6:8	95
1 – 2	110	6:11	95
1:1–2	91	6:13	91

6:14	95
7:1–3	94
7:1 – 9:10	91
7:4–6	94
7:7–9	94
7:17	95
8:1–14	94
8:2	95
8:5	93, 102
8:6	93
9:1–10	94
9:8–10	95
9:11–15	91, 95–6

Obadiah

10	111
13–14	111
15	199

Jonah

1	109
4:2	13, 109

Micah

2:1–5	24
2:12	77
3:1–2	96
3:8–12	96
4:4	24
5:4	77
6:3–5	49
6:6–8	73
6:8	16, 97, 98
7:3	97

Nahum

1:2	110

1:3	110
3:1	111
3:4	111

Habakkuk

1:2–4	108
1:13	9
2:2–17	108

Zephaniah

1:14–18	113
2:4–15	66, 110
2:10	111
2:15	111

Haggai

2:9	33

Zechariah

3:10	24
7:8–12	59, 103
7:9	80
9	115
9:1–8	66, 110
9:9–10	115
10:2	77
11	77
14	113

Malachi

2:16	62
2:17	10, 108
3:2–3	9
3:5	103
3:6	4
4	113

New Testament

Matthew

2:1–2	115
2:6	120
3:15	128
4	120
4:3	119
4:6	119
4:8–9	132
4:8–10	117
4:17	115
4:23–24	118
5:1 – 7:29	120
5:12	120
5:17–20	123
5:21ff.	123
5:21–22	124, 151
5:21–37	122, 128
5:27–28	124, 151
5:39–48	128
5:45	22, 29
6:10	115
6:24	132
6:33	132
7:12	128
8:5–12	139
9:9–13	23
10:26	192, 194
10:34–38	39
10:39	34, 37
11:4	118
12:18–20	119
12:36	200
12:48–50	39
13:24–30	190
13:36–43	190
15:7–9	121
15:10	194
15:11	124, 151, 194
15:16–20	124, 151
15:17–20	124, 151, 194
16:16	117
16:17–21	117
16:25	37
16:27	12

19:7–8	62
19:19	48, 129
19:29	34, 37, 39
21:9–10	117
21:12–17	137
22:15–22	159
22:37–40	48, 129
23:1–36	121
23:23	104, 202
23:27	152
25:31–33	193
25:31–46	12, 120, 162, 190
26:36–46	19
28:16–20	139
28:18	132
28:19	132

Mark

1:14–15	115
2:13–17	23
3:32–35	39
4:22	192
8:27–33	117
8:35	34, 37
10:19	126
10:29	37, 39
10:30	34, 39
11:8–10	117
11:12–19	137
12:29–31	126
14:61–64	117
15:26	117
16:15–18	139

Luke

2:14	115
2:28–32	139
4	118
4:5–6	117
4:16–21	121
4:17–19	191
4:17–21	118

4:18	57	5:24–30	122
4:21	191	5:45–47	121
5:27–32	23	6:15	117
8:17	192	8:11	128
9:18–22	117	8:12	10
9:24	34, 37	8:36	34
10:5	180	8:37–44	121
10:27	129	10:10	33, 34
11:37–52	121	10:11	120
11:42	104	10:14	77
12:3	194	12:12–13	117
12:15	58	12:35	10
12:51–53	39	12:47–48	122
13:29	139	13:34	129
14:26	34, 39	14:6–13	193
16:19–31	197	14:9	4
17:11–19	23	14:15–17	144
17:26	195	15:12	129
17:33	34	15:12–17	47
18:9–14	121	16:8–11	143–4
18:29	37	16:13–14	143
18:29–30	34	17:3	33
19:1–9	23	18:33–40	116
19:37–40	117	18:36	117, 123, 126,
19:45–48	137		161
20:25	132	21:15–17	120
22:25–26	120		
22:27	120	*Acts*	
22:31–38	132	1:6	139
23:1	117	1:7	139
23:4	190	1:8	139
23:42	190	4	186
24:46–47	121	4:12	186
		4:18	186
John		4:19	186
1:1	143	4:32–35	24
1:1–3	144	10:42	122
1:5	10	12:20–23	141
1:18	144	14:17	29
1:49	115	15	125, 151
2:13–17	137	15:5	124
3:14–17	121	15:8–11	124–5
3:18	190	15:19–20	125
3:16	7, 25, 26	16:22–39	159
3:19–20	10	17:28	3
4:1–42	23	17:31	115, 122, 196

24:2–25	140		13	158–61, 180,
24:26	159			181
24:14	151		13:1	31
25:1–12	140		13:1–7	158, 159, 160,
25:23 – 26:32	140			167, 168
			13:3–5	160, 169
Romans			13:4	37, 167
1:3–5	140		13:4	181
1:4	104		13:6–7	160
1:18	14, 27		13:7–8	37–8
1:20	27, 163		13:8–9	127
1:29	27		13:8–10	159, 160
1:29–32	125		13:9	129
2:5	195		13:10	127
2:5–6	192		14:10–12	12
2:6–7	195		14:17	180
2:14–15	27, 163		14:19	180
2:16	104, 122			
2:29	148		*1 Corinthians*	
3:20	201		1:10 – 2:10	146
3:23	25, 201		1:24	146
3:24	104		1:30	146
3:25	104		2:8	153
4:25	103		2:10	146
5:1	103		3:10–15	9, 12
5:6–11	7, 33		3:12–15	10
5:11	103		4:5	10, 122, 194
5:12–19	20		4:10	37
5:12–21	195		4:12	198
6:9–10	104		5:1–2	125
6:15–16	125		5:7	103
6:23	22, 29		6:18	125
7	147		7:15	180
7:6	148		8:6	143, 144, 146
7:7–11	147		13:12	199
7:10	147		14:33	17, 179, 180
7:11	147		15	196
7:14	145, 148		15:19	196
8:3	147		15:20–28	104
8:4	151		15:22	20
8:9	147			
8:18	196		*2 Corinthians*	
8:32	103		3:5–6	148
8:38	153		3:7	148
12:9–21	159		4:11	37
12:18	180		5:10	12, 190

5:14	103
5:18–20	7
5:21	103, 104
8:9	103
10:3–6	175

Galatians

3:13	104, 121
3:13–14	199
3:19	126, 152
3:24–25	125
4:5	104
5:1	34
5:14	48, 129
5:19–21	125
6:16	180

Ephesians

1:17	147
1:21	153
2:18	103
3:10	153
4:3	180
4:25–31	125
5:8–13	10
5:21 – 6:9	34
5:22–32	26
6:9	197
6:10–18	156
6:12	153, 155

Philippians

1:29	37
2	131
2:6–11	20
3:20	185

Colossians

1:15–20	146
1:15–23	144
1:16	153
1:16–17	143
1:20	128
1:24	37
2:10	153

2:15	122, 138, 153, 192
2:16–17	124
3:5–10	125
3:12 – 4:1	34
3:15	180

1 Thessalonians

4:3–8	198
4:6	192
4:17	195, 196
5:13	180

2 Thessalonians

1:5	198
1:7	192
1:7–9	195
1:9	196
1:10	196

1 Timothy

2:1–2	156, 180
2:2	177
2:3	180
2:4	191
2:16	104
5:10	58
5:24	194

2 Timothy

2:3	198
2:12	198
2:13	4
4:1	122

Titus

3:1	158

Hebrews

1:2–3	143, 144
1:3	3, 103
1:10–13	144
7:26–28	103
8:10	163
9:14	103
9:15	104

9:23–28	103	4:3	125
9:28	190	4:17	93
10:1	123	5:2–3	120
10:3–14	123	5:4	120
10:12	103	5:14	180
10:14	103		
10:18	123	*2 Peter*	
10:31	9	3:3–4	191
12:14	180	3:6	191
12:29	9	3:7	195
13:8	4	3:9	32, 110, 191
13:20	77	3:10	195
		3:11	195
James			
1:17	22	*1 John*	
1:27	57, 105	1:5	10
2:5–6	57	2:9	125
2:8	48, 129	3:4	19, 125
2:9–11	125	3:16	5
2:13	12	4:8	5
3:18	180	4:16	5
4:12	194	5:3	127
4:13–15	37	5:11	196
5:1–6	55		
5:4	113	*Jude*	
5:10	198	2	180
		4–8	125
1 Peter		7	111
1:16	9, 44	16	125
2:1	125		
2:13	160	*Revelation*	
2:13–14	158	6:9–11	197
2:13–17	30	7:17	77
2:13 – 3:7	34	13	181
2:14	167	18	111
2:19	159	19:11	113, 193
2:19–20	198	21	196
2:25	77	21:3	196
3:11	180	21:22–23	196
3:14	37		
3:22	153		

General Index

agape   *see* Christian love
Ahab, king   89–90
Amos, the prophet   79, 90–6,
    111–12
Anderson, Norman   41
Anselm of Canterbury   3
Aquinas, Thomas   20–1
Aristotle   26
St Augustine   126–7, 175, 179
Authority   *see* human government

Barth, Karl   135
Berkhof, Hendrik   154–5
Blenkinsopp, Joseph   78, 82
de Blois, Matthijs   39
Bruce, F.F.   116

Calvin, John   20, 103, 135–6,
    159–60, 164
Chantry, Walter   51, 125–6
Chesterton, G.K.   19
Christenson, L.   155
Christian love   162
church
    and human legal systems   182–8
    and Roman empire   130–2, 158–60
    and sin   155–6
    and state   Ch. 6 *passim*, 133–7,
        161, 164, 174–5, 185–8
Colson, Charles   168, 178–9
Colwell, John   138
community   *see* human beings,
    relationships between people
de Connick, Frédéric   4–5, 55, 166,
    178, 182–3, 202
covenant relationship   *see* Mosaic
    law
Cranfield, C.E.B.   127, 159–60
Creation   Ch. 2 *passim*
    goodness   17, 26–7, 33–5

Daniel, the prophet   158
death   14–16, 19–20, 157
Denning, Lord   178
Deuteronomy   46–8, 148–9
    and kingship   76
divine revelation   Ch. 1 *passim*
Donne, John   38
Dumbrell, W.J.   35
Dunn, J.D.G.   79

Elihu, Job's comforter   11
Ellison, H.L.   95
eternal life   196
Ezekiel, the prophet   8, 72, 77,
    99–100, 111, 150–1, 196

Fall   18–22, 25–7, 33–5, 157
Foster, Richard   155
freewill   17–18, 24–5, 198

Genesis   17, 40
Gladwin, John   57
God
    and human law   16, 178, 182–4
    as dynamic   3
    as light   10
    as sovereign   7–8, 11
    as ultimate reality   2–5
    character   Ch. 1 *passim*
    constancy   4–5
    creator   1–2, 17, 19
    freedom   2
    good gifts   33–5; *see also* creation
    holiness   8–10
    judgement   13, 19, 29, 32–3,
        92–6, 105–112, 149, 195–6;
        see also Last Judgement
    justice   10–13, 70, 112–3, 192
    love   2, 5–7, 12–13
    mercy   12–13, 95–6, 198–9

otherness 8–9
righteousness 10–12
self revelation *see* divine
     revelation
wrath 13–16, 110, 167, 192
good 162–74
     and individuals 169–71
     discerning what is good 162–4
grace 6–7, 29, 32–3

Habbakuk, the prophet 108
Harte, David 152
Haugen, Gary 21, 34, 83, 183
Hell 195–6, 199
Henry, Carl 10
holiness 101; *see also* God *and*
     Mosaic Law
Holy Spirit Ch. 7 *passim*
     and creation 143–5
     and law Ch. 7 *passim*
     and revelation 143–4
     righteousness 147–53
     wisdom 145–7, *see also* Mosaic
          Law and the Holy Spirit
Hosea, the prophet 32, 90, 96
human beings
     dignity 22–4
     image of God 2, 17–18, 20,
          22–5, 60, 176
     liberty *see* freewill
     relationships between
          people 25–6, 35–6, 48–9,
          171–4
     relationship with God 7, 9, 15,
          18, 46–8, 198
human government Ch. 8 *passim*;
     see also justice
     accountability to God 161–2,
          180–2, 201
     and the common good 36–8,
          175–8
     authority from God 30–32, 186
human legal systems 16, 31, 40,
     178–80, 187–8
     as provisional 192, 200–1
     limitations 156, 188, *see also*
          Mosaic Law and human law

human society *see* human beings,
     relationships between people
human work 25, 37

injustice Ch. 5 *passim*, 112–13,
     189–90; *see also* justice, social
Isaiah, the prophet 81, 97, 100–2,
     105, 108–9, 111, 113, 146
Israel *see* Mosaic Law
     and judgement 93–5

James, the apostle 104–5
Jehoshaphat, king 11, 64
Jeremiah, the prophet 75, 90, 97–9,
     105–7, 149–51
Jeroboam I, king 72
Jesus
     and creation 144–5
     and justice 103–5, 137, 193–4,
          197
     and power 120, 132, 136–8
     and revelation 144
     and the cross 16, 103–4, 146,
          189–90
     ascension 122, 191
     as good shepherd 77, 120
     as servant 120
     Messiah 116–19, 121–2, 145–6
     resurrection 122, 196
     Son 6, 143
     teachings 29, 48, 62, 104, 118,
          120, 128–9, 132, 137, 143–4,
          159, 162, 168, 191, 197–8;
          see also kingship, Mosaic Law
John, the apostle 5, 10, 127
John the Baptist 118
Jonah, the prophet 13
jubilee 53–4, 58
judgement *see* God *and* Last
     Judgement
justice 20–1, 35–40, 174
     and bribery 86–7, 96–7
     and deliverance 12, 70–1, 79–80,
          198–9
     and false witness 85–6
     and human government 30–2,
          177–8

and order 178–80
and pagan kings 105–10
and the poor 83–5, 98
and the prophetic call Ch. 5
    passim
and wisdom 81–3
criminal justice 167
in the new testament 103–5
social justice 35–6, 166–80, 184–7
see also God, Jesus, Kingship,
    Mosaic Law *and* State
Justinian 20

Kant, Immanuel 23, 175
kingdom of God 118–20, 132,
    139–41, 156, 161
kingship Ch. 4 *passim*
and covenant 74, 79–81
and Jesus Ch. 6 *passim*, 158,
    193–4
and justice 70–1, 73, 78–88
and wisdom 81–3
king as shepherd 76–7, 120
righteousness *see* kingship and
    justice
within Israel 71–88, 157–8

Last Judgement Ch. 9 *passim*
as revelation 193–6
law *see* human legal systems, Mosaic
    Law
and Holy Spirit Ch. 7 *passim*
natural law 27–8, 163–4
Lebacqz, Karen 83
Leviticus 38, 44–6, 49
Lewis, C.S. 196
Liberalism 169–71
love *see* God, love
human love 26
Luther, Martin 133–5

Malachi, the prophet 103
Marshall, Christopher 14, 60, 128,
    159, 168
Mawhinney, Brian 161
McAdam, Caroline 172–3

McConville, J.G. 149
Micah, the prophet 90, 96–7
Montgomery, J.W. 184
Moore, Thomas 198
morality 15, 65–6, 152–3
and nature 27–8
Mosaic Law Ch. 3 *passim*
administration of justice 62–4
and ceremony 52, 124–5
and covenant relationship 41–8
and criminal justice 59–61
and divorce 61–2
and equality 52–3
and family 53–4, 59–60
and holiness 44–6, 48–9, 66–7,
    124–5
and Holy Spirit 145–8, 151
and Jesus 122–30
and landholding 53–4
and morality 126–9, 152–3
and social justice 52–9
and those who work 55–6
as guidance 50–1
insufficiency 147–53
Moses 3, 41–3, 50–1, 63, 69–70,
    81, 84, 148

Nahum, the prophet 111
Nebuchadnezzar, king 106–7
Nehemiah, the prophet 101
new covenant 47, 125–6, 150–1
Numbers 46

Obadiah, the prophet 111
Oestreicher, Paul 57

Paul, the apostle 10, 14–15, 17, 27,
    29, 116, 125, 127, 140–1,
    144–7, 151–3, 156, 158–60,
    167–9, 179, 192, 195, 196
Peter, the apostle 124–5, 191
Pope John Paul II 38, 58–9
prophets of the Old Testament
    Ch. 5 *passim*
Proverbs 82–7

von Rad, Gerhard 78
Rawls, John 36–7, 169–70, 172, 176
redemption 33, 102
Rehoboam, king 81
Reisinger, E. 127
relationships *see* human beings
repentance 149
resurrection *see* Jesus
revelation *see* divine revelation, Holy Spirit, Jesus, Last Judgement, Scripture
righteousness *see* God, holiness, Holy Spirit, justice, kingship
Rose, Tom 188

Samuel, the prophet 71–2
Sandel, Michael 171–2
Scripture *see* Mosaic Law *and* Index of Biblical References
    as revelation 163–4
    second coming 190, 191–3
Shakespeare, William 4
Shalom 12, 48–9, 55, 75, 79, 179–80
sin 9, 14–16, 19–20, 27, 147–8, 157
    and its punishment 16, 192
    original sin 19
    structural sin 153–6
Sider, Ronald 57–8

Solomon, king 75–6, 81
state
    and church *see* church
    as instrument of God's justice 167–8
Suggate, A.M. 79

Tawney, R.H. 58
Temple, William 23–5, 93, 173, 179, 185
Ten Commandments 28, 41–3, 51, 125–7, 164–5
Thompson, Alwyn 172–3
Torah *see* Mosaic Law
Trinity, doctrine of 143
two swords theory 132–6

utilitarianism 169

Wilberforce, William 19
Wink, Walter 154–5
Witte, John 133–5
Wright, Christopher 10, 39, 56, 67, 124, 130
Wright, N.T. 147, 181, 186

Yoder, J.H. 160

Ziesler, J.A. 20
Zechariah the prophet 102–3